NEXT

YOUNG AMERICAN WRITERS ON THE NEW GENERATION

ERIC LIU

EDITOR

W·W· NORTON & COMPANY

NEW YORK

LONDON

The text of this book is composed in 11/13.5 Berkeley Book
with the display set in Gill Extra Bold Condensed Caps
at 150% horizontal scale.
Composition and manufacturing by
the Maple-Vail Book Manufacturing Group.
Book design by Margaret M. Wagner.

Library of Congress Cataloging-in-Publication Data
Next: young American writers on the new generation / Eric Liu,
editor.
p.   cm.
1. Young adults—United States.   I. Liu, Eric.
HQ799.7.N39   1994
305.23'5—dc20   93-38794

ISBN 0-393-03585-9
ISBN 0-393-31191-0 (paper)

W. W. Norton & Company, Inc.
500 Fifth Avenue, New York, N.Y. 10110
W. W. Norton & Company Ltd.
10 Coptic Street, London WC1A 1PU

1 2 3 4 5 6 7 8 9 0

CONTENTS

PREFACE

Over the last few years, there has been no shortage of disparaging commentary about Americans in their twenties and early thirties. Neither has there been a shortage of negative labels for us, from "Generation X" to "Twentynothings" to the "Lost Generation."

There has, however, been a shortage of insight about our lives and perspectives. Mainstream media coverage of this age group has been a study in caricature. Are we drifters or career-obsessed young fogies? Are we spoiled whiners? Apathetic slackers? These heavy-handed, often conflicting stereotypes have only two things in common: they mock us, and they rob us of our voices.

That is why, in 1991, I started *The Next Progressive*, a journal of political and cultural opinion produced entirely by women and men of this generation. And that is why I feel a book like this one is necessary.

Next is an anthology that—by its variety of opinions, personalities, and points of view—defies simplistic efforts to categorize this age group. The contributors are individuals, not archetypes. We do not pretend, singly or collectively, to be the "voice of the generation." We range in age from twenty-four to thirty-two. We hail from all parts of the country. We are black, white, Asian, Latino, straight, gay, liberal, conservative—and, each of us, independent.

At the same time, we are brought together by a certain sensibility. We share an outlook—media savvy, worldly-wise, conscious of our diversity—that derives not only from our youth but also from our place in history. Just as many people describe today's world as "post–Cold War," so do many of my peers see this generation as "postboomer." That is, we were born behind the baby boom—"after it all happened." After Vietnam. After the civil-rights movement. After the women's movement.

Taken simply as historical fact, these statements are true. We are indeed "postboomers." But, as William Safire has written, "*post* identifies a time only by what preceded it." *Next,* on the other hand, looks forward.

What does it mean to be our age in this day and age? On issues ranging from politics, race, and culture to feminism, courtship, and sex, how do the unique conflicts of our times affect us? What aspirations and anxieties do we have? These are questions that each of us addresses in this collection, in very different ways—sometimes complementary, often contradictory.

These personal essays are written not just for our peers but for our elders as well—for those who may not understand us but who want to search beneath the superficial stereotypes. The purpose of this anthology is not to bash our elders or to worry aloud about the future—although various contributors do both. Our larger purpose is to speak for ourselves.

By making our voices heard in so unfiltered a manner, we invite rebuttal, skepticism, and criticism. But by deliberately avoiding a sound-bitten, graphics-laden, eye-popping style, we challenge readers to pay close attention, to avoid the snap judgments, unburdened by reflection, that have characterized most reports on the "twentysomething" crowd. We have thought hard about these essays. And we invite readers to do the same.

This book would not have been possible without the efforts of many people. Henning Gutmann, my editor at Norton, believed in this project from the time it was a bare-bones book proposal. His instincts, editing talent, patience, and commitment to this book made it possible. Rafe Sagalyn, my literary agent, conceived of the leap from *The Next Progressive* to *Next*. I also want to thank: Carroll Haymon, whose encouragement and crystal-clear commentary on these essays were invaluable; all those who have made *The Next Progressive* a success; and, of course, the fifteen contributors who joined me in this venture. Finally, thanks to my mother, whose strength and courage inspire me every day; and to my father, whose voice still guides me. To all these people, this collection is dedicated.

Eric Liu
Washington, D.C.
October 1993

**N
E
X
T**

LARGER THAN LIFE

Jenny Lyn Bader

When my grandmother was young, she would sometimes spot the emperor Franz Josef riding down the cobbled roads of the Austro-Hungarian Empire.

She came of age so long ago that the few surviving photographs are colored cream and chestnut. Early on, she saw cars replace horses and carriages. When she got older, she marveled at the first televisions. Near the end of her life, she grew accustomed to remote control and could spot prime ministers on color TV. By the time she died, the world was freshly populated by gadgetry and myth. Her generation bore witness to the rise of new machinery created by visionaries. My generation has seen machinery break down and visionaries come under fire.

As children, we enjoyed collecting visionaries, the way we collected toys or baseball cards. When I was a kid, I first met Patrick Henry and Eleanor Roosevelt, Abraham Lincoln and Albert Einstein. They could always be summoned by the imagination and so were never late for play dates. I thought heroes figured in any decent childhood. I knew their stats.

Nathan Hale. Nelson Mandela. Heroes have guts.

Michelangelo. Shakespeare. Heroes have imagination.

They fight. Alexander the Great. Joan of Arc.

They fight for what they believe in. Susan B. Anthony. Martin Luther King.

Heroes overcome massive obstacles. Beethoven, while deaf, still managed to carry an unforgettable tune. Homer, while blind, never failed to give an excellent description. Helen Keller, both deaf and blind, still spoke to the world. FDR, despite his polio, became president. Moses, despite his speech impediment, held productive discussions with God.

They inspire three-hour movies. They make us weepy. They do the right thing while enduring attractive amounts of suffering. They tend to be self-employed. They are often killed off. They sense the future. They lead lives that make us question our own. They are our ideals, but not our friends.

They don't have to be real. Some of them live in books and legends. They don't have to be famous. There are lower-profile heroes who get resurrected by ambitious biographers. There are collective heroes: firefighters and astronauts, unsung homemakers, persecuted peoples. There are those whose names we can't remember, only their deeds: "you know, that woman who swam the English Channel," "the guy who died running the first marathon," "the student who threw himself in front of the tank at Tiananmen Square." There are those whose names we'll never find out: the anonymous benefactor, the masked man, the undercover agent, the inventor of the wheel, the unknown soldier. The one who did the thing so gutsy and terrific that no one will ever know what it was.

Unlike icons (Marilyn, Elvis) heroes are not only sexy but noble, too. Unlike idols (Gretzky, Streisand), who vary from fan to fan, they are almost universally beloved. Unlike icons and idols, heroes lack irony. And unlike icons and idols, heroes are no longer in style.

As centuries end, so do visions of faith—maybe because the faithful get nervous as the double zeroes approach and question what they've been worshiping. Kings and queens got roughed up at the end of the eighteenth century; God took a beating at the end of the nineteenth; and as the twentieth century draws to a close, outstanding human beings are the casualties of the moment. In the 1970s and 1980s, Americans started feeling queasy about heroism. Those of us born in the sixties found ourselves on the cusp of that change. A sweep of new beliefs, priorities, and headlines has conspired to take our pantheon away from us.

Members of my generation believed in heroes when they were younger but now find themselves grasping for them. Even the word *hero* sounds awkward. I find myself embarrassed to ask people who their heroes are, because the word just doesn't trip off the tongue. My friend Katrin sounded irritated when I asked for hers. She said, "Oh, Jesus . . . Do people still have heroes?"

We don't. Certainly not in the traditional sense of adoring perfect people. Frequently not at all. "I'm sort of intrigued by the fact that I don't have heroes right off the top of my head," said a colleague, Peter. "Can I get back to you?"

Some of us are more upset about this than others. It's easy to tell which of us miss the heroic age. We are moved by schmaltzy political speeches, we warm up to stories of pets saving their owners, we even get misty-eyed watching the Olympics. We mope when model citizens fail us. My college roommate, Linda, remembers a seventh-grade class called "Heroes and She-roes." The first assignment was to write about a personal hero or she-ro. "I came home," Linda told me, "and cried and cried because I didn't have one. . . . Carter had screwed up in Iran and given the malaise speech. Gerald Ford was a nothing and Nixon was evil. My parents told me to write about Jane Fonda the political activist and I just kept crying."

Not everyone feels sentimental about it. A twentyish émigré raised in the former Soviet Union told me: "It's kind of anticlimactic to look for heroes when you've been brought up in a culture that insists on so many heroes. . . . What do you want me to say? Lenin? Trotsky?" Even though I grew up in the relatively propaganda-free United States, I understood. The America of my childhood insisted on heroes, too.

Of all the myths I happily ate for breakfast, the most powerful one was our story of revolution. I sang about it as early as kindergarten and read about it long after. The story goes, a few guys in wigs skipped town on some grumpy church leaders and spurned a loopy king to branch out on their

own. The children who hear the story realize they don't
have to believe in oldfangled clergy or a rusty crown—but
they had better believe in those guys with the wigs.

I sure did. I loved a set of books known as the "Meet"
series: *Meet George Washington, Meet Andrew Jackson, Meet
the Men Who Sailed the Seas,* and many more. I remember
one picture of an inspired Thomas Jefferson, his auburn
ponytail tied in a black ribbon, penning words with a
feather as a battle of banners and cannon fire raged behind
him.

A favorite "Meet" book starred Christopher Columbus.
His resistance to the flat-earth society of his day was
engrossing, especially to a kid like me who had trouble trying new foods let alone seeking new land masses. I identified with his yearning for a new world and his difficulty
with finding investors. Standing up to the king and queen
of Spain was like convincing your parents to let you do stuff
they thought was idiotic. Now, my allowance was only
thirty-five cents a week, but that didn't mean I wasn't going
to ask for three ships at some later date.

This is pretty embarrassing: I adored those guys. The
ones in the white powder and ponytails, the voluptuous
hats, the little breeches and cuffs. They were funny-looking,
but lovable. They did outrageous things without asking for
permission. They invented the pursuit of happiness.

I had a special fondness for Ben Franklin, statesman and
eccentric inventor. Inventions, like heroes, made me feel as
though I lived in a dull era. If I'd grown up at the end of the
nineteenth century, I could have spoken on early tele-
phones. A few decades later, I could have heard the new
sounds of radio. In the sixties, I could have watched black-
and-white TVs graduate to color.

Instead, I saw my colorful heroes demoted to black and
white. Mostly white. By the time I finished high school, it
was no longer hip to look up to the paternalistic dead white
males who launched our country, kept slaves and mis-
tresses, and massacred native peoples. Suddenly they
weren't visionaries but oppressors, or worse—objects. Sam-
uel Adams became a beer, John Hancock became a building,
and the rest of the guys in wigs were knocked off one by

one, in a whodunit that couldn't be explained away by the
fact of growing up.

The flag-waving of my youth, epitomized by America's
bicentennial, was a more loving homage than I know today.
The year 1976 rolled in while Washington was still reeling
from Saigon, but the irony was lost on me and my second-
grade classmates. The idea of losing seemed miles away. We
celebrated July fourth with wide eyes and patriotic parties.
Grown-ups had yet to tell themselves (so why should they
tell us?) that the young nation on its birthday had suffered
a tragic defeat.

Historians soon filled us in about that loss, and of others.
Discovering America was nothing compared to discovering
the flaws of its discoverers, now cast as imperialist sleaze,
racist and sexist and genocidal. All things heroic—human
potential, spiritual fervor, moral resplendence—soon
became suspect. With the possible exception of bodybuild-
ing, epic qualities went out of fashion. Some will remember
1992 as the year Superman died. Literally, the writers and
illustrators at *D.C. Comics* decided the guy was too old to
keep leaping buildings and rescuing an aging damsel in distress. When rumors circulated that he would be resurrected,
readers protested via calls to radio shows, letters to editors,
and complaints to stores that they were in no mood for such
an event.

A monster named Doomsday killed Superman, overcom-
ing him not with Kryptonite but with brute force. Who
killed the others? I blame improved modes of character
assassination, media hype artists, and scholars. The experts
told me that Columbus had destroyed cultures and ravaged
the environment. They also broke the news that the cow-
boys had brazenly taken land that wasn't theirs. In a way,
I'm glad I didn't know that earlier; dressing up as a cowgirl
for Halloween wouldn't have felt right. In a more urgent
way, I wish I had known it then so I wouldn't have had to
learn it later.

Just fifteen years after America's bicentennial came
Columbus's quincentennial, when several towns canceled
their annual parades in protest of his sins. Soon other festiv-
ities started to feel funny. When my aunt served corn pud-

ding last Thanksgiving, my cousin took a spoonful, then said drily that the dish was made in honor of the Indians who taught us to use corn before we eliminated them. Uncomfortable chuckles followed. Actually, neither "we" nor my personal ancestors had come to America in time to kill any Native Americans. Yet the holiday put us in the same boat with the pilgrims and anchored us in the white man's domain.

I am fascinated by how we become "we" and "they." It's as if siding with the establishment is the Alka-Seltzer that helps us stomach the past. To swallow history lessons, we turn into "we": one nation under God of proud but remorseful Indian killers. We also identify with people who look like us. For example, white northerners studying the Civil War identify both with white slaveholders and with northern abolitionists, aligning with both race and place. Transsexuals empathize with men and women. Immigrants identify with their homeland and their adopted country. Historians proposing a black Athena and a black Jesus have inspired more of such bonding.

I'll admit that these empathies can be empowering. I always understood the idea of feeling stranded by unlikely role models but never emotionally grasped it until I watched Penny Marshall's movie *A League of Their Own*. For the first time, I appreciated why so many women complain that sports bore them. I had enjoyed baseball before but never as intensely as I enjoyed the games in that film. The players were people like me. Lori Petty, petite, chirpy, wearing a skirt, commanded the pitcher's mound with such aplomb that I was moved. There's something to be said for identifying with people who remind us of ourselves, though Thomas Jefferson and Lori Petty look more like each other than either of them looks like me. I'll never know if I would've read the "Meet" books with more zeal if they'd described our founding mothers. I liked them as they were.

Despite the thrill of dames batting something on the big screen besides their eyelashes, the fixation on look-alike idols is disturbing for those who get left out. In the movie *White Men Can't Jump*, Wesley Snipes tells Woody Harrelson not to listen to Jimi Hendrix, because "White people can't hear Jimi." Does this joke imply that black people can't hear Mozart? That I can admire Geena Davis's batting but never appreciate Carlton Fisk? Besides dividing us from one another, these emotional allegiances divide us from potential heroes too, causing us to empathize with, say, General Custer and his last stand instead of with Sitting Bull and the victorious Sioux.

Rejecting heroes for having the wrong ethnic credentials or sex organs says less about our multicultural vision than our lack of imagination. By focusing on what we are instead of who we can become, by typecasting and miscasting our ideals—that's how we become "we" and "they." If heroes are those we'd like to emulate, it does make sense that they resemble us. But the focus on physical resemblance seems limited and racist.

Heroes should be judged on their deeds, and there are those with plenty in common heroically but not much in terms of ethnicity, nationality, or gender. Just look at Harriet Tubman and Moses; George Washington and Simón Bolívar; Mahatma Gandhi and Martin Luther King; Murasaki and Milton; Cicero and Ann Richards. Real paragons transcend nationality. It didn't matter to me that Robin Hood was English—as long as he did good, he was as American as a barbecue. It didn't matter to Queen Isabella that Columbus was Italian as long as he sailed for Spain and sprinkled her flags about. The British epic warrior Beowulf was actually Swedish. Both the German hero Etzel and the Scandinavian hero Atli were really Attila, king of the Huns. With all this borrowing going on, we shouldn't have to check the passports of our luminaries; the idea that we can be like them not literally but spiritually is what's uplifting in the first place.

The idea that we can never be like them has led to what I call jealousy journalism. You know, we're not remotely heroic so let's tear down anyone who is. It's become hard to remember which papers are tabloids. Tell-all articles promise us the "real story"—implying that greatness can't be real. The safe thing about *Meet George Washington* was that you couldn't actually meet him. Today's stories and pictures bring us closer. And actually meeting your heroes isn't the best idea. Who wants to learn that a favorite saint is really just an egomaniac with a publicist?

Media maestros have not only knocked public figures off their pedestals, they've also lowered heroism standards by idealizing just about everyone. Oprah, Geraldo, and the rest turn their guests into heroes of the afternoon because they overcame abusive roommates, childhood disfigurement, deranged spouses, multiple genitalia, cheerleading practice, or zany sexual predilections. In under an hour, a studio audience can hear their epic sagas told.

While TV and magazine producers helped lead heroes to their graves, the academic community gave the final push. Just as my peers and I made our way through college, curriculum reformers were promoting "P.C." agendas at the expense of humanistic absolutes. Scholars invented their own tabloidism, investigating and maligning both dead professors and trusty historical figures. Even literary theory helped, when deconstructionists made it trendy to look for questions instead of answers, for circular logic instead of linear sense, for defects, contradictions, and the ironic instead of meaning, absolutes, and the heroic.

It was the generations that preceded ours who killed off our heroes. And like everyone who crucified a superstar, these people thought they were doing a good thing. The professors and journalists consciously moved in a positive direction—toward greater tolerance, openness, and realism—eliminating our inspirations in the process. The death of an era of hero worship was not the result of the cynical, clinical materialism too often identified with my generation. It was the side effect of a complicated cultural surgery, of an operation that may have been necessary and that many prescribed.

So with the best of intentions, these storytellers destroyed bedtime stories. Which is too bad for the kids, because stories make great teachers. Children glean by example. You can't tell a child "Be ingenious," or "Do productive things." You can tell them, "This Paul Revere person jumped on a horse at midnight, rode wildly through the dark, figured out where the mean British troops were coming to attack the warm, fuzzy, sweet, great-looking colonists, and sent messages by code, igniting our fight for freedom," and they'll get the idea. America's rugged values come gift wrapped in the frontier tales of Paul Bunyan, Daniel Boone, Davy Crockett—fables of independence and natural resources. Kids understand that Johnny Appleseed or Laura Ingalls Wilder would never need a Cuisinart. Pioneer and prairie stories convey the fun of roughing it, showing kids how to be self-reliant, or at least less spoiled.

Children catch on to the idea of imitating qualities, not literal feats. After returning his storybook to the shelf, little Billy doesn't look around for a dragon to slay. Far-off stories capture the imagination in an abstract but compelling way, different from, say, the more immediate action-adventure flick. After watching a James Bond film festival, I might fantasize about killing the five people in front of me on line at the supermarket, while legends are remote enough that Columbus might inspire one to be original, but not necessarily to study Portuguese or enlist in the navy. In tales about conquerors and cavaliers, I first flirted with the idea of ideas.

Even Saturday-morning cartoons served me as parables, when I woke up early enough to watch the classy Superfriends do good deeds. Sure, the gender ratio between Wonder Woman and the gaggle of men in capes seemed unfair, but I was rapt. I wonder whether I glued myself to my television and my high expectations with too much trust, and helped to set my own heroes up for a fall.

Some heroes have literally been sentenced to death by their own followers. *Batman* subscribers, for example, were responsible for getting rid of Batman's sidekick, Robin. At the end of one issue, the Joker threatened to kill the Boy Wonder, and readers could decide whether Robin lived or died by calling one of two "900" numbers. The public voted overwhelmingly for his murder. I understand the impulse of those who dialed for death. At a certain point, eternal invincibility grows as dull and predictable as wearing a yellow cape and red tights every day of the year. It's not human. We get fed up.

My generation helped to kill off heroism as teenagers, with our language. We used heroic words that once described brave deeds—*excellent, amazing, awesome*—to describe a good slice of pizza or a sunny day. In our everyday speech, *bad* meant good. *Hot* meant cool. In the sarcastic slang of street gangs in Los Angeles, *hero* currently means traitor, specifically someone who snitches on a graffiti artist.

Even those of us who lived by them helped shatter our own myths, which wasn't all negative. We discovered that even the superhero meets his match. Every Achilles needs a podiatrist. Every rhapsodically handsome leader has a mistress or a moment of moral ambiguity. We injected a dose of reality into our expectations. We even saw a viable presidential candidate under a heap of slung mud, a few imperfections, an alleged tryst or two.

We're used to trysts in a way our elders aren't. Our parents and grandparents behave as if they miss the good old days when adulterers wore letter sweaters. They feign shock at the extramarital exploits of Thomas Jefferson, Frank Sinatra, JFK, Princess Di. Their hero worship is a romance that falters when beloved knights end up unfaithful to their own spouses. People my age aren't amazed by betrayal. We are suspicious of shining armor. Even so, tabloid sales escalate when a Lancelot gives in to temptation—maybe because the jerk who cheats on you somehow becomes more attractive. Other generations have gossiped many of our heroes into philanderers. The presumptuous hero who breaks your heart is the most compelling reason not to get involved in the first place.

Seeing your legends discredited is like ending a romance with someone you loved but ultimately didn't like. However much you longed to trust that person, it just makes more sense not to. Why pine away for an aloof godlet who proves unstable, erratic, and a rotten lover besides? It's sad to give up fantasies but mature to trade them in for healthier relationships grounded in reality.

We require a new pantheon: a set of heroes upon whom we can rely, who will not desert us when the winds change, and whom we will not desert. It's unsettling, if not downright depressing, to go through life embarrassed about the identity of one's childhood idols.

Maybe we should stick to role models instead. Heroes

have become quaint, as old-fashioned as gas-guzzlers—and as unwieldy, requiring too much investment and energy. Role models are more like compact cars, less glam and roomy but easier to handle. They take up less parking space in the imagination. Role models have a certain degree of consciousness about their job. The cast members of "Beverly Hills 90210," for example, have acknowledged that they serve as role models for adolescents, and their characters behave accordingly: they refrain from committing major crimes; they overcome inclinations toward substance abuse; they see through adult hypocrisy; and any misdemeanors they do perpetrate are punished. For moral mediators we could do better, but at least the prime-time writing staff is aware of the burden of having teen groupies.

Heroes don't have the luxury of staff writers or the opportunity to endorse designer jeans. Hercules can't go on "Nightline" and pledge to stop taking steroids. Prometheus can't get a presidential pardon. Columbus won't have a chance to weep to Barbara Walters that he didn't mean to endanger leatherback turtles or monk seals or the tribes of the Lucayas. Elizabeth I never wrote a best-seller about how she did it her way.

Role models can go on talk shows, or even host them. Role models may live next door. While a hero might be a courageous head of state, a saint, a leader of armies, a role model might be someone who put in a three-day presidential bid, your local minister, your boss. They don't need their planes to go down in flames to earn respect. Role models have a job, accomplishment, or hairstyle worth emulating.

Rather than encompassing the vast kit and caboodle of ideals, role models can perform a little neat division of labor. One could wish to give orders like Norman Schwarzkopf but perform psychoanalysis like Lucy Van Pelt, to chair a round-table meeting as well as King Arthur but negotiate as well as Queen Esther, to eat like Orson Welles but look like Helen of Troy, and so forth. It was General Schwarzkopf, the most tangible military hero for anyone my age, who vied instead for role-model status by claiming on the cover of his book: *It Doesn't Take a Hero*. With this title he modestly implies that anyone with some smarts and élan could strategize and storm as well as he has.

Role models are admirable individuals who haven't given up their lives or livelihoods and may even have a few hangups. They don't have to be prone to excessive self-sacrifice. They don't go on hunger strikes; they diet. They are therefore more likely than heroes to be free for lunch, and they are oftener still alive.

Heroism is a living thing for many of my contemporaries. In my informal poll, I not only heard sob stories about the decline of heroes, I also discovered something surprising: the ascent of parents. While the founding fathers may be passé, actual mothers, fathers, grands, and great-grands are undeniably "in." An overwhelming number of those I polled named their household forebears as those they most admired. By choosing their own relatives as ideals, people in their twenties have replaced impersonal heroes with the most personal role models of all. Members of my purportedly lost generation have not only realized that it's time to stop believing in Santa Claus, they have chosen to believe instead in their families—the actual tooth fairy, the real Mr. and Mrs. Claus. They have stopped needing the folks from the North Pole, the guys with the wigs, the studs and studettes in tights and capes.

In a way it bodes well that Superman and the rest could be killed or reported missing. They were needed to quash the most villainous folks of all: insane communists bearing nuclear weapons, heinous war criminals, monsters named Doomsday. The good news about Superman bleeding to death was that Doomsday died in the struggle.

If the good guys are gone, so is the world that divides down the middle into good guys and bad guys. A world without heroes is a rigorous, demanding place, where things don't boil down to black and white but are rich with shades of gray; where faith in lofty, dead personages can be replaced by faith in ourselves and one another; where we must summon the strength to imagine a five-dimensional future in colors not yet invented. My generation grew up to see our world shift, so it's up to us to steer a course between naïveté and nihilism, to reshape vintage stories, to create stories of spirit without apologies.

I've heard a few. There was one about the woman who taught Shakespeare to inner-city fourth graders in Chicago who were previously thought to be retarded or hopeless. There was the college groundskeeper and night watchman, a black man with a seventh-grade education, who became a contracts expert, wrote poetry and memoirs, and invested his salary so wisely that he bequeathed 450 acres of mountainous parkland to the university when he died. There was the motorcyclist who slid under an eighteen-wheeler at full speed, survived his physical therapy only to wind up in a plane crash, recovered, and as a disfigured quadriplegic started a business, got happily married, and ran for public office; his campaign button bore a caption that said "Send me to Congress and I won't be just another pretty face. . . ."

When asked for her heroes, a colleague of mine spoke of her great-grandmother, a woman whose husband left her with three kids in Galicia, near Poland, and went to the United States. He meant to send for her, but the First World War broke out. When she made it to America, her husband soon died, and she supported her family; at one point she even ran a nightclub. According to the great-granddaughter, "When she was ninety she would tell me she was going to volunteer at the hospital. I would ask how and she'd say, 'Oh, I just go over there to read to the old folks.' The 'old folks' were probably seventy. She was a great lady."

My grandmother saved her family, too, in the next great war. She did not live to see the age of the fax, but she did see something remarkable in her time, more remarkable even than the emperor riding down the street: she saw him walking down the street. I used to ask her, "Did you really see the emperor Franz Josef walking down the street?"

She would say, "Ya. Walking down the street." I would laugh, and though she'd repeat it to amuse me, she did not see what was so funny. To me, the emperor was someone you met in history books, not on the streets of Vienna. He was larger than life, a surprising pedestrian. He was probably just getting some air, but he was also laying the groundwork for my nostalgia of that time when it would be natural for him to take an evening stroll, when those who were larger than life roamed cobblestones.

Today, life is larger.

AIDS AND THE APOCALYPTIC IMAGINATION

Stephen Beachy

TWENTYSOMETHING

We have MTV attention spans, right? We think in sound-bite images. More interested in mood and suggestiveness than sustained, logical argument. We grew up with punk, take corruption for granted. We're more frightened of boredom than violence. We use television as a toy or a clock: when the second commercial break in "Donahue" ends, we know it's time to go to work at our temporary telemarketing job. We're definable, white, and disaffected. This would obviously be reflected in the essays we write.

POSITIVE

After we tested positive, we became kleptomaniacs. Traveled across the country, shoplifted $1,500 worth of books from B Daltons and Waldenbooks and other Kmart-owned chains. As if now that the figure of DEATH loomed larger, an electronic skeleton in a suit and tie, rattling his scythe over our bed, there was nothing we wanted more than to curl up in a living-room chair for the rest of our lives, reading. Instead of letting go, we became acquisitive, stealing all the things we'd never owned. A blender, toaster, coffee grinder, new shoes, black baggy Levi's . . . Ours was a typical American response to the threat of death, the loss of meaning, collapse. Microcosm of America in the eighties? The whole century? Waste piling up, plastic doohickeys, Styrofoam cartons, last week's fashion, useless things and objects and stuff, food by-products, crap you don't know WHAT it is. Who needs all this shit, really? We started stealing vitamins instead, megadoses of vitamin C, coenzyme Q-10, beta-carotene, blue-green algae, NAC, every nutritional supplement that somebody somewhere has claimed is helpful for HIV infection. 1,000 mcg of B12 a day, garlic extracts, Chinese herbs, we'll try anything. We've never felt healthier, more energized. We only know we're sick because anonymous lab technicians said it was true, but we're virtually vibrating. You can recognize us by that Spirulina glow.

No, it wasn't exactly *The Living End*. Nice premise; two attractive, HIV+ queer boys run amok, rob banks, shoot bigots, but a truly awful film, and we had no desire to live it out. Tennessee Williams is a little more our style, sultry melodrama, with plenty of whiskey and broken dishes. I did wind up in jail for a couple of hours in Des Moines after getting greedy at the Valley West Mall—I'd never owned a $65 pair of pants in my life, why start now?—but was bailed out by my brother's band (Squidboy, "the only Des Moines band to be compared to Samuel Beckett"). My boyfriend nervously waited at the Record Den, stuck without transportation among all those white people, the aesthetic wasteland. Let me play the role of gay aesthete, the horrified queen . . . oh, honey, that civilization has GOT to GO. Postmodern homo boys; what a range of styles to choose from. Angry queers were in vogue for a while, but that's over, right? Kinda tired, kinda cliché. We're dignified now, soldierly, the boys and girls next door. Still, I get testy: I've been promised the end of the world since I was a kid, my Christian apocalyptic heritage, and I'm hoping I won't be disappointed. Please, everything burst.

NOTHING TO LOSE

Actually, that's a blatant lie. We've probably got years ahead of us without any symptoms, three to eight before we even

develop an unsightly rash, and by that time, so we're told,
AIDS will have easily developed into a chronic, manageable
disease. More treatments every day. A hopeful new class of
LTR inhibiting drugs, including curcumin, found in the
spice turmeric. If you could patent it, drug companies might
spend money on the needed research, but in the meantime
there're alternative therapies, Chinese medicine, acupunc-
ture, psychic surgeons. We put this photography chemical
called DNCB on our skin to stimulate the immune system,
leaving splotchy red circles here and there on our bodies.
I'm planning to participate in a voodoo ceremony soon, to
get possessed by OMOLU (also known as Babalu'-Aye'),
lame old god, god of plagues and their cure, master of time
and death. Wear white, head uncovered, the drums, *thump,
thump, thump,* a temporary loss of individual consciousness
as my body's mounted by a force or forces sweeping
through the quivering throng . . . Snakelike, undulating . . .
Meanwhile, we're advised to reduce our stress, keep holding
on, meditate, creatively visualize healing. HIV infection is in
no way, at this point, the same thing as a death sentence. If
it ever has been. How it functions in our imaginations is a
different story. We've been expected to die for so long that
we believe it ourselves, and live accordingly. We dream
about airplanes crashing, rotting trees, architecture in
flames. We want to kiss serpents and explode into fragments
in one final, glorious moment.

GENERATION X

Like everything else, we either are or aren't a myth,
depending on whose statistics you choose. We're called the
"second wave"—young gay men still seroconverting at an
impressive rate. Seroconversion, sort of sounds like a weird
religious ritual, doesn't it? Are you going to the seroconversion tomorrow night in the basement of the abandoned
church? Be sure to wear black. What we lose in peace of
mind, we gain in credibility at Act Up meetings. At this
point, let's face it, we're the least "innocent" of "victims," we
have no excuse, the barrage of safe-sex information, the free

condoms, *blah blah blah . . . Well, rubbers break. (Use two or three.) Maybe oral sex without ejaculation or fingerfucking isn't as safe as you thought. Maybe the antibodies take more than six months to show up in your bloodstream, so your negative test is no guarantee. The answer? Celibacy, of course. Masturbation, maybe, but be sure to wear rubber gloves. Fantasy. But we, the second wave, we obviously aren't sublimating very well. Maybe the image of death, a dark, sexy man in black, is something we find exciting. That's death as metaphor, of course, not sickness and putrefaction.*

STAR WARS

It's a hopelessly pervasive metaphor, this dark/light thing. Darkness is death, evil, matter, madness, femininity, and anyone who's not Caucasian. Light is the symbol for life and reason and stress-free evolutive New Age consciousness. What we're evolving into, the cyberspace cheerleaders will tell you, is something more akin to light. We'll leave our dark old apelike bodies behind, merge with information. There's a promise of something approximating immortality in there somewhere, as well as a subtle, but fairly obvious racist ideology. The body's a dying form, especially poor and non-Caucasian bodies, AIDS is just part of the *natural* evolutionary process. You have to take a broad general view of things . . .

Meanwhile, our bodies, Jonathan's and mine, are slowly being undermined. His is only twenty-three years old and covered by a silky golden skin. I can't tell how much pain it's received, just by touching it, I only know that from hearing his stories, lying next to him, night after night. Perhaps you know what it's like to be so in love with a handsome, dying young man, because you've seen it on TV. You had to dab the moisture from your eyes with a Kleenex, sniffle, blow your nose. Well, it isn't like that at all. It isn't a cathartic moment of tragedy, a mediated shorthand for grief. Here, in our lives, it is always happening. There are textures, smells, fevers. There are days when we don't even remember that it's there, so wrapped up in the real tragedy, which is not in our dying, but in our living: applying for ridiculous jobs, filling out forms, selling books to buy food, stealing vitamins. Shoplifting is hard work, so is applying for food stamps, and every pathetic moron of a boss with a part-time temporary position licking out toilet bowls wants a résumé, two interviews, work experience, and an associated degree: with two hundred applicants for every pitiful job, he gets them. The bullshit is getting us down. We are sad so often.

We lie together in the late afternoon. Jonathan's pale brown chest, my creamy arms, a penis, a thigh. Other than this, not much is going well. He's even more expendable than I am, because his skin's more brown. When I brush my lips against the darkest part of his body, the back of his neck, I feel skin, not darkness.

We aren't members of the General Population. I've never met the General Population, but I assume they're all white heterosexuals with money, who don't shoot speed. Here in my life, I hear it from friends and acquaintances (the non–General Population? the Specific Populations?) all the time: the idea that somebody's already got the cure, that AIDS is a designer syndrome. There's something eugenic in the air, something genocidal. Accusations are thrown about, that Native Americans are being infected through hepatitis vaccine on reservations, CIA experiments in the seventies, ties to swine fever. Paranoia mutates into new strains as quickly as the virus itself. Whether the death of huge numbers of "social undesirables" in this country is a conspiracy or simply a result of the way our society is structured may be irrelevant. The simple fact is: we are dying, and this makes a lot of people happy.

PUBLIC SPACE

We live in San Francisco, we're twenty-eight and twenty-three, we're in love. Last summer, we're sitting in a park on the top of Nob Hill, holding hands, smooching. We're accosted by this Christian, who follows us around the park, spewing hate and reading the Bible at us. Something about our pairing offends him, obviously. That we represent only

one gender? Two races? Two heights, two styles of dress, do
our musical tastes clash? Both of us have penises, it's true,
one's Caucasian, one's mulatto, one's tall, one not really, one
dresses like a street person with taste, one like an off-duty
cop, one listens to too much Sonic Youth, the other to D-
Train. Whatever it was that disturbed him, he suggested we
should "get out from underneath the sun." He taunted me
with "Are you giving your lover AIDS?" Well, despite the
necessary correction—you don't give anyone AIDS; you give
them the HIV virus, which is *probably* one of the most
important factors leading to AIDS—I may have been doing
just that, unawares. The idea made him so happy, who
wouldn't have wished a painful death on the man?

We tried to ignore him, moved away, he followed. This
went on for a good half hour. He was gleefully reading at us
about the destruction of Sodom, occasionally reminding us
that AIDS is punishment from "god." We just wanted to
relax and talk about Clarice Lispector, this wacky Brazilian
fiction writer. Finally, he got so offensive that my excellent
lover (I'll confess, he's the tall one) grabbed a bottle out of
the trash and raised it into the air, ready, so it seemed, to
bash the pesky little Christian's skull right into the pave-
ment, watch blood oozing this way and that. Go ahead, he
said; kill me. He wasn't afraid to die; he was expecting Jesus
to meet him at the pearly gates with cookies and milk and a
merit badge for harassing queers.

It's something that makes Christianity such a formidable
opponent, despite the fact that it's so obviously going
through its death throes; death is perceived as a reward, life
as a trial or war. Unfortunately, Christianity's death throes
could drag on for another few centuries and carry us along
into its own prescripted apocalypse. The man in the park
practiced Tai Chi with his equally tolerant friends, as training to combat the forces of darkness. I, one of those forces,
held my lover back; we didn't kill him, although we could
have, Tai Chi notwithstanding. Morals? Conviction? Thou
shalt not kill? No, simply the knowledge that my one true
love'd end up in some prison, where condoms are not made
available because the state of California doesn't want to promote sexual immorality among the inmates. It wants to

promote death. If I could have killed that man with no threat of reprisal, I certainly would have. As that overhyped band Jane's Addiction sang, back in their heyday in the early nineties: Some people should die; it's just common knowledge . . .

THE SCRIPT

I grew up in a heavily Christian environment, an avid fan of endtime ideologies. Plenty of guilt, salvation, repressed sexuality, and fire from above. Oh, I know not all Christians are morons; I've read Kierkegaard and Tillich. But I have an uncle who lives in the Ozarks, got on the Tomorrow Show back in the seventies when he stored his dead mother in a refrigerator, trusting that God would bring her back to life. Other relatives are Amish, sweet people really, pacifists who don't beat up anyone except their children. My parents were nice Mennonites; we lived in the suburbs and strip malls which could have been most anywhere but were, in fact, in Iowa. What a guilt-ridden, unhappy little twelve-year-old gay-boy I was. I believed in Jesus, both the mellow hippie version and the apocalyptic conqueror. Now, I know a teen-ager who begs for spare change on Polk Street; he's got a leather jacket with a depiction of the crucifixion on the back and the single word SILLY. Yeah, it's hard to take the whole melodrama seriously, isn't it? But it does live on, outside and in.

The idea of apocalypse still obsesses me. I learned a pretty standard version from reading best-selling author Hal Lindsey as a kid, wildly stretched interpretation of the book of Revelations, as well as fragments of Ezekiel, Daniel, and the Gospels. It was exciting. The profit to be made by predicting doom is not surprising, nor is the ability to weasel out of past predictions once the deadline has passed. What may be surprising is how many of us seem to want the world to end. You can almost picture us, a whole nation of men and women, standing in cornfields, along highways, in public parks, erect penises, moist vaginas, watching the sky and waiting. Waco, Texas; need I say more? But there's a more institutionalized version. Here're the signs and markers for those of you curious to keep score as the holocaust unfolds: First, a Jewish state had to be reconstituted and the city of Jerusalem recaptured by that state. Next we get a united European confederacy, to correspond to the ten-headed beast of Revelations, the temple being rebuilt in Jerusalem, wars in the Mideast involving Russia, all leading up to the rapture (when all the good Christians just sort of vanish, meet Jesus in the sky or another dimension or someplace) and the mark of the beast (probably the Universal Product Code) implemented under a semiglobal culture headed by a false messianic savior. And then, it all goes up in smoke, trumpets, angels, chariots, and nuclear bombs . . .

Simply quaint folklore if we hadn't watched our nation slip dangerously close to the status of theocracy during the eighties.

> Israel is the only stable democracy we can rely on as a spot where Armageddon could come.
>
> —*X-President R. Reagan*

Return of the Repressed

Christian apocalypse is hardly the only version we have to contend with. Everybody's anxious for destruction or rebirth. The current vogue is to look past the year 2000, to the year 2010 (dawning of the age of Aquarius) or 2012 (end of the Mayan calendar). The spectrum of New Age thought is rife with a lust for catastrophic revitalization, renewal, an evolutionary leap. But 2012? Just in time for the boomers to evade death, I guess, but kinda disappointing if you ask me. Who can wait twenty years?

All the loose ends tied up. How convenient. A final confrontation of good vs. evil, black vs. white, darkness vs. light. Dividing things in two, looks like I'm in the column under DARKNESS; I'm not only sexually unclean, I'm infected, I'm a walking symbol of DEATH. Liberation movement for the nineties: I am DEATH, hear me roar.

TENDER

Sometimes I wake up early in the morning and watch Jonathan sleep. Most people look especially lovable, fragile, when asleep and it makes me feel tender. I want to stroke his head softly, comfort him. I don't want to hurt people, most of the time. Other times, however, I dream of this city in ruins, gunfire, explosions, the whole mess bursting wide open. I don't want my dying to be cut off from everyone else. I'm nauseated by the General Population. I admire the stereotypical image of violent young African-American males. Jonathan says that the glamorization of that violence, the whole gangsta image, is stupid and tired and usually self-destructive. He'd know better than I would; he grew up with men like that and suffered because he was a sweet boy and kind and gay. Now he's six feet four and takes no shit from anyone. But my fantasy, my very Caucasian fantasy, is of darkness, of violence unleashed on the land: the suburbs I came from, the strip malls, the Christian churches going up in flames, at the hands of young African-American males. Jon says those gangstas aren't burning down any malls; they are the malls. Still, to me, this fantasy is sexually exciting.

POSTMODERN

Another identity to try on:

We, queer men, have sometimes understood our particular role in society as being about the exploration of freedom and its limits. Pursuing a kind of knowledge tied up with death and sexuality. Is this true? I hate it when people use the first-person plural; it assumes too much: that one can be a spokesperson, that one can represent the "gay perspective."

Try it again: I, a queer man, have sometimes understood my role as being about the exploration of freedom and its limits. Pursuing a kind of knowledge tied up with death and sexuality. Something about expending energy, impermanence, a mobility free from the constraints of breeding.

Granted, I missed out on the carnival of sexual exploration
that took place in the seventies. It's been raised now to the
status of a mythic age—ah, the bars! the baths! There's this
real generational thing here that the boomers have about
informing us we missed the party, we got here too late, and
it goes way beyond gay culture. The "golden age" of rock
and roll, when white musicians learned how to rip off black
R & B artists and market their ideas. Sex, drugs, and music
neatly wrapped up in a package touted as being about political activism. Back when young people still had ideals, and
so on. I could care less about the bars and baths, really.
Promiscuity and anonymous sex are hardly the only avenues
for exploration, and the exchange of bodily fluids isn't necessary either. What's lacking may just be a mood. Of festival,
of pushing limits. It's not death itself that's dampened that
energy; it's the particular manner of dying, slow, drawn out,
the sickness of it. We've witnessed the body's gradual decay,
the stench and memory loss and unsightly rashes. No fireworks, no implosion, no James Dean car crash. What if the
disease involved instead the possibility that one might spon-
taneously combust during intercourse? If anything, there'd
be an increase in the attendance at the bars and baths, and
not just among gay men.

What am I saying? The apocalypse, like violent individual
death, is, and has always been, an erotic idea. At the same
time, if AIDS has robbed us of certain freedoms, certain avenues for exploration, it has provided us with others. It has
the potential to free up the imagination—my imagination,
the imaginations of gay and queer men, of all those living
with HIV, and of the culture at large, by tying death, real,
visible, physical death as a driving force to that imagination.
I don't want to make the mistake of celebrating the renaissance in the arts that is sometimes attributed to AIDS, at the
expense of the lives of actual artists. But serious thought
about death should tie us somehow to ideas of freedom,
shouldn't it? Arguably the most interesting North American
queer male writing fiction these days is Dennis Cooper, with
his intense, obsessional narratives about, among other
things, the desire to open the bodies of handsome young

men and find out what's inside. Figuring out what the limits to individual freedom are: whose freedom and at whose expense? Pursuing a kind of knowledge tied up with death and sexuality, but well aware of the position, and freedom, of the other, through whose dead body this kind of knowledge has traditionally been acquired. He's emerged from the debris of punk culture with a hard, focused vision of emptiness and a yearning for something like transcendence. Yet behind his cloak of amorality he may represent a sort of moral vanguard, someone who is at least seriously asking these questions, and championing a new space in which to explore our obsessions with death and mass destruction.

> I have very early memories of an absolutely threatening world, which could crush us. To have lived as an adolescent in a situation that had to end, that had to lead to another world, for better or worse, was to have the impression of spending one's entire childhood in the night, waiting for dawn. That prospect of another world marked the people of my generation, and we have carried with us, perhaps to excess, a dream of Apocalypse.
>
> —*Michel Foucault*

NOSTALGIA

I remember masses of bodies bouncing into one another, the music so loud you could feel your inner organs trembling with the sound waves. Smoke and beer stench and sweaty bodies voluntarily receiving and inflicting pain in the pit in front of the stage. Some singer writhing with pain and loathing, and then, once in a while, among all the collective moods we're experiencing, a little rage, a little despair, a little euphoria, a lot of irony, nobody really takes this slash-and-burn stuff very seriously anymore, still, there's this moment, some chord or plateau of sound, and maybe, for just a second, you wanna cry. Something like transcendence. Destroy everything, mock everything, even your own emotions and poses, toss out all history and faith and future, dance to that sound, writhe to it, the sound of collapse. Even though nobody paid attention to the lyrics, nobody had too many illusions by that point about some great purity or honesty to hardcore, it was just energy, just music, just fun, background noise to meet sex partners by, whatever. But somewhere, in the heart of all that, I seem to remember something, some moment, at the very least. Give me that illusion, at least. A space so pure and empty that it slightly resembled the conception of Being that some of those Eastern religions use. You know, those religions our elders were so fond of, back in that decade they're always going on about. The fifties? I forget; I don't think I was born yet. Back when they wore bell-bottoms, you know.

DEFINED

"We," as a generation, have a particularly vivid relationship to the apocalypse. Yeah, I'm using the first-person plural AGAIN; even in quotation marks it's bad news. Pretty soon I'll be talking about THEM as well, as if the most important struggle going on in this country wasn't about class or race, but about generation. I'm warning you beforehand, ironically distancing myself from my own statements, so I can still have the pleasure of saying things that are ridiculously simplistic and lumping all sorts of diverse individuals into the category of "twentysomething" or "baby boomer." Like this: Think of how many simulations we watched on TV in our "formative years," how often the year 2000 has been evoked as some sort of crucial doorway. We take the nihilistic energy of punk for granted; we've been slam dancing all these years as preparation for the riots to come. With AIDS, sexuality has been tied more strongly in our imaginations to the idea of death. Our elders have been busy trying to theorize their way out of subjectivity, escape from the confines of the self, a possible solution to the apparent uselessness of individual existence, the apparent pointlessness of history. They've rendered beforehand anything we might try as already done, obsolete, unoriginal. Now, they're desperately trying to tell us who we are: we're either slackers, or we're "Beverly Hills 90210," sideburns, as easily defined by our hair as THEY were THIRTY years ago. Here, grab onto Kurt Cobain and Courtney Love as easy symbols to get a handle on us. Baby boomers have never been known for an ability to deal with complexity, despite their fawning over chaos theory and all those colorful fractals.

It's kind of great, isn't it, talking about human beings as if they only existed in groups, experienced only collective moods, could be statistically graphed and measured according to norms and generational trends. It's easy to buy into such definitions; after being told for so long that we have nothing of our own, no original youth culture or lifestyle, we'll jump at the opportunity: yeah, that's who we are, Seattle, flannel, grunge! I went to see the movie *Slacker* with my boyfriend; it said absolutely nothing to or about him, dealt only with Caucasians. His status as marginally employed isn't voluntary, and he'd never dream of raising it to the level of art form or ideology. He craves a little bit of luxury, some squandering and excess. As ideology, slacking is about minimalism, refusing to join in the orgy of consumption, if more cynically than the naive "tune in, turn on, drop out" of THIRTY years ago. But voluntary slacking is a small subculture, even within the larger group of the Caucasian middle class. It's sometimes mistaken for subversion, as if politely stepping aside from the feeding frenzy will bring late capitalism to its knees.

There are potentially subversive structures being put into place, it's true: the cassette culture that grew out of punk, bypassing the channels of the music industry, as well as the recently burgeoning zine culture, bypassing the censors and tastemakers of the publishing industry. A democratic proliferation of communication that's been receiving so much attention lately, it's threatening to break out into the vision of the "culture at large," taking with it the voices of runaway teenagers, black drag queens, S & M dykes, anarchist punks, pedophiles, and even some pissed-off heterosexual white boys. Any structural foundation to help us proliferate communication, set up networks of resistance, or at least potential resistance, is a "good" thing: these are positive, proactive steps, which are giving voice to tons of interesting fringe types (such as postboomers) who might otherwise be trapped in the invisibility that in our culture is virtually the same thing as nonexistence.

If everyone would rely on such networks for their information we might be getting somewhere, but meanwhile, there're Rupert Murdoch and what's-his-face Hearst buying up newspapers, there's Jerry Falwell bidding on the UPI. This storming of the reality studios the baby boomers were supposed to do has mostly resulted in watered-down images of the past, images and ideas that were supposed to be revolutionary THIRTY years ago. Designs that look pretty when you're on hallucinogens won't necessarily help create some great change in consciousness if you stick them on a billboard for Macy's. That people who used to protest authority, war, and other equally vague concepts have now mastered the propaganda machine is not particularly reassuring. We've recently watched our grandparents' generation hand over power to our parents' generation. Break out the champagne. As the excellent, yet barely THIRTY poet Joshua Clover put it: Fleetwood Mac, houseband of the revolution. Meanwhile, if you'll allow me to be melodramatic for a moment, I'm dying.

SLACKING

For now, it's fine. Nobody really gets hurt and white kids can feel as if they're experiencing poverty. Which they certainly are—poverty: 1. being poor—want; 2. scarcity or lack; 3. inferiority, poorness. Yeah, really, it's pretty excellent; buy your clothes off the street, work as little as possible, get food stamps, dabble in the sex industry, temp jobs, this or that scam, always rip off your employers. Then you discover that you need health insurance, that every therapy and medication you need to stay healthy is part of some enormous profit-generating industry feeding off sick bodies. This is not a metaphor. Take a short walk through our pleasant hospital hallways, take a tour through all the scrubbed and stinky structures of our health-care systems and the metaphorical quality of vampirism will elude you: our sick bodies are literally feeding thousands.

WHILE I'M ON THE SUBJECT OF HOSPITALS...

What is wrong with hospitals is not only that they are places where human bodies are treated as just that—bodies, to be probed, researched, and fondled—but that in the process of trying to put a cheery face on death and dying, they've eliminated all life, all difference. Following a very Caucasian aesthetic of "pleasantness" in decor, an environment so bland and homogeneous that it pretends to be universal, a space has been created akin to a spiritual void. It might be more interesting and more explicit to design them to resemble medieval torture chambers. Why not rock-and-roll wings, literate wings, wings being overtaken by vegetation, wings for people who hate Muzak and paintings of sunsets? With all the talk of health-care reform, we might consider serious reform of the whole idea of what hospitals are, how they function, whom they serve. Hospitals encourage us to die. How many times in the past few months alone have I heard somebody living with HIV say that they won't die in a hospital, they won't die after a prolonged illness, they'll do it themselves. I feel the same. My fear is not so much of death—whatever that whole business is about, I'll end up there anyway—it's of hospitals. It's the scene from all those TV melodramas that have so shaped my idea of what I don't want "reality" to resemble. The family and doctors gathered around the bed, the machines that go PING, the tasteless flowers and paintings. Bad carpeting, no doubt. Oh, no. No, really, not for me.

OTHER OPTIONS

Slack away, my friends: isn't time what life is made of? Or wait, no, time is money. Weird, if you really think that's been said in complete seriousness, by somebody who's dead now. As for me, I've got three and a half years before I even get that first unsightly rash, I'll be over THIRTY by then, well past the age when I'll worry about physical appearance, sex appeal. Oops, wait, latest blood tests are in, T-cells dropping faster than predicted, revise that estimate . . . Maybe simply refraining from consumption is losing some of its charm as lifestyle. I'm no longer so entertained by simply excusing myself from the table of excess, excess cars, excess nouvelle cuisine, excess information, excess entertainment, excess money to be made from AZT studies, excess appliances, excess malls, retail outlets, high-rise condos, espresso outlets, gentrified neighborhoods, banks, computerized corporations . . . Maybe it's time to start destroying.

APOCALYPSE NOW

A little festival night of madness? An orgiastic carnival, à la Rabelais, the Dark Ages, tying death back in to collective ritual, the community, the superabundance of the ever-regenerating Earth? Cool, dude. A little rampage? A few riots? Arson, looting? Dead cops, curfews, the National Guard, a nuclear blast. Imagine the awesome visuals, the feelings of UNITY and TOGETHERNESS and GLOBAL BROTHERHOOD as we all die together. Sort of like the harmonic convergence with napalm.

> I believe that the catastrophe story, whoever may tell it, represents a constructive and positive act by the imagination rather than a negative one, an attempt to confront the terrifying void of a patently meaningless universe by challenging it at its own game, to remake zero by provoking it in every conceivable way.
>
> —J. G. Ballard

CHANGE

It's a commonplace that we live in a death-repressing culture. Another commonplace is that our cultures are in need of vast structural changes, our ideas of government, medicine, gender, science, the family. And another: The nineties will make the sixties look like _____. (Fill in the blank with whatever metaphor of tameness and stability and ineffectuality you prefer.) If we repeat it enough, it just might come true; chant it like a mantra: RADICAL CHANGE RADICAL CHANGE RADICAL CHANGE. As we approach the end of the millennium, or even the year 2012 if you like, we'll likely witness, and take part in, an increase in apocalyptic thinking, radical thinking, frenzies and orgies and violence, too. Will riots just become further justification for genocide? *Dude!* Evolution, not *revolution* . . . But wait. Could we use that apocalyptic energy to create positive social change? What does "positive" social change consist of? More entitlement programs, bigger welfare checks? Tiny percentage cuts in defense spending? A strong leader who'll use the Marines to protect the rain forests instead of protecting the interests of oil companies? A new world order of global, environmentally concerned fascism?

I could easily lose myself in conspiracy theories, render myself incapable of action, decide that anything I do is what THEY want me to do. They're waiting for any excuse to implement the control mechanisms, more surveillance cameras everywhere you turn, a public more and more willing to do away with civil liberties in the face of carefully manipulated panics about crime and drugs and missing children. And AIDS. Or, I could try to step past all that, in the freedom that the idea of death, my death, even a highly unlikely global death holds out to me. Render myself capable of most anything, call everything open to question, right now. Refuse to accept the idea that exploration is really about a love of the boot, coming down to squash it. Refuse to accept the idea of too much freedom. Embrace that risk, for the sake of something, a temporary autonomous zone, as Hakim Bey says, of the spirit. Build alternative spaces and networks that might endure, or might endure only as legend, or might not leave any trace at all—and maybe that's the point.

I know these are words, and easy to write. Really, alone late some afternoons, Jonathan out looking for work or stealing vitamins, I fall asleep slowly, exhausted, feeling my self disintegrate, drifting so far away from everything in the dimming light. Outside it's sunny and windy and cold and I feel that I never want to leave this room again. I wake up in the dark, a couple of hours later, my throat burning, confused, not knowing who or where I am. Everything seems bleak and horrible. If I could crumble the "existent order" by telephone at those moments, as easily as ordering out for Chinese food, you could consider it done. I just feel weak and tired.

The word *freedom* is tossed around so much, what can it mean in a body like this? Always temporary, and even that bought with a prosperity built on the dying bodies underneath us. The word's virtually meaningless. Would you die for freedom? Your own, somebody else's, or some abstract concept that could exist in some imagined future? Sacrifice yourself for the building of this great global structure that will give each and every one of us a comfortable, if claustrophobic space? Build, build, build.

One important function that slackers are serving is to question this whole idea of "work" as something to be valued. That crazy French guy, Bataille, was always opposing the concept of work with that of eroticism. One was slowly building, saving, looking toward the future. The other was expending what had been saved, wildly, with abandon, denying the reality of work, the future, anything but RIGHT NOW. The central question, then, becomes NOT how to maintain our standard of living, how to make sure we have as much stuff as our parents did, not even how to keep on progressing toward an EVER MORE JUST society. The central question becomes individual, cultural, global DEATH.

I Think about Death

We've attended these workshops on how to stay healthy with HIV, my boyfriend and I, and the main thesis I've come away with is one of PRESERVATION. Nothing excessive, no stress, a soothing daily ritual without drugs or coffee or angry pulsing rap music. Just stay cool, and keep existing. In the hopes, I suppose, that a cure will be found and we'll be able to go back to our old ways, the tension that is the source of most of our pleasure. So, I've been thinking about this a lot. At what point do I want to give it up, burn myself up in some final burst, pursuing "something like transcendence," some sort of ecstasy? Here we all are, relentlessly marching toward nonexistence, forced to think about something as weird as time in terms of quality vs. quantity.

PROPAGANDA

I get busted shoplifting again, some E, some C, some garlic extract. The only irritating thing is the self-righteous security guard, convinced that everyone who steals is on drugs. He thinks I'm selling the vitamins on the street to buy heroin or speed.

Afterward, we wait for the bus, my lover and I, arms full of information about this syndrome, these diseases we're at risk for. On the bus stop, a poster educates us about gay bashings: FOUR TEENS STAB GAY MAN ON VAN NESS, and it relates the details of the crime, the man's horror, the escape by the perpetrators without punishment. This is not an education I want for myself or anyone else. Gays as victims, easy targets, pathetic and abused. I don't want heterosexuals to feel sorry for me; I don't want anyone's pity. I'm looking to form alliances, not to cry in public and have my grief "acknowledged." If there's anything I'd like to do in public, it's die, when the time comes, not as spectacle, to be analyzed, explained away, added to tallies, showing up on T-shirts or baseball caps or quilts. Listen, some of my relatives are Amish, those people make quilts, NOT my friends, NOT my lover. Knitting in the face of death? How about an AIDS memorial TIME BOMB, an AIDS memorial RIOT? When I die I want to unleash something into the environment, some sort of energy, an explosion. Of freedom? Revolt? The concept's still kind of abstract, but I'm working on it. Maybe what's needed is a lesson, to institutions, religions, medical bureaucracy, all this bad structure we're surrounded with, HOW TO DIE, preferably with a certain sense of style. I want to smash those bus stop posters, if somebody's trying to do ME a favor, put up some posters that say: BASHERS ATTEMPT TO BEAT UP GAY MAN. HE SHOOTS THEM. THEY'RE DEAD NOW. I don't care if the images aren't "true"; give me a break. After Reagan, Desert Storm, the reporting of the L.A. riots, you want the facts, please, nothing but the facts?

The presentation of this threat in the media, however, can play a decisive role as a possible genuine threat. For firstly, the fear of a real end of the world on a global scale is public mischief. Anyone who insists that this might happen has no idea of biochemistry, that is, of the power of organic matter to regenerate itself; and when he talks of apocalypse he is referring rather to his own chances of survival than to those of the universe.

—Dieter Lenzen

In Retrospect, a Blur

What am I saying? That we should promote destruction, if not for political reasons, because it's fun? But in the meantime, build a better health-care system? Apocalypse is good? Death makes us free? Twentysomethings are poised to wreak havoc on the world? I feel this essay disintegrating, losing its focus. At least in this way, it too can serve as metaphor. For my body? Our culture? So dispersed that only death or apocalypse can give it back a sense of unity? My life, our history, now that it's over, it's clear enough, there always was a point and that was it. To end.

But the world won't end, even though I might like it to, fireworks to amuse me on my deathbed. They say that males have this problem, particularly, of being unable to identify with anything or anyone beyond their own ego. No, nothing should end, things should multiply, fluctuate, proceed in a sly, continuous mutation. Snakelike, undulating. Shedding the skin when its time is over, just like that.

"WHAT SET YOU FROM, FOOL?"

Paul Beatty

For my homeboys and me, Los Angeles summer afternoons meant running from baby Crips, asking the police why they were frisking us, and sneaking across the border into ritzy Cheviot Hills, where we would climb fences to look at backyard pools. "Hey, check out that slide!" We quickly learned that the world is gang related. Each of us, whether we like it or not, rolls with a multiplicity of identity posses, which leapfrog into position depending on the situation. My principal identity is antiestablishment black man, but if I get caught with a bag of hashish in Turkey, you can bet money I'll be shouting "American citizen! *Soy un Americano!*" Some identity gangs we join wittingly, finding affirmation in visions and goals shared by others. You remember the shirts "Black by Popular Demand." Other social sets jump us in against our wills, forcing us to submit to burdensome expectations and legacies. I think of Crips putting in work for a 'hood they'd rather not live in, white people steadfastly dissociating themselves from a torrid history of brutality, and Al Pacino in *The Godfather, Part I.* The gangs that hold down our neighborhoods shape our identities by establishing and enforcing boundaries, behavioral and psychic. They use territorial graffiti to convey messages of belongingness to residents, prisoners, and intruders.

Westside Crip   18th Street Vatos Locos   Beverly Hills 90210
Girls' Gym   Employee Entrance   By prospectus only   No
money down   Exact change required   We take food stamps
No tennis shoes   No hats   No khakis

The pain-in-the-ass aspect to running with any of the
American ethnic gender sexual-preference class gangs is that
each cultural clicka follows a different set of rules. In gyms
and playgrounds across the country b-ballers run through a
stock list of questions in order to familiarize themselves with
the local ground rules. The ceremonial staccato bantering
starts when the ball is put in play. "What's game?" "Everything back or airballs and steals straight-up?" "Is the pole
in or out?" A versatile player learns to adapt to different
neighborhood hegemonies without compromising individual style. In seventh grade, my best friend, Toi, got bussed
to an all-white junior-high school. My friends and I used to
trip watching Toi answering the phone, metamorphosing in
and out of social standards, depending on who called. If an
affluent, split-level Tudor-style white kid was on the line,
Toi slouched and went into his California Caucasian drawl:
"Fer sure, I'm stoked. We'll party. Later days, dude." When
it was one of the local heads calling with the haps for the
weekend, Toi dropped his voice a couple of octaves: "You
know thaaat. That jams gonna be live as fuck. Awwwight
later, cuz." Though we mercilessly teased Toi about being a
cultural chameleon, he was only trying on the colors of different gangs until he found a jacket that fit.

Sometimes even your skin doesn't fit. I remember my first
day of school after moving from hippy white Santa Monica
to black Los Angeles. I walked into Ms. Glucksman's fourth-
grade class wearing a smile and a brown pair of size
slim Sears Toughskins. I'd never seen so many Afro-Amer-
icans in my life. My rhythm was strange. I walked funny.
I talked funny. Sheepishly I underwent the new kid third
degree.

"Where you from?"

"Santa Monica."

"Where's that at?"

"Where you stay at?"

"Hunh?"

"Stay" sounded very transitory. I didn't live in no home or nothing.

"Where do you live?"

"Oh, right across the street."

"Damn, nigga, check out your pants. When's the flood? This fool sportin' some serious highwaters."

I started thinking, "I get it, these is the niggers the white folks in Santa Monica thought I was." I finally had a reference group for the slurs and bullshit I had tolerated for nine years. I didn't know what a nigger was, only that I shouldn't be one. The only things remotely black about me then were my skin color and out-of-control Afro, which looked like the sun's corona around my head, solar flares n' all. I knew I was black; I just didn't behave black. I did have an idea of the consequence of being black, and it had nothing to do with Martin Luther King's "Content of a Man's Character" speech. In third grade Ms. Freeman chose not to place me in the top-secret after-school group for advanced readers, despite my having passed the number-two pencil tests. My uppity mother complained to get me, one of two Negroes in the entire school, into the class. All this so I could learn words like *serape* and *sombrero*. In second grade this tow-headed Dennis the Menace cowlick white boy called me a "nigger." I knew enough about being black to jump his ass at the sound of the three-o'clock bell. After that I was hostile toward my rock fight partners David, Steven, and Ralph. Attempting to cool me out, Ralph and I looked up *nigger* in the dictionary. It wasn't in there. To our kid logic that meant that *nigger* wasn't a word.

"See, Paul, there is no such thing as a nigger."

"Yeah, but *snot-boogieman* isn't in there either and we call Erik that every day. What about, *niggardly,* and *niggle?*"

"Those words mean 'cheap' and 'stingy.' They have nothing to do with color."

I calmed down, and the next day we returned to our walking-to-school skulduggery. We'd act as if we were catching the Ocean Park bus. Nonchalantly we'd wait for the doors to open and then unload on the driver with a fusillade of paper clips, rubber bands, and spitballs.

I didn't have a black boot camp to teach me how to deal with Los Angeles. I walked into battle unarmed. Moms was like, "If you get lost, show someone this note with your address on it." The only thing Pops ever taught me was the shake. Los Angeles's playground rules were different, and I felt myself reassessing who I was. "Your mama so old she farts dust." It was no longer my bodysurfer pals and I having contests to see who knew the most dinosaur names. Friendship was now about being somebody's partner or their boy. Friendship carried responsibilities. I had to learn who had and didn't have backup. Backup was a complicated, surreal, reinforcement network of friends, attack dogs, and hoodlum relatives. You never knew when someone might stick a finger into your best friend's burrito. Forcing you to make a quickfast cost/benefit analysis whether it was an incident worth fighting over. Niggas can organize when they wanna. When I learned in middle school that no motherfucker is an island, I was like, "What, that's not obvious?" For the most part my friends and I kept our backs pressed up against the walls.

If you believe the pervasive hyperbole in hip-hop music, today's young black male doesn't have an identity problem. These neo–Stagger Lees with beepers are simply baaaad muthafuckahs. Viewed by society as impulsive, kinetic criminals and turbulent hip-hop icons, young people find it hard to construct a sense of self, independent of negative racial expectations. Holding on to our self-esteem is priority one. "Real niggaz" stroll the neighborhood never changing hats, unfadeable, unleashed, and uncompromising—belying any hints that constant police harassment and early-morning phone calls to your mother can shake an eighth grader's hardrock persona. "Hello, Ms. Beatty. Your son was in a confrontation with an Officer Barbella earlier this evening. Can you come down to the station and straighten this out?" "Ma, me and Toi didn't do nothing. This fucker called us turds and niggers. He opened the back door to his car and told us to get in 'cause he was going to kick our asses and not do any paperwork." Back in the day I knew who I was; I was a scared, nervous motherfucker looking for the red exit sign over the door of opportunity.

Stretching through young adulthood, Ronald, an L.A. homey for life, used his popularity with women to develop a sense of self that transcended race and class. Using inductive reasoning; Ronald explained his image as a cross-cultural player: "I'm a no-money, ugly motherfucker, so women must like me for me, my personality. That's a beautiful feeling to know that someone likes you for you." Ronald keeps his friends on their identity toes. If you don't fit into his cultural schematic perceptions, if he thinks you're frontin', get ready. He'll hit a jay, sip a Colt 45 forty, turn down the car stereo, and with Roger Daltryesque nonsequitur didacticism ask, "Who the fuck are you? Who are you really?" Ronald's self-assuredness comes from belonging to a strong family of persevering achievers who interpret blackness as a birthright. For his family, blackness is a proud legacy. It's an everlasting gob stopper to be sucked on forever and then passed on to the children, so that every generation grows up with a sweet taste in their mouths. In my family black was a fact, simple as that. Not a scientific fact like "Objects at rest tend to stay at rest" (some might argue that this also applies to black people) but a folk fact analogous to "What goes around comes around." The Beattys didn't embrace blackness; we dealt with it. I received most of my early formal race training at Ronald's house. When most black homes featured velour-upholstered corner groups and rack stereo systems, Ronald's parents decorated their apartment with African artifacts. They had all the black accessorial stuff, tapestries, shields, charcoal sketches depicting everyday black folk. On the bookshelf in front of James Baldwin was a small framed poster that read:

> black ball
> black magic
> black death
> black sheep
> black cat
> black mail
>
> white lies

Al, Ronald's brother, once told me that when they lived in an all-white Chicago suburb Moms would turn it around whenever their blue-eyed-devil friends came over to play.

Between touch-football games we kvetched about the unfairness of being poor young black Americans. "When I get rich I'm going to hire a bunch of white people to do the three C's: cook, clean, and chauffeur." Race preceptor that he is, Al would set us straight. "You would hire some whities, fool. When I get rich I'm going to hire some niggas. Why give some racist crackers a job?" Oh shit, you're right. Deep, cuz. I was two shades darker and poorer than Al, but I realized that Al was blacker than I. He had been to Muslim school, celebrated Kwanzaa, his uncle David was a Panther. I had read some comic books about Benjamin Banneker, Harriet Tubman, and Charles Drew, and my mother got caught in the middle of a Black Panther/LAPD shoot-out.

It wasn't until my junior year at Boston University that I underwent my first consciously positive identity transformation. I took Howard Zinn's The Lily-White Upper-Middle-Class Liberal Musings of a Tenured Professor 231, a course world famous for being an easy "A." The students learned a little racism, sexism, classism, then went back to the dorms thinking they were Ghandhi and John Brown reincarnate. "Gee, Paul, I didn't know you had it so bad." "Yeah, dude, it's terrible. Can I get one of those Heinekens?" Out of the small library of assigned texts I bought two, Emma Goldman and The Autobiography of Malcolm X. A lazy student interested only in entries for my course journal, I thumbed through Emma Goldman, but The Autobiography refused to be skimmed. With the agonizing presence of a pissed-off grandparent The Autobiography grabbed me by the earlobe and pulled me in the right direction. My shit (black for psyche) was radically and permanently altered. I couldn't talk to any white folks without a resounding "goddamn" echoing in my head. I stopped hanging with my white friends. The racist contradictions and indulgences were too deep. My departure wasn't about their being white Beelzebubs, it was about acknowledging their base attitudes of white supremacy and my uneasy acquiescence in it. Mr. X was speaking about hypocrisy and self-awareness, American and black.

It didn't matter if parts of the book were lies and exaggeration; the direct application of the text to my life was downright scary. In grade school Malcolm's teacher suggests that he give up dreams of becoming a lawyer and concentrate on carpentry, a more appropriate vocation for a black man. I knew exactly where Malcolm was coming from. On my first visit home from college I was walking back from a friend's house when I noticed that my old elementary school was having an open house. Deciding it would be a gas to visit Mr. Edmunds, my sixth-grade teacher, I popped into his classroom just as he was preparing to leave. Old Man Edmunds remembered me and seemed happy to see me. He told me he was penning a how-to educational guidebook on teaching inner-city youths by emphasizing discipline and good citizenship. He asked me what I thought of his teaching methods. My fingers stiffened as I remembered the hand cramps from writing "I promise to be a good citizen and not talk in class" five hundred times. I promptly made up some bullshit on how his lectures on maturity and citizenship had become the fundamental tenets of my life. I said he was the reason I was the docile eighteen-year-old Negro he saw before him. He asked if he could quote me on that and what did I do for a living. I said yes he could quote me and told him that I wasn't working, I was attending an overpriced eastern college with hordes of white folks. Shocked, Mr. Edmunds shook my hand and congratulated me on exceeding his expectations. I couldn't figure out why he was so surprised. I was a good student; gifted, class president, a little trouble with my nines tables, but otherwise I had rocked sixth grade. Mr. Edmunds explained to me that based on my "jive character" he had predicted I would be an electrician and a moderately well behaved citizen. He didn't think I had the discipline or fortitude required for college. Not wanting to hear any more of his nostalgic slander I said good-bye and turned to leave. As I left, Edmunds reminded me that I still hadn't graduated from college. Feeling insulted, bitter, and guilty for my low opinion of electricians, I ran home and told my mother instead of spitting in his face.

You may know my name, but look you don't know me.

—*Positive K*

Reading *The Autobiography of Malcolm X* closed the book on one segment of my life and opened the cover to another. I had some history to relearn. I wasn't the only one undergoing an identity transmogrification. Large numbers of black youths wandered around America asking directions to that amorphous area on the map called the Black Community. "Let's see, the Black Community? You want to go straight down Carthage until you get to Diaspora. Make a left at The Middle Passage and bear right till you get to the intersection of Colonialism and Self-determination." For the nineties black generation, *The Autobiography* is a starter's kit for exploring the boundaries and mysticisms of color. It's a book of spells that has influenced a nation of young necromancers to practice a hip psuedoscience that I call Malchemy. Malchemy is a black deconstructionist experimental method composed of P-funk, country gris-gris, the jitterbug, nationalism, and collard greens. Determined to unearth dead legacies, Malchemists use magical incantations and three-quarter truths to turn base metalheaded rusty tin Negroes into gold-plated sunpeople prideful of their histories and themselves. America is on the verge of being cast into a nigrescent Dark Age, because the freaks come out at night and Africans are bodyrocking black to the future.

The downside to this crescendo of community actualization is its usage by the black identity cabals as a garrote to strangle women's rights and self-expression. You should see me saddle the racial high horse, a black knight jousting the rock-and-roll Metallica Negroes. I walk through New York sucking my teeth and looking disdainfully at the squeaky-voiced tory collaborators who sip miso soup at sidewalk Greenwich Village cafes surrounded by the honky enemy. "Stop smiling, acting so harmless, and put your pinky back on that spoon you integration-at-all-costs jerk." But, there but for the grace of God go I, when my white friends are in town. The problem is that one African-American's brainwashed luxury-car-driving food-stamp-cashing hair-straightened nigga is another's pedigreed true African. To help clarify this predicament, I developed the Beatty Scale of Quintessential Blackness. Unlike the ancestry-based octaroon, quadroon, zebra-roon, fullroon race-purity measure, the Beatty Scale has a degree of Africaness equivalent to Kelvin's absolute zero. Unfortunately, the only absolute Africans were those primordial sunfolk. Those earthlings who as Richard Pryor stated were the first people to have thought "Where the fuck am I and how do you get to Detroit?" At the risk of alienating every colored person on the planet, here is my celebrity spectrum of Quintessential Blackness.

In the nineties Black is a religion with no ecclesiastic grand poohbah but plenty of clergypersons and missionaries. Friday nights the urban contemporary Reverend DJs lead the congregations and proselytize the backsliders. "Sistren and brethren, tonight's sermon concerns communication. Let us turn to vinyl scripture *A Tribe Called Quest*. Rap apostle Q-Tip sayeth unto Phife-Dog in freestyles "Check the Rhime" Song 9 verse 6, 'If knowledge is the key, then show me the lock.' " Although hip-hop sermons are thematically black, many faithful radioland parishioners are white. Ardent believers who say their "amens," "true indeeds," and "parley parleys" at the breakbeats in the benediction. White listeners should be ever mindful of EMPD's hardcore admonition, "Don't act too cool or you might get shot." Tipper Gore and the rest of the censor police are also wary of angelic white youth adopting radio/street values—afraid their naive progeny might emulate a cool ghetto stutter and in the process develop a permanent stammer.

Dubbed Oreos, Apples, and Bananas, colored kids who don't fit into the conventional playground cubbyholes get treated like broken crayons trying to shove themselves into the Crayola box. But there are no stinging epithets for the black at heart, Marguerite Duras, mambo-fevered white racial misfits. When whites act like people of color it comes off as shallow caricature. A coolout of mine and I went to a house party with some of his prep-school friends. The affair wasn't a house party in the sweat-on-the-walls, fogged-

THE BEATTY SCALE OF QUINTESSENTIAL AFRICAN-AMERICAN BLACKNESS*

Jet Black	*Flat Black*
Billie Holiday	Thurgood Marshall
Malik El-Shabazz	Charles Barkley
Anita Hill	Any Negro League baseball player
Charles Barkley	Rosa Parks
Wilma Rudolph	Mary McCleod-Bethune
Mrs. Rudolph	Parliament-Funkadelic
Mudbone	Marcus Garvey
Mary McCleod-Bethune's shoes	Joie Lee
Nat Turner	Angela Davis
Harriet Tubman	Flo Hyman
Julie Dash	Fishbone
Bruce Lee	Wynton Marsalis
Crazy Horse	Robin Givens
Geronimo	Richard Pryor
U.S. Rep. Maxine Waters	Black Gummed Canines
Son House	*Jet* magazine
Toni Morrison	
Big Mama Thornton	

Glossy Black	*Gray*
En Vogue	Clarence Thomas
Charles Barkley	Rae Dawn Chong
Any roller derby queen	Charles Barkley
Public Enemy	Diana Ross
Spike Lee	John Doggett
Yo-Yo	Atlanta politicians
W.E.B. DuBois	Bill Cosby
Booker T. Washington	Shadow Senator Jesse Jackson
Rev. Jesse Jackson	Any black members of
Michael Jackson	Marky Mark's Funky Bunch
Bo Jackson	Spike Lee's *Malcolm X*
Rebe Jackson	*Ebony* magazine
Action Jackson	
Branford Marsalis	
Rap video dancers	
The Congressional Black Caucus	
Essence magazine	
Emerge magazine	

*Degrees of Blackness are subject to change without prior notice.

windows, red-light sense. It was more of a condominium
party. Willie and I weren't in the spot for five minutes when
a punch-drunk stereo disc jockey figured that he knew what
the colored guys wanted to hear. He dimmed the lights and
proceeded to play every rap record in the collection. Whities
commenced to headbobbing. Putting into practice the dance
and mannerism lessons learned from "Yo! MTV Raps." All
the while looking out of one eye toward me and Willie. Am
I doing this right?

There are deviations from the norm. One such exception
is white rapper MC Serch. Serch's story of b-boy Romulus
wolf-child raised and adopted by the brothers receives
much press in the hip-hop periodicals. Like early jazz's Bix
Beiderbecke, Serch has become rap's white *auténtico* wun-
derkind. Serch grew up in Jewish environs, leaving his
neighborhood to pal around with the homies and sit in on
blackness. In Mr. Serch's case, Bix's dixieland New Orleans
was a housing project in Queens, New York, and the New
Orleans Rhythm Kings were Run-DMC. While respected for
his microphone skills, MC Serch merits props from the hip-
hop cognoscenti for being introspective about the ramifications of being a white artist in a black art form. Thankfully,
Serch appears to shun the role of hip-hop cultural attaché,
goodwill ambassador to the ghetto.

I rarely read about white folks who grew up in all-black
neighborhoods and attended schools that were not 60 percent black, but 99.9 percent black. The aptly named Louis
Pasteur Junior High in Los Angeles had the reputation of
being a daytime home for the fermented youth of West Los
Angeles. At Pasteur the administration treated the few white
kids like pampered curios. Most of them were in the aca-
demically enriched classes and had a special bus to whisk
them up Airdrome back to Cheviot Hills after school. One
white cat who didn't board that bus was Todd. At three
o'clock Todd walked south, the direction of the notorious
Hoover Crips. Born and raised in the 'hood, Todd didn't
need a Ghetto Pass or a black Family Circle Seal of
Approval.

Black folks dole out respect in curious ways. Some whi-

ties get undue respect just because they are white and act a
creditable black. Todd got a different respect. I vividly recall
white boy Todd at cutting contests, saggy gray khakis gangster creased and starched, out poplocking some challenger
juiced with electric boogie. My mom loved Todd. He used
to take karate classes with her at a Shotokan dojo on Pico
Boulevard. Two green-belt apprentices with crispy sharp
form and nasty roundhouses, Todd and my mother became
fast friends. She would come home telling me how Todd
praised and respected my basketball game and how I should
come down to the dojo and improve my chi. I took a couple
of lessons, but I wasn't with gojo breathing, getting kicked
in the stomach, and slapped around with bamboo sticks.
Bushido could kiss my ass. Todd and I became friends for a
quick second, but our posses were different. Mine was academic goof-off make out party cool. His was a hardcore set
of survivors just trying to get over. Soon our friendship rele-
gated itself to hellacious pickup basketball games during
lunch. You only had forty-five minutes and niggas including
Todd got busy. After school we parted ways. Todd traveled
south. Me, Anthony, Jerry, and Fred backpacked northwest,
getting into lightweight trouble on the way home. "Fuck,
the police. Which way you goin' to run?"

Nowadays, I run into would-be Todds. Fab Five Freddy
Frankenstein creations outfitted in the expensive accoutre-
ments of young blackness. The fashions are exact. The collo-
quialisms forced, but passable. The street saunter pops. The
stitches concealed by adopted roughhouse attitudes.
"Wassup, nigga?" The first "nigga" flies out of their mouths,
a test pilot on reconnaissance for any queer looks and reac-
tions. "See niggas don't know me. Even though I'm from
around the way and back in the day. They can't see this.
Know what I'm sayin'?" No. Appreciation for culture is cool,
but I am skeptical that it will lead to any significant change
in the status quo. I can see an uptown white boy sitting in a
plush swivel chair behind a black marble desk rubbing his
chin as he tells an ex-con single-parent superlover nigga-
with-attitude job applicant that he's not qualified and can't
be trusted behind the register. "You criminal-minded, reme-

dial, alternative high-school dropout. Get your unfinished-job-application-filling-out ass out my office. Step the fuck off and break dodge B. Security!"

Damn it feels good to see people up on it.

—*Biz Markie*

More than a few Negroes enjoy having the white folks jocking their athletic grace, their cool resiliency to strife. You can see the watermelon smiles on their faces, nodding yes to every white wannabe attempt to scale the Berlin Wall of cultural difference. *"Ich bin ein Negro."* Given a tacit runway clearance these vicarious niggers fly loop-de-loops through identity, one hand on their joystick and the other around a forty-ounce—holding on to the two white folkloric symbols of black manhood.

Over the past five years malt liquor consumption in the United States has increased by over one million barrels of brew. I'm no market researcher, but I would guess that rap culture has had much to do with this growth. Rappers have introduced malt liquor to the music's underaged and white fanbase, two previously untapped markets. Under twenty-ones stand in front of the dance clubs arms crossed waiting for the doors to open sipping from the give-a-way large brown bags. Except maybe in Oregon, you never saw whities drinking malt liquor until rap and forty-ounce images became *de rigueur* for any artist with a ghetto street bent.

The dry weight of a forty-ounce bottle is three pounds and twelve ounces. I believe its weight changes depending on whose hands hold the bottle. Drinking in the ghetto is like drinking on Jupiter. The gravitational pull in the inner city is different. There a bottle of Midnight Dragon weighs close to ten pounds. Catching a buzz can be a precursor to serious consequences beyond bitter words, double-dog dares, and fistfights when everyone carries a lead paint chip on his shoulder. Never did a forty look heavier than when I realized that during lunch my male GED prep students went over to the deli for roast-beef sandwiches and beer. Circus strongmen drinking on the sun, washing down life with hundred-pound forties.

In the hands of white college hepsters at the University of Mercury, a forty weighs a shade over one-half pound. I watch them, brand-new book bags and bank cards cruising the fast-food joints planning the night on the town. "Let's drink some Brass Monkey, some Olde English, some Cisco." What do they know about Cisco?

Whites aren't the only folks to jump on the forty-ounce bandwagon. I know some Aspen-ski-vacation, company-car-drivin' niggas who, two years ago, never drank malt liquor because it was too "ghetto." Now these bougie black men who ride a runaway stagecoach christened "Corporate America," use Colt 45, rap, and speech as tenuous reins tied to the spooked horses of black manliness.

The malt liquor stigma used to scare me shitless. Malt liquor was something that your Pops and his loud friends drank while playing cards and dominoes in the kitchen. Occasionally somebody's aunt would sit in the front seat of a burgundy Buick Regal sipping Pink Champale waiting for someone to pop a dime bag into her hand. I downed my first forty with Al, walking the streets, checking out the faux marble stars inlaid on Hollywood Blvd. "Al, how in the fuck Nipsy Russell get a star?"

"*Hunh?* Nipsy Russell, yeah. The motherfucker who makes people lose on "The $20,000 Pyramid," yeah. Let's go get a forty." I was bit reluctant, but peer pressure from a best friend goes a long way. "What kind of cat ass nigga don't drink malt liquor? Swing up, cuz." With my race loyalty at stake, I put two hands around this glass dreadnought and swung up thinking "Forty fucking ounces—that's damn near a gallon." I don't think I even finished. I feared I was on the road to handout vagrancy, headed for a lifetime of hanging outside Thriftown Liquors, grizzled and oily, bumming dimes. "Brothermanbrothermanbrotherman."

It wasn't long before I acquired the taste, sneaking an occasional Imperial Quart of Colt 45 into the movies, burp in people's faces at Brooklyn Brandy Alexander buppy get-togethers. Everything was mellow until a fateful winter in

Los Angeles when Ronald introduced me to the hemlock of ghetto brews, St. Ides. On my first night back Al and I were discussing what beer to buy to help us reacquaint ourselves with each other and the L.A. police state. Ronald starts gushing and bubbling about this new hard-to-find shit that is liquid LSD. The one sip pissy drunk shit, called St. Ides. So we rolled to the Korean market next to the Dum-Dum Donuts on La Cienega. Some local hoods known as the PBGs (Playboy Gangsters) were buying their Tuesday night libations. Shoulder to shoulder at six one, six four, and six five, me, Ronald, and Al are too old and too tall to go the long way around. We held our ground in the stare contest that traditionally takes place between urban unknowns. Soon the young band of angels parted to let us through muttering face-saving effronteries, "Who is these Lurch motherfuckahs?" We lurched our way toward the refrigerator, and I picked up my first forty of St. Ides. It had a bright red sticker on the label, "World's Strongest Beer! $1.49." Shit, maybe I shouldn't be fuckin' with this.

We made our ritual drive to Malibu and as we had done hundreds of times before, parked off the Pacific Coast Highway on a bluff overlooking the ocean. An hour and a half later we had missed the sunset and were swimming in the fifty-degree Pacific Ocean in late December wearing Calvin Klein skivvies. The next day we scoured the Westside looking for our newfound dopamine. That night parked next to the Santa Monica pier things started as they usually do; 1580 KDAY, who is seeing whom, what niggas is fucking up. Then everything outside the car just melted away and we all started speaking at once. What began as casual conversation became a polyphonic drunken confessional. We opened our chest plates and real emotions about tragedy, our fathers, and one another rushed out past our macho sentries. Three grown-ass niggas crying, lost, and blubbering in sin and sorrow. We looked at the half-empty bottles going "What the fuck is in this?" We drove home trying to figure out why niggas are so retarded. Los Angeles blurred by, a blue-and-gold-flaked Jean-Michel Basquiat painting, a wave and spray-paint landscape.

Now that I'm a righteous sun person I've stopped drinking malt liquor—not because of any rumors concerning the mishegas of toxic ingredients put into malt liquor in a plot to sterilize and exterminate the black race. I didn't quit because the life expectancy of blacks is a steadily decreasing 69.2 years, six years less than that of whites. I stopped because I tired of being party to Madison Avenue's boogedy-boogedy shuffling stereotyped target marketing. St. Ides's shrewd advertising campaign is a major reason behind its popularity. Their hip-hop radio jingles are light-years ahead of the Schlitz Malt Liquor Bull and Olde English 800 ads that feature baritone Amos 'n' Andy soundalikes searching for an ice-cold *raison d'être*. I remember the old Schlitz Malt Liquor television commercials. Silk-and-sequined black party-goers politely mingled at an upscale rhythm-and-blues get-together. Then some fool opened a can of the Malt Liquor Bull and things got funky. The same bull that marched down Wall Street in the Merrill Lynch commercials was now rampaging through the black community. Schlitz malt liquor had the power to turn a staid soiree into a bug-eyed ghetto Pamplona in sixty seconds.

St. Ides's radio spots are strictly on the hardcore tip. Backed up with DJ Pooh's dope production Ice Cube, Yo-Yo, EMPD, and the Geto Boys parody their Billboard hits into driving ads whose bumping samples come diddy boppin' out of Compton and Houston's Fifth Ward. There is no subtlety to the ads; the jingles gangster lean and dare the consumer to drink. The product is 5.5 percent alcohol, so why bullshit? St. Ides is decidedly blunt about establishing a direct link between the product's alcohol content, sexual potency, felon cool, and the sheer profundity in being a drunken slob. Here is a small sample of lyrics that on the surface are fun lovin' but disturbing in light of real-life connections between violence, sexual abuse, and alcohol.

> . . . drink St. Ides and the boots are ass out. Ice Cube is 5000 as I pass out.
> The S-T. crooked I-D-E-S guaranteed to get a big boody undressed.
> . . . drink it, drink it, then I burp. After I slurp Ice Cube'll put in much work.

	Colt 45	Sparkling Pink Champale	Haffenreffer Private Stock
Taste	Smooth only because it's so watery. Rolling Rock in a big bottle.	Hey, Kool-Aid! Sweet. Tastes suspiciously close to a red version of its G. Heileman cousin, Colt 45.	Robust. Bitter enough to let you know you're about to get busy.
Complexion	Pale gold.	Looks like saliva after you've sucked on cherry popsicles all afternoon. If it sparkled, I missed it.	Color of honey in the cute little bear-shaped plastic squeeze bottles.
Bouquet	None.	Smells like day-old spilt beer.	Aromatic. Reminiscent of a wheat field at harvest time. You could drink this all night and kiss your lover in the morning.
Description	Traditional 40 dog. Barbecue beer. Good for getting up the nerve to ask for a slow drag. Minus: The omnipresent Billy Dee Williams aura.	An early experimental wine cooler. Puts you in a virile supercool funky seventies adult mood. Bad jazz, Pam Grier, and Fred Williamson in various states of undress. If you like the "Beauty Shop" plays you will love Pink Champale. Go 'head with your bad self.	A nice beginner's malt. Goes well with most cannabis generas. Good beer for drinking with friends and talking about one another's shortcomings.
Potency	Not the Mike Tyson of beers. More like the Rock 'em Sock'em Robot of malt liquor. Knocks your block off, but it takes awhile. Allows you to maintain cool in touchy situations (e.g. getting busted by the cops, Moms, or Pops).	Weak. Goes well with frozen Mexican food. According to Daryl, "Part sham, part pale."	Muy genérico.

Midnight Dragon Special Reserve	Schlitz Malt Liquor Bull	St. Ides
Swill. Extremely harsh. Goes down like sharp and bent rusty nails. Nasty aftertaste.	No nonsense. Crisp and to the point. Nice malty flavor and body.	Crazy smooth, but who cares; that's not why you drink it.
Murky urine.	Amber-gold.	Depends. Could be goldenrod on Tuesday and copper brown on Friday.
Smells like napalm in the morning.	Nice hickory scent. Redolent of a spring breeze.	Rocket fuel with a hint of ammonia.
The Riunite of malt liquors. 75¢/16oz. can. Remember when your college chums replaced your Mountain Dew with piss? Here's your chance for revenge.	A good accompaniment to potato salad. It should come with a foldout lawn chair and some shit-talking relatives.	The cutting edge of beer. Popular among the thrill-seeking crowd. Never the same drunk twice. Might set a belligerent tone, might turn your life into a Fellini movie. Guaranteed to flip the script.
No Joke. Little known, but must be major cause of black-on-black crime. As for the ad campaign, I fail to see how anyone can suck on anything if you are passed out in the gutter.	Decent kick. Stings, because that's what it's supposed to do.	Strictly for professionals. Never drink it alone. Psilocybic. Liquid antimatter. Never mind about operating heavy machinery, you'll have trouble lighting a cigarette. Good thing, too, because St. Ides is flammable.

Funky as the St. Ides commercials are, the poster campaign for Midnight Dragon, the inner city's discount malt
liquor, has taken target marketing to a new level. The poster
shows a white woman clad in a string bikini and wearing
high heels sitting backward in a chair. She is drinking from
a forty-ounce bottle of Midnight Dragon, her crimson lips
pursed around a thick black straw. The caption reads, "I
could suck on this all night." Niggas is still buggin'. I'm no
longer on the malt liquor trip. I have tired of tigers, blue
and red bulls, reptiles and gargoyles on my beer bottles.
Long after the cooptive forces of capitalism dilute hip-hop
into elevator music, St. Ides will still be on the shelves.
Delivered to your corner stores, bodegas, y tiendas by a dev-
ilish imp in a black truck—dry-ice smoke swirling around
the cases stacked on his hell red handtruck. For those of
you who don't mind submitting to racial mockery and niche
marketing, here is a survey of premium malt liquors tasted
by me and certified Beermaster, DCP. We didn't test Crazy
Horse because a line has to be drawn somewhere.

Since Columbus got blown off course, the history of cultural exchange in the Americas has been one of inequity and
injustice. Had the Indians put the Pilgrims on a Reaganomic
self-help plan, America might be the home of a different
kind of brave. When indigenous kindness and self-preserva-
tion became heathen savagery, America constructed a
flawed image of itself. Like the narcissistic witch in *Snow
White,* America looks at its ugly countenance in the mirror
and sees beauty—oblivious to identity's dualistic nature.
Identity is a construct determined not only by how you see
yourself but also by how others see you. A poet I know with
a serious drug problem has lost almost all sense of who he
is. He walks around the neighborhood avoiding those who
know him because he can see in their expressions that he
is no longer the stylish, together person he thinks he is.
Communities in America behave similarly. We travel in
packs, cautious of outsiders, knowing that how they see us
affects how we see ourselves. By the year 2000 most of this
nation's population will have spent entire lifetimes looking
into funhouse mirrors that reflect distorted images of self.
We pay to see inaccurate, two-dimensional depictions: the

colored sidekick, the understanding mammy, the blond bimbo, the drunken Indian, the bubbling queer, the homicidal homosexual, the Latino mugger, the dragon lady, the tragic mulatto, Mr. Moto, Charlie Chan, the faithful retainer, the faithful wife.

Despite multiculturalism's good intentions, stereotypes continue to be our primary framework for interpreting social interaction. We have not learned to see cultural plurality in the United States for what it is, a survival technique in a society where difference is something to be feared and ridiculed. Those wishing to confront this legacy of xenophobia must realize that cultural gangs have a genuine depth to their experience beyond the stereotypic signifiers of music, sex, dance, and malt liquor. The world has been force-fed the historical vicissitudes of the white man from Alley Oop cave dweller to rocket scientist. The marginalized others are forced to erect cultural mausoleums that blow up the importance of ethnic collectiveness and deemphasize the role of personal struggle. Our chosen histographers carry on about Stonehenge, the Great Wall, Machu Picchu, and the pyramids without any thought for the motherfuckers who carried the bricks.

How many identifiers of shoot-'em-up rap studio braggadocio think of the real-life victims of black-on-black crime and societal ostracism? On the streets there are no rehearsals, sound checks, remixes, and do-overs. The background sound of oppression is the metronomic hum of a machine inflating an AIDS patient's chest with the hot air of civic concern. The percussives of prejudice are the squeaky wheels of an IV bottle pushed around the intensive-care unit by a wounded veteran of ghetto skirmishes recovering from bullet wounds and thanking a visitor for bringing the latest issue of *Guns & Ammo* to help pass the time. When white America bothers to ask me anything, it asks only about those cultural manifestations that fit into their notions of black life: "What did you think about the *Boyz 'n the Hood*?" Can a member of the privileged posse understand that when I called home to ask Ronald the same question, there was automatic fire in the background and Ronald was facedown on the floor, carrying on about how real it was? When you

walk through your gentrified neighborhood, a prideful yuppie pioneer of urban manifest destiny and you hear the
locals speaking in undecipherable rhythmic hip-hop codes,
do you understand? "Yo, G-Mac, they blind, baby they blind
to fact . . ." "If you could see what I could see?" ¿Entiendes?
At the local Rodney King insta-unification rally you probably thought you was down, marching next to niggas banging
clenched fists against their thighs. Allow me to enlighten
you before you get lit up. We weren't keeping time with
"Hey Hey! Ho Ho! Whatever I don't like has got to go!"
chants but waiting for an excuse to give remedial lessons in
Schwerner, Goodman, and Cheney civil disobedience and
teamwork.

When you're a Jet you're a Jet . . .

—Steven Sondheim

I once told Kevin, a white friend of mine, that he would
make a good black man. It was a helluva compliment, but
he didn't understand. The high signs of our respective cultural gangs clashed. His Jim Morrison fingers "weaving
secret minarets, speaking secret alphabets" couldn't translate
my faux gangbanger, "Crip here" hand signals. We slapped
palms and went our separate ways. The soul kitchen is
closed.

MIXED LIKE ME

David Bernstein

I am a twenty-six-year-old man, half black and half Jewish, who founded and edits a conservative magazine that deals with race relations and culture. Such a statement would have been extraordinary thirty years ago; today we treat it with mild interest and move along. No one would argue that my life has been typical—typical of the "black experience," of the "Jewish experience," or of any other dubious paradigm associated with a particular race or ethnicity. I have not overcome racism or poverty, and people become visibly disappointed when I tell them that my mixed background has not been a cause of distress, or any other difficulty for that matter.

However, my story may be of some interest. For better or worse, America is going to look more and more like me in the next century—that is to say, individuals are going to be walking embodiments of the melting pot. The argument over whether America is more like cheese dip or the multi-culturalist "tossed salad" (Are you getting hungry yet?) will be made moot by the increasing incidence of mixed marriage and of the growing class of mutts like me who have more ethnicities than the former Yugoslavia.

My parents married in 1965, in Washington, D.C. If they had lived then in the comfortable suburb where they now reside, they would have been breaking the law—miscegenation, as marriage between blacks and whites was known in those days, was still illegal in Maryland. My mother was a native Washingtonian who, until her teen years, felt sorry for the few white people who lived near her, her mother, and two siblings; she thought they were albinos. Her parents—both of whom had moved from the country to Washington when they were teenagers—were separated when my mother was just a toddler. She was raised, along with an older sister and brother, in a small brownstone apartment in downtown D.C. Her brother, the oldest child, went off to fight in the Korean War, one of the first black airmen to participate in the integrated armed forces. While in Korea, he fell in love with and married a Korean girl. Meanwhile, my mother attended segregated public schools until senior high school, when she was in the first class that integrated Eastern Senior High School in the wake of the Supreme Court's *Brown* decision. After graduation, she opted not to attend college, because she didn't know what she wanted to do—and "didn't want to waste" my grandmother's money.

My father grew up in North Philadelphia, one of those old working-class neighborhoods where there were Jewish blocks, Italian blocks, Irish blocks, and so on. His parents were second-generation Americans: Grandpa Bernstein's family was from Poland; my grandmother's family from Leeds, England. (I understand the Blasky family still lives there, apparently running a successful wallpaper-hanging business.) My grandfather and my father's two brothers fought in World War II; my father, who was too young to go, became a paratrooper soon after the war ended. After leaving the Army in the early 1950s, he moved to Washington, where he and my mother eventually ended up working at the same furniture-rental place.

Despite the rich possibilities for mischief making presented by their union, my parents did not marry to make a political statement. While their contemporaries marched for civil rights and held sit-ins, they hung out with a mixed-race group of cool cats at various jazz nightclubs in downtown D.C. Most of these establishments were burned to the ground after Martin Luther King's assassination in 1968, bringing to an end that unique era of naive integration.

Since those riots, race relations in this country have been tinged with guilt, fear, and lies.

In 1970, my father's company transferred him to the redneck mill town of Reading, Pennsylvania. My mother hated it; my father tolerated it; and I went about the business of growing up. I went to a mostly white private school and Monday afternoons attended Hebrew school with the children of Reading's prosperous and assimilated Jewish community. My Cub Scout group and summer camp were at the local Jewish community center, which had been bombed recently by Reading's prominent community of neo-Nazis.

It was also at the center that I was first called a "nigger." My mother had been preparing me my entire life for that to happen, but when it did, I was hardly bothered at all. I actually felt sorry for the kid who shouted it at me during a softball game; he genuinely felt bad afterward and apologized about six times. (Even though it's out of sequence in our little narrative, I should recount the only other time I have been called a "nigger." A couple of years ago, I was riding on D.C.'s Metro with two white liberal friends when a white homeless person approached me and stated, "You niggers get all the jobs." My friends were horrified and silent. I laughed and told the bum that he was right; that was how it should be.)

We moved back to Washington in 1977. Again, I attended private school, this time at Georgetown Day School, a place founded in the 1940s as Washington's first integrated school. Despite the forty-year tradition, there were still not many blacks at GDS. The students were largely from well-to-do, secular Jewish families with traditions of liberal political activism. My family, though secular, was not well-to-do or politically active. My parents were somewhat liberal, but it was a liberalism of function rather than form; in other words, they might be considered budding neoconservatives. I inherited from my parents a healthy suspicion of conventional wisdom—which, in the case of my teachers and peers, was overwhelmingly on the left. By 1980, I was one of six kids in my junior-high class to vote for Ronald Reagan in our mock election.

My "political awakening" was just beginning. In high school I cowrote a piece in the school newspaper on what it meant to be conservative, an awfully crafted piece of literature that nearly caused a riot, despite its (by my standards today) extremely mushy conservatism. I started to realize that you could make liberals mad just by saying the "c" word. On election day 1984, I wore a jacket and tie to school to celebrate President Reagan's impending victory. One friend didn't talk to me for a week.

It never dawned on me that, as a "person of color," I ought to be "mortally" opposed to this Reagan guy. All I ever heard come out of his mouth just sounded like good sense to me. I heard over and over again on TV that the man was a racist and that he was bad for black people. But what stuck with me from all this was that the people who repeated this charge were buffoons. Early on, the idea of race was not central to my view of politics. This would change rather sharply later on.

My freshman year in college was spent at Allegheny College in lovely Meadville, Pennsylvania. Within weeks, it was apparent to me and several of my friends there that the school was lousy. A group of us dedicated our lives to the idea of transferring out of that freezing mud hole of a campus. In one of our brainstorming sessions on how to make our transfer applications look beefier, we locked onto the idea of starting a "Conservative Club," which would be a forum for discussing ideas on the right. It sounded like fun, and more importantly, we would all be made vice presidents of the club, an ideal way to bolster our extracurricular résumés.

Once again, just using the word *conservative* nearly brought the campus down around our ears. Two of the conspirators in our résumé-building scheme went before the student government in order to get the necessary recognition, supposedly just a formality. Forty-five minutes later, after shrieks of outrage from the so-called student leaders of this $13,000-a-year institution of higher learning, we were told that the student government was afraid to get involved in "neo-Nazi" groups and that we should come back in a month with a detailed statement of just what we stood for.

Only one member of the SG stood up for us—a young woman who pointed out that on a campus with absolutely no political activity, people who showed some initiative to do something, anything, ought to be encouraged.

But this was a college where political discourse was typified by this statement from the school's chaplain: "We should divest from South Africa. Harvard and Princeton already have, and if we want to be as good as them, we must do so as well." In this kind of environment, which is now typical at liberal-arts colleges around the country, it should have come as no surprise that conservatism was associated with evil. It wasn't the last time that the supposed characteristics of conservatives like me—that we were narrow-minded, ignorant, and shrill—were to be embodied better by our critics.

I did finally escape from Allegheny College, going back home to the University of Maryland. At UM, I decided to make politics a full-time vocation. I worked in Washington afternoons and evenings at various political jobs, first at the Republican National Committee and later at a small, conservative nonprofit foundation. In between, I took a semester off to work for Senator Bob Dole's ill-fated presidential campaign. Returning to Maryland, I was soon elected president of the campus College Republicans, a position that occasionally put me at the center of campus political attention.

This was not because I was a vocal, articulate (some would say loudmouthed) conservative but because I was a *black* conservative. Conservatives are a dime a dozen, smart ones are common, but a black one? "Nelly, wake the kids! They have to *see* this!"

Other conservatives loved having me around. After all, most of them were presumed to be Nazis from the get-go by the ultrasensitive P.C. crowd; having a black person say you're okay was temporary protection from the scholastic inquisition. Further, as a black conservative, I was thought to have special insight into why more blacks didn't identify with the Republican party. Again and again, I was asked how conservatives could find more blacks (or African-Americans, if the petitioner wanted to be sensitive). After a while, I think I actually began to believe that, somehow, I had special understanding of the souls of black folk, and with increasing confidence I would sound off about the political and social proclivities of African-Americans.

In a perverted way, liberals and left-radicals liked having me around as well—because I helped justify their paranoia. I was living proof that imperialist, racist forces were at work, dividing black people and turning us against one another. How else, they theorized, could a black person so obviously sell out both his race and the "progressive" whites who were the only thing standing between him and a right-wing lynch mob? The ardor (and obvious pleasure) with which they alternatively ignored and condemned me demonstrated their belief that I was more than just the opposition: I was a traitor, a collaborator in my own oppression. Finally, one particularly vitriolic black militant suggested in the school newspaper that black conservatives ought to be "neutralized." I took it personally.

And I got fired up. There comes a time in every conservative activist's life when he gets the heady rush of realization at how much fun (and how easy) it is to annoy liberals. Indeed, it was something I had been doing for years. People on the left, with their self-righteousness, humorless orthodoxies, and ultrasensitivity to their own and everyone else's "oppression" are only fun at parties if you get them pissed off. Naturally, then, it is something that conservatives spend a lot of time doing.

Rush Limbaugh, R. Emmett Tyrell, P. J. O'Rourke, hundreds of editors of conservative college newspapers like the *Dartmouth Review,* and thousands of College Republican activists turned the 1980s into one long laugh for conservatives at the expense of the P.C. crowd. The staleness of liberal beliefs, the inability of the campus activists to move beyond sloganeering to real thought, and the creation of a regime on campus by college professors and administrators that treats open discussion as anathema offered fertile ground for conservative humorists.

But it also allowed many conservatives to dismiss leftism as a political force, and they were unprepared when it was resurrected as such in the person of Bill Clinton—thus in 1992, it was the right that too often degenerated into empty

sloganeering. The intellectual stagnation of liberalism con-
tributed to the intellectual sloth of too many conservatives,
concerned more with one-liners than actually formulating
policy.

I was no exception. I slipped easily into the world of left-
ist haranguing. I was always good for a sound bite in the
school newspaper, and as a unique case—a black Jewish
conservative—I had opportunities to comment with some
built-in authority on a range of issues. Controversy with the
Black Student Union? I would have a comment. Someone
wants the university to divest from South Africa? I would be
there with other conservatives holding a press conference
presenting the other side. Controversy between Arab students and Jewish students? The College Republicans would
uphold the Reagan tradition of unswerving support for
Israel as long as I was in charge. Tensions rising between
black and Jewish students? I was there to denounce genuine
bigots brought to campus in the name of "black awareness"
and "free speech" like Louis Farrakhan and Stokely Carmi-
chael (this, of course, did not further endear me to the radical black students).

I tried not to lose sight of why I was doing this; that
annoying liberals was just a means, not an end. But like
every young right-winger, I'm sure that more than once I've
annoyed just for annoyance's sake. There are worse sins, but
this is the only one I'll admit to in print.

Since those heady college days, I have become a magazine
editor. *Diversity & Division* looks at race relations in America
from the perspective of young people, particularly of its
black Jewish editor and white male managing editor. Do I
still go after liberals? Yeah, sure. But the issues we talk
about—those bearing on the future on how we are all going
to get along—are not very funny. And the things that leftists
advocate on these issues, from radical multiculturalism to
quotas, promise to make it next to impossible for us to sur-
vive as a multicultural society.

There are two lessons, I think, that my little autobiography teaches. First is my comfort in moving between worlds
of different cultures and colors. The conventional wisdom
about us mixed-race types, that we are alienated, never feel-

ing comfortable in either culture, is baloney. I am black. I am Jewish. I am equally comfortable with people who identify themselves as either one, or neither one. Why? Because to me the most defining characteristic of who I am is not my race, ethnicity, religious beliefs, political party, or Tupperware club membership. Rather, I see myself as an individual first, part of the larger "human family" with all the suballegiances reduced to ancillary concerns.

This is obviously a very romantic and idealistic notion. It is also, equally as obviously, the only ideology that will allow us to overcome prejudice and bigotry and enable everyone to get along. In me, the melting pot the idea has become the melting pot the reality, with (I must immodestly say) reasonably positive results. My commonality with other people is not in superficial appeals to ethnic solidarity—it is far more fundamental.

That is why I am sickened by people who continue to insist that we must all cling to our ancestors' "cultures" (however arbitrarily defined at that moment) in order to have self-awareness and self-esteem. The notion of "self" should not be wrapped up in externalities like "culture" or "race"—unless you want to re-create the United States as Yugoslavia, Somalia, or any other such place where people's tribal identities make up their whole selves. Indeed, true self-awareness stands opposed to grouping human beings along arbitrary lines like race, gender, religion, weight, or preferred manner of reaching orgasm. Groupthink is primitive. It is not self-awareness; rather it is a refuge for those afraid of differences.

At the contemporary university, students are exhorted to "celebrate diversity" by people who practice just the opposite. There is nothing "diverse" about having racially segregated housing (black students at many colleges have their own dorms), tribalized curricula (Black Studies, Women's Studies, Gay Studies, etc.), or any of the numerous other pathological policies that enlightened administrators foist off on students in the name of tolerance.

What we ought to teach kids to celebrate is their individuality and their accomplishments, not to take phony pride in what their ancestors did. So what if a black man invented the traffic light? Do I really shine in his reflected glory? If so, then I really do have a self-esteem problem.

Those who preach about diversity believe that tolerance means not exulting one class of human being over another, by recognizing that every race and culture has made a contribution to modern civilization: a worthy goal, especially if this were true. But this way of thinking ignores a powerful truth, an obvious solution to the bigotry and suspicion that these sensitivity warriors say they are out to eliminate. The reality is that groups aren't equal; individuals are. If it is "self-evident that all men are created equal" isn't it even more self-evident that blacks and whites, men and women, Christians and Jews are created equal?

Granted, we haven't lived up to this absolute ideal. But we are beginning to see the implications of setting our aspirations below what we know to be the best. Here's the second lesson I think my story tells.

Despite my obvious distaste for the entire notion of group politics, I have become wrapped up in it. By editing a magazine that deals primarily with racial issues, I am not doing what I would most like to be doing. But I am doing what is expected. Under our phony system of racial harmony, college-educated blacks are expected to do something that is, well, black. Black academics are concentrated in Afro-American studies, sociology, and other "soft" fields where they can expound at length about the plight of the American Negro. Everyone, it seems, needs an expert on what it means to be black. Corporations need human-relations specialists to tell them about the "special needs" of black employees. Newspapers need "urban beat" reporters. Foundations, political parties, unions, and any other organizations you can name all need black liaisons to put them "in touch with the community." And, of course, conservatives need a magazine that reassures them that many of the ideas that they have about race relations are not evil and fascistic. These jobs are generally somewhat lucrative, fairly easy to do, and carry just one job requirement—you have to be black.

No one is forced to follow this course; there should be no whining about that. But in life, as in physics, currents

flow along the path of least resistance. As long as it is easy
to make a living as a professional race man, the best and
brightest blacks will be siphoned off into this least-
productive field in our service economy. The same is true,
of course, of Hispanics, Asians, or whatever minority group
is in vogue in a specific region or profession. Our educational system, our country's entire way of thinking about
race, is creating a class of professionals whose entire raison
d'être is to explore and explain—and thus perpetuate—the
current regime. All the preaching of sensitivity, all the Afro-
centric education, all the racial and ethnic solidarity in the
world will not markedly improve race relations in America.
Indeed, the smart money says that this obsession with our
differences, however well-meaning, will make things much,
much worse.

But this is a point that, blessedly, may well be rendered
moot for the next generation. Intermarriage is the great
equalizer; it brings people of different races together in a
way that forced busing, sensitivity training, and affirmative
action could never hope to—as individuals, on equal foot-
ing, united by common bonds of humanity. Four hundred
years ago Shakespeare wrote of intermarriage:

> Take her, fair son, and from her blood raise up
> Issue to me; that the contending kingdoms . . .
> May cease their hatred; and this dear conjunction
> Plant neighbourhood and Christian-like accord
> In their sweet bosoms . . .

Eventually, if all goes well, America's melting pot will be
a physical reality, bringing with it the kind of healing Shakespeare had in mind. Let's just hope we don't file for an ethnic divorce before then.

IN THE SHADOW OF THE SIXTIES

David Greenberg

"Reverend," a student asks a grizzled veteran of the sixties in the first frame of a "Doonesbury" cartoon, "what were the protesters during the sixties really like?"

"What do you think they were like?" the reverend responds.

"I think of them all as larger than life, bonded and driven by commitment, putting their lives on the line for a great cause."

Silence. The reverend gazes blankly. The student raises his eyebrows in hope.

"Uh, right," the reverend finally says. "You got it exactly."

"I knew it!" cries the student. "God, I missed everything!"

Not many pop commentaries about my generation ring true, but for me this comic strip does. I've rarely been able to identify with the popular-culture portraits of my generation, which usually depict young conservatives rebelling against their parents' liberalism or indifferent cynics unaware of any history before last week. But the student in the "Doonesbury" cartoon, with his wistfulness toward the sixties, captures the feelings and yearnings of any number of people I know and gets to the heart of what I think animates much of my generation.

Like many of my peers, I have for a long time been captivated by the sixties—that kaleidoscopic decade that really ended somewhere around 1973—by its triumphs, its daring, and its sense of urgency. I've listened to every Dylan album, studied Nixon and the antiwar movement, read lots of Mailer, gleaned obscure details of the Chicago Seven trial. During my senior year of college, amid job searches and farewells, I spent three months putting together a student magazine about the much-celebrated May Day demonstrations at Yale—which had happened twenty years earlier. The campus activity of that season marked a time that seemed to brim with excitement, and by dissecting and reassembling that historic period, I fancied, I could transpose myself back to the same streets, buildings, and classrooms I now inhabited. If I couldn't make history myself, I could at least enjoy its thrills vicariously.

To myself and others enchanted with the sixties, no other recent time seems so exciting. The formica-encrusted fifties evoke images of appliances, patio furniture, and men with nine-to-five jobs—the picture of ordinariness. The seventies we view sarcastically, with derision masquerading as mock nostalgia; it's fun to laugh at the Village People, "The Love Boat," and bell-bottoms, but few want to relive them. The magical sixties, however, still spark the imagination: the Mississippi Freedom Summer and the San Francisco Summer of Love, the 1963 March on Washington, and the 1968 Democratic convention, Monterey, and Woodstock. Great strides were made against poverty, racism, sexism, for liberty, justice, creativity.

The sixties seem to me to embody ideals that were almost realized but then slipped away. The pursuit of these ideals— the importance of individual predilections over societal norms; equality and fairness for women and blacks and the poor (so obviously now a noble goal that it feels trite even to speak of it); a spirit of love and acceptance—these pursuits were somehow left unfinished. We're still chasing these dreams in our own time, but the grand, dizzying revolutionary fervor has given way to a painstaking, if not boring, daily struggle.

So even as the sixties inspire us, they also daunt us. It's hard to live in such a long shadow. The 1992 L.A. riots are instantly likened to Watts. The gay rights movement invites analogies with the black civil rights movement. We reflexively compare virtually every contemplated foreign-policy venture to the quagmire of Vietnam. These comparisons arise, perhaps, because so much progress was realized either during the sixties or as a result of its movements, so much tumult caused by its activity, that we're still seeing the consequences play out.

In the realm of pop culture, too, the sixties linger, like a carved-up Thanksgiving turkey still sitting at the table years later. Every other issue of *Rolling Stone* magazine in the last several years, it seems, marks the twentieth anniversary of some great event from that time: Sgt. Pepper's, Woodstock, or, lest we forget, the founding of *Rolling Stone*. And once the wave of twentieth anniversaries passes, on come the twenty-fifths. Classic-rock stations proliferate. Jagger, McCartney, Dylan, Pete Townshend, and Neil Young all seem in a perpetual comeback phase. *Tommy* and *Layla* are winning Tonys and Grammys. Where Dylan once went electric, now Eric Clapton goes acoustic. And don't think my generation doesn't listen to this stuff. Either Nirvana pales next to Led Zeppelin, or I'm over the hill at twenty-five (a distinct possibility, I grant you). My generation is replaying the sixties LP, but it's lost its fidelity.

We're getting the sixties again, but always as some rehash, reprise, or recycling of the original. Whereas John F. Kennedy is alleged to have smoked pot in the White House (which helps explain his enthusiasm for sending a man to the moon), Bill Clinton denied inhaling to get there. When people in my generation light up, they might play a Jimi Hendrix or Jefferson Airplane CD, as though replicating the full sensory experience will open the gateway to the feelings of liberation that the activity once afforded. Still, they can't enjoy it as freely, since a thickheaded backlash tries to link recreational use with crack addiction and gang warfare.

Campus protests, though fairly common when I was at school, were nonetheless difficult to get excited about. The rallies on the main plaza, with their microphone feedback and smatterings of halfhearted applause, usually seemed deliberate but limp imitations of the sixties efforts, lacking the cultural context or conviction to ennoble them. Whereas Vietnam was a war worth protesting, the Gulf War targeted a tyrant so menacing and indefensible that even a lot of one-time isolationists supported it. The anti–Gulf War movement, for the most part, ended up just another self-conscious sixties reprise. Once more, without feeling.

The list continues:

They had the Free Speech Movement; we get political correctness.

They had "Turn on, tune in, drop out"; we get "Just say no."

They had communes; we get Melrose Place.

They had *Apollo;* we get the *Challenger*.

They had the Pill; we get AIDS.

Restive, we itch to act anew, to create something of our own, fresh and vital. Magazines devoted to defining our generation's thinking pop up everywhere, trumpeting the need for a new politics or a new aesthetic. We're constantly hearing familiar refrains: that we need to form a new community, to transcend the old political labels, to forge grass-roots reform. At a recent gathering of politically aspiring young writers who wanted to craft a "generational statement," people spoke of breaking from the ways of the past, of setting a new direction, of "postideological politics," whatever that might mean. In all these efforts, the promise of our generation is held out: a new movement; a new beginning.

But wait. These words and sentiments, too, sound eerily familiar. Where have we heard them before? Ah, yes! The complaints and frustrations of these magazine founders and manifesto drafters could easily have been uttered by the members of Students for a Democratic Society, the organization of the sixties' New Left. Just like today's young activists, the SDS members, at the sixties' outset, chafed under the constraints of the imperfect world forced upon them. They, too, complained of having no voice in the world of their elders. Indeed, the participants at last year's generational gathering knew they were working in the shadow of SDS's Port Huron statement. Some even passed around copies of that famous credo. Despite the talk of transcending ideology, a lot of the group was well aware that the "end of ideology" was a generation-old concept. Acting anew, then, turned out to be quite old.

Thus our crippling paradox: We try to escape history only to find that escaping history is a trap. Forging the future is a thing of the past. A nagging fin-de-siècle voice reminds us of the seemingly all-encompassing sweep of our predecessors. We are left wondering how we can initiate anything, intellectual, artistic, or political, without the innovation feeling like a cheap replica. No Copernican revolution seems conceivable.

Far from a dispassionately analyzed era, a discrete historical entity easily removed and held up to the light, the sixties have become an emotionally charged symbol. Those who lived through (created?) the sixties clearly want to revisit the era to restore order and meaning to this jumble of their lives' events. But my peers missed it all; why should we be fascinated by the time? Simple envy or disappointment at having missed the fun can't explain it, for all eras offer tantalizing romantic images.

I think it's because we missed the sixties just barely. Might we have enjoyed it all firsthand if only we had set the alarm clock a few years earlier? The nearness of the era enlivens the prospect of having lived through it. Popular culture, along with vague childhood memories of the era's residue that flit about in the recesses of our minds, invest the period with an inchoate, preconscious sense of acquaintance.

In Proust's *Remembrance of Things Past,* the narrator, Marcel, meditates on memory and notes how his actual memories blended with one he never really experienced: "All these memories, superimposed upon one another, now formed a single mass, but had not so far coalesced that I could not discern between them . . . that veining, that variegation of coloring, which in certain rocks, in certain blocks of marble, points to differences of origin, age, and formation." Similarly, my impressions of the era do not bear the exact coloration of memories of my actual experiences. Yet I do possess a keen, if fleeting, sense of the time, more than a historical familiarity. To my generation, the sixties lie between memory and history, a memory at a remove. Our search for lost time dwells on the sixties, figuring out precisely what it was we just missed.

To say the sixties shaped us all is not to say it shaped us all the same way, and I won't attempt to extrapolate from my view of the era to manufacture a skeleton key that unlocks the mystery of all people under the age of thirty. I'm not even going to try to describe or speak for my whole genera-tion—a pointless task. Recently there has been a spate of journalistic attempts to pigeonhole us—books, magazine cover stories, marketing strategies—and it has been my con-temporaries, more than anyone else, who have derided them. "I am twenty-two, but I am not a member of your ridiculous and trite 'twentysomething generation,'" reader Bo Brock wrote in a letter to *U.S. News and World Report* after the magazine ran a typically daft generation piece. "I am not to be banded with any group so widely codified by its self-proclaimed 'members' and in the press." I share that resentment, which I think is prevalent among people my age.

At bottom, members of this generation just don't see our-selves as a cohesive group the way we imagine youth in the sixties did; the attempts to force that paradigm to fit might be yet another illustration that we walk in the sixties' shadow. Some resent the media generalizations because they patently omit huge chunks of society, focusing on a narrow segment of relatively affluent, educated people. Even among the affluent and educated, there are those who don't see themselves in the popular portraits—like me, for one. The media mandarins, in their thirst to generalize, have overlooked those of us who don't fit their schemes.

I don't consider the entire generational exercise a wash. Up to a point, these generalizations can offer insight into how people at certain ages responded to common events of their lives. But when carried too far, they resemble the zodiac on a Chinese restaurant place mat, ascribing the same characteristics to all roosters, monkeys, or pigs simply because of the incidence of their birth year. Besides, a moment's reflection makes it obvious that someone's eco-

IN THE SHADOW OF THE SIXTIES

nomic, intellectual, ethnic, or psychological background has far more influence on his or her worldview. The broad generational groupings forget that we react *differently* to what are indeed common events of our lives. To avoid such crude distortions myself, I won't make sweeping generalizations about all people born in a certain time-frame. Instead, I'll make sweeping generalizations about three different groups of people born in a certain time-frame—and about how our different views of the sixties color our lives today.

Some of my contemporaries have reacted to the sixties and its lasting legacy with anger and venom. Indeed, this group was the first of my peers to enthrall the mass media: the Reagan Revolutionaries they were dubbed. During the Reagan heyday, our generation was deemed one of young Michael J. Fox conservatives, rebelling against our liberal parents. Statistics were thrown at us about college graduates heading to Wall Street as the death knell of humanitarian ideals supposedly rang out.

This assertion always seemed to me vastly overstated. Sure, a lot of people bought into the Reagan presidency for its spirit of acquisitiveness, but I always took the materialism of 1980s youth to be just another manifestation of the overall zeitgeist. After all, our parents voted in large numbers for Reagan, too.

Still, I see around me a new type of conservative in my generation, even if they don't dominate our ranks the way the pop culture would have had us believe. These peers of mine fiercely resent those who enjoyed the sixties and hold them responsible for bequeathing a legacy of problems, attributable, in various cases, to the Great Society, Vietnam War protesters, drug use, feminism, and modern art. And although ideologically aligned with those who opposed the sixties changes, they try to portray themselves as the inheritors of the sixties mantle, as an insurgent conservative vanguard fighting the status quo of softheaded liberalism.

The most visible and extreme representatives of this group populate the dark alcoves of universities, publishing newspapers with the words *review* or *spectator* in the title—

the *Dartmouth Review* being the most notorious example. These papers subsist on the hundreds of thousands of dollars funneled to them annually by right-wing foundations allegedly doing "charitable" work. From these broadsides, they regularly torch the overstuffed strawman of political correctness, which they see as a product of the excesses of the sixties.

At the expense of betraying a political bias, I'll call this group reactionaries. I mean this in a descriptive, not pejorative, sense; they're reacting against the changes of the sixties. To them the sixties represent the source of the myriad problems of today's sophisticated world, and they look to icons like William F. Buckley, the senior sixties conservative champion, as role models. (It was even considered a mark of ascension among the ranks of one conservative group at my college when Buckley himself invited you to sail with him.) These reactionaries revel in highbrow language and smarmy clubbiness. To quote a phrase of journalist Sidney Blumenthal, they have "the rare ability to deal exclusively in invective and derision without achieving satiric effect."

How do these conservatives differ from their predecessors? What makes them a generational type, not just a political stripe? Campus papers like the *Dartmouth Review* seem to me to be distinguished, above all, by an unabashed viciousness; there have been a number of infamous incidents of publishing openly racist, sexist, and anti-Semitic articles or editorials. This anger stems in part, I think, from our generation's relationship to the sixties.

Older conservatives who battled against sexual and personal liberation, and against the notion that all was not well with Eisenhower America, saw society change around them. Perhaps in the course of their fight, they learned to accommodate. Today's reactionaries, growing up after the deluge, got stuck with the results of a more permissive and sophisticated society. They imagine a prelapsarian Norman Rockwell America. It's easier to fulminate for a return to that myth than actually to undo the perceived damage. From the women's and civil rights movements to environmentalism and consumerism, many changes of the sixties are here to stay. The reactionaries' venom, if I may hypothesize, comes from frustration with that reality.

Another segment of my generation does not actively despise the sixties yet nonetheless disdains the period's starry-eyed idealism. This type—the apathetic and disaffected "Generation Xer" of current cultural discourse/hype—has been the latest pretender to emerge in the media to "explain" or encapsulate my generation. (To some extent, this type is just a mutation of the Wall Street money glutton, reshaped for the leaner, meaner nineties but still hedonistic and without intellectual or moral aspirations.) Like the young Reaganite stereotype, this cliché has some truth to it, but it simply can't explain the generation as a whole. Given the attributes of the cynic stereotype—lazy, smart-assed, brain-dead from TV—it would be a miracle if we achieved anything so much as reading an issue of *USA Today* in our lifetimes. We'd be grazing our endless field of cable channels, ignoring the world around us, drinking and sleeping our way into oblivion. (*Hmm . . .*)

Nonetheless, I know my share of cynics. They see themselves in movies like *Singles* and read books by "writers" such as Douglas Coupland and Bret Easton Ellis. The extent of their political passion is feeling ticked off by the burdens of debt and environmental depredation they'll have to carry. They favor quixotics who promise to shake up the system, the Jerry Browns and Ross Perots, if they care to vote at all. They include the *Wayne's World* buffs who can subdivide heavy metal into all its taxonomic subgenres and the black-clad neo-beatniks who speak about moving to San Francisco or Seattle as if it will change their lives. Slackers, hackers, moaners, loners, losers, lollygaggers, Lollapaloozers, anarchists, anachronisms, shifters, drifters, dropouts, cast-outs, castaways, and "Gilligan's Island" junkies all share a lack of ambition and a forced disengagement from society.

These cynics may studiously avoid all appearances of being influenced by anything older than themselves. But they, too, owe a debt to the sixties (exhibit A: the Dead-

head). They have their precursors in the sixties counterculture, those who disdained the political process for acid
dropping and public frolicking. Like today's cynics, people
in the counterculture seemed unbothered by the turmoil
around them—or, if bothered, saw no point in doing anything about it. They mostly wanted to have fun, finding in
music and the pursuit of leisure a refuge from a disappointing world. The sixties—the time when this counterculture
dropout ethos infiltrated mass culture—now allows today's
cynics to get away with their cavalier attitudes toward sex
and drugs, work and play.

Popular attempts to define my contemporaries have failed
in part because they've ignored a third group: the idealists.
These idealists—who seem to me to be the most numerous
type of my generation—see the sixties as a time when
mostly, though not entirely, positive change was wrought.
They celebrate the era as a fount of inspiration and a
reminder of the possibility of a cultural and political
reawakening. They take great interest in the sixties for what
they might learn from them. They'll squander their free time
to publish magazines about campus protests that happened
twenty years ago. They're the ones "Doonesbury" carica-
tures.
    Idealists range in ideology from the mostly leftish com-
munity-service activists to the nonreactionary yet free-
market types who (vainly?) try to dream up private-sector
solutions to environmental destruction and poverty.
Whether they admire SDS members and their participatory
democracy or Yippies who tried to run a pig for president,
Martin Luther King or Malcolm X, idealists hearken to the
sixties for their heroes and role models. They've inherited a
certain ethic that the sixties brought to bear on our times
and share a basically heroic view of the decade as a time
when youth seized control of its own destiny. They admire
the activists' enthusiasm for political engagement and tend
to forgive its excesses. In the last election, many idealists
were among the ranks of the young Clinton boosters, wanting to believe in the promise of change.

As the Reagan youth boomlet might have reflected only a multigenerational turn toward conservatism, might not the Clinton kids represent only a general societal shift toward activism? What distinguishes the current crop of idealists from their predecessors, I think, is a less-romantic view of political progress. In the sixties, so much happened so fast; protesters suffered an enormous letdown when they couldn't eradicate racism or pull us out of Vietnam overnight. Having come of age after Vietnam and Watergate—and here, alas, we must resort to fuzzy generational theorizing—today's idealists have had more realistic expectations from our government and society. Having grown up only among Republican presidents, unless you count Jimmy Carter, they figure anything Clinton offers is a bonus.

The popular portrayals of my generation give no hint of the existence of these young idealists. It's easy for scribes to seize upon the embrace of conservative ideology and dash off a facile contrast with our supposedly idealistic predecessors. Similarly, there's a measure of condescension in the portrait of the new generation as blasé. But the idealists challenge their forebears in a different way. They threaten to beat them at their own game. They've been overlooked, it seems to me, because they aspire to do what the previous generation's idealists did not do: finish building the dream of a better culture and country. In that sense, they are the inheritors of the sixties mantle.

To be sure, a good portion of my generation hardly considers the sixties important at all. But I think it's fair to say that, collectively, we're all frustrated by the achievements of the sixties. Whether we realize it or not, we're in its shadow. The decade looms before us all as an imposing precursor to our own age, whether we want to recapture it, escape from it, or slay it. There's nothing wrong with that—it's natural, like a generational Oedipal complex—so long as we see that each of these selective interpretations retains some truths and omits others, perhaps an inevitable result of the anxiety of influence we feel toward the time.

Eventually, the sixties will of necessity recede further and further in the rearview mirror, and we twentysomethings will devote ourselves increasingly to steering through the present. The sixties will be with us for a while, in the Kennedyesque poses of our public leaders, in the Beatlesque and Dylanesque influences of our music, in the rhetoric of race, the polemics of class, the trappings of fashion, the fear of senseless war, and the ongoing quest for utopia. But if the ideas and debates are old, the people who engage in them are new, and we can develop them and shape them in ways that can't be foreseen or planned.

So perhaps the generational mavens, trying to find what unites us, have missed the most obvious characteristic of all: our age. If we're constantly comparing our times to the sixties, it's because that's when young people took center stage. If we seem by turns rebellious, self-consciously indifferent, or naively idealistic, it might be because those are the timeless hallmarks of youth. And if we haven't moved the world, maybe it's because we're only in our twenties.

MY "BOURGEOIS" BRAND OF FEMINISM

Paula Kamen

I always knew that coming out as a feminist wouldn't win me any popularity contests. So I played it cool at a party a few years ago when one of my former high-school acquaintances asked me about the subject of my book, *Feminist Fatale*. I told him the subtitle: *Voices from the "Twentysomething" Generation Explore the Future of the "Women's Movement."* Then, his words lubricated by alcohol, he inquired why I had written it: "What bad thing had happened" to make me into one of those *feminists?*

I even laughed at a joke made by an old friend and coworker during a temporary job as a copy editor at a suburban newspaper. He and I were walking back into the newsroom together when he suddenly struck a zombielike pose, stretched out his arms before him, and stared blankly ahead. He droned: "Patriarchy. Sixty-nine cents to the dollar. Misogynist society. It's better in Sweden."

He explained to the rest of the newsroom that I had brainwashed him during lunch.

But I wasn't as prepared for a confrontation on the feminist activist front, which was much more unsettling. After a speech I gave at an Ohio university, a graduate student in the audience made reference to my "bourgeois brand of feminism."

Of course, I could have shrugged it off and joked, "Bourgeois? But I'm not even French."

Her comment, however, reflected an alarming attitude. She was reacting to one of my concluding points that feminism must become accessible to the masses of people not ensconced in activist communities. I had suggested that feminists make a greater effort to *supplement* "radical-sounding" voices with more moderate-style forms of expression in order to make the movement more marketable.

The word *bourgeois* particularly bothered me because it reflects a common refusal on the part of many radical and academic feminists to communicate with those who exist outside the rigid borders of campus life. It implies that feminism is an elite and exclusive philosophy that would be demeaned if allowed to fall into the hands of the great unwashed masses.

Yet, as I thought about this term, I viewed it in another light—not as an insult but as something to aspire to. What's wrong with creating a more "bourgeois" brand of feminism for communicating with the great Blockbuster-renting, Egg McMuffin–eating, Greyhound-riding mass of the population? Creating a bourgeois brand of feminism can be a lofty goal. It means making the ideas of feminism more accessible, without sacrificing their integrity or trivializing them. It means making the movement a cause for uniting women—and not dividing them.

This task demands more than just conventional marketing; after all, promoting a set of social ideas is a lot trickier than selling a simple consumer product. But marketing is essential, a necessary evil that all of us must practice to get anywhere in the public consciousness.

I was a college student when I first recognized that better communication was needed to confront feminist stereotypes. As a senior, I was given a chance to write an opinion column for the *Daily Illini* at the University of Illinois. I naturally drifted toward "women's issues," partly because the overwhelmingly male staff of that section wasn't covering them.

Instantly, I was branded as a radical feminist. People I met seemed fearful that I would chew them out for using a politically incorrect word or for naively opening the door for me; certain family members warned me that I was jeopardizing my once-in-a-lifetime opportunity to meet guys in college, where the pickings were plentiful. I was suddenly busy defending myself as a nonradical; coworkers joked about why I hated men so much; one called me "the feminist fatale." When going out in a group or on anything even vaguely resembling a date, I found myself hiding the painful truth of my feminist affiliations—as if I were harboring some grisly genetic disorder or family curse that would test even the truest and most faithful of loves.

The label stuck even though my columns were militantly middle-of-the-road. There was nothing revolutionary about my stances. Instead of bug-eyed, hysterical radicals, I interviewed seemingly more credible people, like university administrators and Greek system officials. In my first column, I defined a newly discussed phenomenon called "acquaintance rape" and concluded that males had the ultimate responsibility for prevention. In an analysis of the 1988 election's impact on abortion rights, I conveyed a standard prochoice view.

Even after such tame columns, I vowed to shift to some less-controversial and standard topics, like making fun of cafeteria food, a college writer's staple material. I tried to buffer any column on any topic remotely connected to any "women's issue" with other commentaries—which attracted only a fraction of the attention.

But while everyone else was treating me like one, I didn't consider myself a feminist. I, too, had my stereotypes. After all, I was bourgeois to the bone—not on the vanguard of anything in particular.

Like millions of others in my demographic group, through high school I wore clothes from the Limited, was equipped with a steady series of orthodontic apparatuses, and read *Seventeen* as carefully and rigorously as if it bestowed Talmudic wisdom. My parents were unswervingly traditional in lifestyle, with my mother staying at home and my father working two jobs.

Even when my interest in women's issues grew in college, I was still passive. As a sophomore, I transferred to a historically progressive residence hall, the center of activism on the campus. I interviewed a visiting guest-in-residence, a feminist artist, who shocked me with her radical (from a mid-eighties Reagan-era perspective) philosophies. She pointed out, for instance, how society's expectations for women to be impossibly thin were related to the eating disorders I was witnessing around me. I learned, but did not act. It wasn't until senior year—when I was forced in my column to dig beyond the surface reporting about these issues, defend my views, and take a public stand—that I identified myself as a feminist.

I noticed this same phenomenon among other women. I could ask almost anyone whether they supported the progress of the women's movement and the most basic of feminist principles, and they would say "yes." They agreed that we should respect women's choices, humanize the workplace, give women equal opportunity and compensation for equal work. But, when asked if they were feminists, anyone familiar with the word would automatically and emphatically respond "no."

These young women often feared being associated with the feminist stereotype—the exact opposite of the image that many peer-pressured young heterosexual women want to convey. This fear was so overwhelming that I chose to discuss it in the beginning of the first chapter of my book:

I asked them, and they answered, with some slight variations:

"What do you associate with the word *feminist?*"
"I imagine: bra-burning, hairy-legged, amazon, castrating, militant-almost-antifeminine, communist, Marxist, separatist, female skinheads, female supremacists, he-woman types, bunch-a-lesbians, you-know-dykes, man-haters, man-bashers, wanting-men's-jobs, wanting-to-dominate-men, want-to-be-men, wear-short-hair-to-look-unattractive, bizarre-chicks-running-around-doing-kooky-things, I-am-woman-hear-me-roar, up-tight, angry, white-middle-class radicals."

I guess you get the picture.

As I worked on the book, I started reading about feminism in the public library. But instead of being inspired by feminist literature, I was confused. Many of the readings assumed a consummate knowledge of the past thirty years of feminist philosophy and analysis. ("Of course, this is not to be confused with Gilligan's theories of morality, but rather echo a more *politico* point of view.") The language, left over from more outwardly revolutionary times, was encrusted with manifesto-like terms (like "overthrow the hegemonic capitalist patriarchy"), which seriously blocked my reading comprehension. I remember reading Robin Morgan's *The Demon Lover* about three pages a sitting—and then realizing in the end I didn't know what it was about.

I also felt left out. The available books seemed to describe the specific experience of a limited group of women from past generations. ("Remember when you were at Woodstock breast-feeding your first child, just dropped out of Columbia, and you had that first hit of acid and . . .")

And I was not the only one left out. Consider, for instance, the way black feminist scholar bell hooks takes on *The Feminine Mystique,* the 1963 classic by feminist matriarch Betty Friedan. Friedan spoke of the dramatic plight "that has no name," of the affluent white suburban housewife who was trapped in her mandatory role. Yet, as hooks points out in one of her first books, Friedan hardly recognized the even more limited choices of less-privileged women—working as waitresses, nurses, or maids.

Meanwhile, the feminist figures I saw on television were embarrassing. A spring 1990 "Nightline" episode, "Entertainment or Bad Taste?" featured a debate about the booking by "Saturday Night Live" of notoriously sexist comedian Andrew Dice Clay. When asked about Clay's fans, the radical feminist psychologist who was featured compared them to bystanders that had watched a recent gang rape on a pool table in New Bedford, Massachusetts. She congratulated the SNL cast member and musical guest who refused to perform on a show featuring Clay.

"What they're telling other women is: 'You don't have to stay on the date and take it if you're beginning to feel uncomfortable. If it makes you feel bad, if it makes you feel scared, you can walk off. You don't have to stay on the date.' "

She failed to explain clearly how Clay's comedy, gang rape, and a date rape were connected. The comparison seemed heavy-handed, portraying Clay's fans as mindless savages, as ready to rape as they are to applaud the comedian.

At least I understood, though, what she was trying to say. Even after having spent two years studying and writing about feminism, I am often still confused listening to many academic feminists. In the spring of 1992, on a panel about differences among older and younger feminists at a New York socialist conference, I tried as hard as I could to focus on the speech of one of the women speaking before me. I opened the program periodically—to check if I had wandered in on the wrong panel.

I also felt like a cretin when trying to make sense of a few of the reviews of my own book. Several academics seemed obsessed with trying to peg my single theory of the universe and didn't understand that I was acting as a journalist without a hard-line agenda, reporting many points of view.

One reviewer from a women's-studies journal dismissed the book for its lack of sociological methodology. In the end, she questioned the feminist convictions of the book by referring to the subtitle, "which puts both its subject and the object inside quotation marks, as though uncertain about the ontological status of both the cohort of people interviewed and the movement about which they were asked."

At first, I didn't know what this meant, but I was sure that it didn't sound too good.

Another common failing of the more-visible components of the older generation of feminists is a reluctance to acknowledge the dramatic progress that American women have generally made. The result is that they come off as paranoid, stuck in another era. Radical thinkers and activists often take on the condescending and self-defeating mission of telling people how miserable they are.

Portraying the world as completely oppressive and hostile to women compounds the trepidation among young people that the women's movement is only about recognizing women's victimization. Such a single-minded focus is often overwhelming and distorting. The next generation also needs to hear more positive messages about feminism.

We also need to hear specifics. I'm reminded of a friend's disappointment after going to see an established feminist author at a national leadership conference. When a man in the audience raised his hand and asked what men could do for the women's movement, the author replied, "Give up the power."

What did that mean? Quit his job? Turn his apartment into a domestic violence shelter? Become a eunuch in service to the Goddess?

The vast majority of people of my generation have little patience for anything that seems too ideological, dogmatic, or revolutionary. It smacks of extremist, shortsighted rhetoric from the late sixties. We mistrust such either-or, black-or-white thinking that renders us inflexible to changing conditions. When I was in school, I never took a women's-studies class because I feared being fed a semester-long diet of radical propaganda—and being graded on the extent to which I agreed.

But the fact is that feminism *is* radical. It overturns tradition and age-old notions of women's proper place in society—in religion, law, education, the family, and so on. The challenge, then, is to communicate radical goals using accessible and familiar means of expression.

I have been warned by some radical feminists that voicing a more "moderate" feminism plays into the hands of the opposition. They reason that men have traditionally demanded that women act like "ladies" and have not hesitated to bulldoze right over us. But just because acting with sugar and spice is a traditional female style, it doesn't mean that it cannot be productive. Feminists don't always have to parrot men to be effective.

This more user-friendly approach distinctly appeals to masses of people in this "I'm not a feminist, but . . ." generation. The more than one hundred nonactivists I interviewed for my book in 1990 named as their favorite feminist role model Faye Wattleton, the former executive director of Planned Parenthood. They described her in glowing terms as "articulate," "calm," and "professional." In contrast, just as many described former National Organization for Women president Molly Yard as "abrasive" and "militant." Yet, ironically, I don't view Wattleton as being any less radical or more compromising than Yard, also a solid and dedicated leader. She just conveys the message in a different way.

Consider, too, the style of Patricia Schroeder, a Democratic congresswoman from Colorado. When Schroeder lobbied for the Family and Medical Leave Act, which was finally passed in 1992 after years of debate and Republican presidential vetoes, she talked about a "family-friendly workplace" rather than the more vague "feminization of power." When she met with corporate employees about making the workplace more flexible, she spoke in terms of human values. First, she asked them a question: "How many of you would rather call work and say that your car broke down than admit that your child or spouse was sick?" An overwhelming majority chose the first, and then Schroeder was able to point out society's skewed priorities—we are more willing to accept a breakdown in technology than in a person's health as a valid excuse for taking time away from work.

We will always need militant voices to challenge the status quo, express outrage, and advance women's agendas. And academics play an important role in framing, chronicling, and systematically studying the movement. It was radical feminists who, after all, made the movement a part of popular consciousness and who had the courage to address issues that many considered too extreme for Ma and Pa America. But that doesn't mean that these radical-sounding voices can't be *complemented* by more "mainstream" ones.

The most powerful way to broadcast a more "mainstream" message is through the media. But, as I learned after my book was published, refining and condensing a message require a constant and concentrated effort.

Like most young and unestablished authors, I had no full-time publicist to show me the ropes. So that fall, I was unprepared when a producer from the "Home" show (a mid-morning guide to domestic living) called me. She started with a basic question:

"So, Paula, what are the five main points of your book?"

I panicked, and then thought: Hell, I'll just talk for a while and—sooner or later—I'll come up with a good half dozen or so.

After I rambled on for a few minutes laying the groundwork with some background information, she stopped me abruptly.

"Just answer the question," she said.

"I am. But this is my introduction to the question. I'm giving you a sense of context."

"Forget the context! We don't have context on television! Try again!"

I still rambled on, cluelessly.

"O.K., we'll get back to that one,. Next question: Why do many young people reject the term *feminist?*"

Then I launched into the same epic narrative and analysis.

Needless to say, I did not get a callback from the "Home" show.

After that, I sat down at my computer to learn the elusive art of the sound bite. Laboring all day, I tried to sum up the five main points. They came out to about ten pages. Then I called my old editor, who had transferred to another publisher to work as a publicist.

Lisa had me read my two-page-long attempts at single sound bites and then further whittled them down. For example, as I was blustering on with my explanation of how the older generation has failed to pass the torch, she stopped me at one unusually snappy sentence explaining why this generation doesn't identify with feminism: ". . . the women's movement has an older woman's face on it."

"Say that and cut the rest," she said.

Ah ha! I realized that the trick was using the most concentrated and catchy language possible—like writing a pop song riff or an advertising jingle.

Of course, I was slightly miffed that I had to advance my socially progressive ideas with the same hackneyed advertising techniques used to hawk wart removers and floor wax.

But, I was learning that was the only way. I slowly came to terms with the ugly fact that this is a media age. Without the resources to create my own alternative networks or newspapers, I had to adapt to this reality. Some embarrassment and distortions were inevitable, but I thought that my efforts were worthwhile because of the mass media's vast potential to heighten awareness and spark dialogue on important issues. Meanwhile, I also knew that I had to consider carefully every word I uttered and be aware—constantly—of the risk of trivializing or oversimplifying feminist politics.

As the calls mushroomed and I became my own publicist, I perfected this art of being media-genic. I could summarize any idea not only in a sound bite but also in a cafeteria-style smorgasbord of many different-sized sound bites. For example, I could pinpoint the focus of my book in as few as four words: "Young women and feminism." Or, if I were allotted a more indulgent span of response time, say anything more than five seconds, I could deliver the deluxe model: "A journalistic documentary of the perceptions of women in their twenties of feminism, and their visions for the future."

I learned always to be ready to deliver a deeply felt and honest opinion—even when I had never before considered the question. One time, a *New York Times* reporter called me out of the blue and asked me for a comment about the pitfalls of modern romance. I just churned out that irresistible sound bite gold, saying something like "That's the sexual revolution of the generation in their twenties: quality in relationships instead of quantity."

While this skill helped me to get out some of my message about young women and feminism, I have come up against my own limitations: chiefly, my age. I was twenty-four years old when the book came out and relatively inexperienced as a public speaker. When reporters want a feminist opinion, they almost always turn to the Rolodex card listing the established and recognizable older activists. At my age, without the luck of nepotism or benefits of bribery, it's nearly impossible to have major-league credentials. I have never headed a national organization or been elected to a major political post. My Pulitzer must have gotten lost in the mail.

One risk in getting out the message is to travel too far in the opposite direction of elitism, beyond good taste, to the bargain basement of ideas. I never felt as cheap or degraded as when I appeared on the "Jenny Jones Show." Syndicated from Chicago, this national talk show is usually broadcast during an infomercial-crammed time slot, sometime during the graveyard shift. The producer called me in the spring of 1992 in response to the *New York Times* feature. She told me she was doing a show about the same topic and was inviting some distinguished academic experts. During our "preinterview," I discussed the influence of acquaintance rape and AIDS, and the producer seemed receptive. I thought that even if the show was sleazy, I'd be reaching a large new mainstream audience normally not exposed to such "progressive" analyses.

To my horror, the entire show made "Studs" look like a PBS "Day at the Met" installment. When I got off the Number Six bus and arrived at the studio downtown, I realized that the producer had never seen a copy of my book. She just knew that I wrote for the twentysomethings—and that she needed someone to represent and embody the experience of the twentysomething swinging single woman. According to the script, which was to serve as a general guide for the guests, I was to be the "captain" of the "women's team," and a suave and outspoken local young newspaper columnist the head of the "men's team." The "teams" would debate the nitty-gritty truth of sex and singledom in the nineties.

I was even dressed wrong. While I wore a formal Margaret Thatcheresque suit cut up to my chin, the women on my "team" were clothed in more casual stretch pants, heels, and dangling jewelry. But all our outfits were uniformly accented with the same pin—a pink circle with a woman's symbol inside, courtesy of the show.

The producer noticed my discomfort (I was trembling in the corner) and took me aside to practice my opening line, which was a variation on the *New York Times* quote. We rehearsed it about twelve times.

As the show started, the camera light and Jenny's smile activated simultaneously. She introduced her guests, including the head of a national video dating service and a doctor from the Kinsey Institute. (Even she was better informed and prepared for the show, sporting a polka-dotted minidress.) Also invited was a mastermind who had made up a "sex contract" for a woman to sign on a date, thereby protecting the man against any future claim of rape.

Then the spotlight went on me. I was so horrified that I literally could not speak. One of my worst lifelong fears, going speechless before a crowd, was coming true for the first time during my media career. Finally, with all my effort, I sputtered out the sentences in an entirely new sequence. Jenny dropped her veneer of effervescence and rolled her eyes at the audience, which froze in confusion.

Later in the show, I tried to make up for my gaffe with another comment. I interjected a line about birth control, which the producer had suggested would be useful. During our "preinterview," I had stated that the responsibility for planning for and using contraception is still that of the woman.

But during the show, when I finally got Jenny's attention, I blurted out something like "Men always expect us to take care of the birth control!" I meant to sound like a cool journalistic observer but instead came across as if I were grousing about the behavior of *all those men* I sleep with.

After the taping finally, mercifully ended, I realized just how useless I had been. Two men from the studio audience approached me and commented, "We were just wondering . . . Who are you and why were you here?"

The next day, when I finally emerged from my catatonic, migraine-dulled state, I plotted how I would stop the show from airing on national television. I could dress up as a page or scale the NBC tower at night to steal and destroy the videotape, like the caped crusader fetching a holy-grail-type prize for Robin Williams's character in *The Fisher King*.

Now I am haunted by one threat that refuses to go away: reruns. For months, many friends and acquaintances have delivered the news that they caught the show, although they, of course, are not regular "Jenny Jones" watchers. At a party last year, my friend's cousin mentioned the show and I tried to play it down, first by blaming it on an evil twin. When that failed to convince him, I just explained that I hadn't had the chance to say much. "No, Paula," he replied. "You said quite enough."

During the past few years, I have noticed more young feminist activists courting the media's attention with style. However, like the older generation of feminists, they are largely sticking with their own kind.

From university rallies to underground teenage zines, young activists communicate largely within their own academic or countercultural enclaves. Young professional elites set up networks for themselves. Militant direct-action groups, while energetic and striking, have a tendency to alienate or downright confound the uninitiated. The ample rhetoric in activist and academic circles about the importance and possibility of an inclusive women's movement has not yet been put into significant practice.

Feminists will take a *truly* radical turn when they make their messages dramatically more accessible and relevant to the rest of society. Bridging the gap with nonactivists requires communication that includes down-to-earth language, provides visible role models from different class backgrounds, tackles the "real life" issues of work and the family, and points out specifics instead of just screaming slogans.

Spreading the word about feminism isn't just the task of elites. More affluent women may indeed have the greatest access to the media and the most time to be activists, but it is still urgent for women of all backgrounds to organize and speak out. Those who have shied away from the feminist stigma can look beyond the stereotypes. Issues like equal pay, sexual harassment, acquaintance rape, and reproductive choice are not confined to any one segment of society.

My generation of pragmatic idealists is prepared to embrace this more "bourgeois brand of feminism." We recognize that it gives us the flexibility and base of support to respond to the challenges facing *all* women. We can look to

feminist activists before us, whose triumphs, disappoint-
ments, and occasional foibles provide invaluable lessons.
And by communicating across class, race, and educational
lines, we can build on the tremendous progress that older
feminists have already made.

After all, making our message more accessible doesn't
mean that we've been co-opted by the hegemonic capitalist
patriarchy—or that we've sold out. It means we're getting
savvy.

And only then will substance prevail over stereotype.

LIVING THE LANSING DREAM

Ted Kleine

I went to high school at J. W. Sexton in Lansing, Michigan, a Depression-era brick fortress that sat across the street from a Fisher Body auto assembly plant. The plant was blocks long on each side and wrapped in a skin of corrugated steel painted a shade of green somewhere between the Statue of Liberty and mold. It loomed so near the high school that on football Fridays, when the Big Reds butted heads in Memorial Stadium, night-shift workers stood on balconies and watched the game.

A few times, I stood on Verlinden Avenue, along the plant's front face, and looked into the row of windows just below the roof. I hoped to see auto bodies jerking along in the progression from chassis to Caddy, but I was too low, the windows were too high, and all I could see were powerful ceiling lamps, beaming yellowish light on rooms full of mysterious auto work. General Motors, Fisher Body's parent company, wasn't releasing any industrial secrets, and they sure weren't letting any Sexton students in to take field trips or use the bathroom.

Back in the Factory Days, when Michigan-made cars ruled the roads, so many Sexton grads went to work for Fisher Body that there might as well have been a tunnel leading from the graduation stage to the Axle Line, or to the Oldsmobile factory, a mile away on Main Street. On a clear day, a Sexton student could see his future, and all avenues led to a secure, middle-class life in a serene city full of UAW lapel pins.

Ransom Eli Olds built his first car in a workshop on River Street, and for years afterward, the city made a good living piecing together the ever-evolving models of R.E.O.'s buggy. A hotel and a freeway are named after Olds, and his initials have become a word: we have a Reo Street, a Reo School, and, until it burned in a spectacular fire in 1975, a Diamond Reo truck plant. R.E.O. Speedwagon, popular in Lansing since their bar band days, took their name from an early Olds car.

Getting hired at a Michigan auto plant in the old days was easier than getting drafted. A few days after his discharge, a World War II vet was walking down a street in Pontiac, in full uniform. As he passed an auto plant, a foreman ran out the front door and yelled, "Hey, Marine! You want a job?"

Even better is the tale of a young Flint gas jockey who did a fill-'er-up for a big shot in GM's personnel department.

"Why aren't you working in the shop?" the GM recruiter asked.

The gas jockey shrugged, so the recruiter took down his name and address. A week later, the young man received a letter in the mail asking him to report for a physical to determine his fitness for duty with the General. That was back in '72; the gas jockey is now a seasoned shoprat.

While Nikita Khrushchev and Leonid Brezhnev bragged about building a workers' paradise in Russia, we lived in one in Michigan: weekly pay stubs the size of Third World annual incomes, two cars in the driveway, and deer-hunting trips each November to the north woods, which were stocked like a royal game preserve. The shops offered blue-collar work at white-collar wages, so the riveter at Fisher Body earned as much as the fisheries biologist at the Department of Natural Resources, and they often lived in matching ranch houses in the same neighborhood.

My family was part of Lansing's other big industry. I was a state government brat. Throughout my entire childhood and adolescence, my dad worked as economist for the Michigan Department of Management and Budget. He took the job in 1966, when he was twenty-four and moved from

Maryland with my mother, who was six months pregnant with me and cried the whole trip.

As the auto industry boomed, so did the state bureaucracy. I always assumed that the state would one day have a place for me, too. If nothing better came along, I figured I could sit in an air-conditioned government cubicle and work as an editor at, say, the Department of Transportation. A state job was my birthright, but I didn't look forward to claiming it any more than the son of a shoprat looked forward to claiming his spot on the line.

Leaving home was never in my plans, though. My youth was spent plotting a way to be a writer and still live in Lansing. Journalism seemed like the best course, since the only time I ever read about Lansing was in the local paper, the *Lansing State Journal*. When I was eleven, I read a boy's biography of Thomas Edison, which described a newspaper he printed himself, then peddled on the train between Port Huron and Detroit. In a single page, it condensed the news of the world, with dispatches from England, France, and more exotic countries. This inspired my first journalistic effort, the *Lansing Eagle,* a lemonade-stand newsletter in which I ran articles on the Arab-Israeli situation, copied out of the *Detroit Free Press,* as well as local stories like "A Big Paint Mess," which began, "Someone dumped a bucket of paint on the sidewalk in front of the Barnes' house." The *Eagle* made me the Hearst of Christine Drive, where my "circulation director," a younger boy named Steve, sold the paper door-to-door for three cents, since I was too diffident for home solicitation.

Growing up in a subdivision on the western edge of town, I had no idea that Lansing was actually a city, with slums and factories. Beyond bicycle thefts, I knew nothing of crime. When a candidate for mayor campaigned on the slogan "For Safe Streets," I assumed he meant to fix the potholes. Although Lansing is stony cold and cloudy most of the year, when I recall my boyhood I am stuck with an image of the city in August. Locusts buzzed in the hot grass, and I sat out in the backyard reading *Baseball's Greatest Pennant Races,* the perfect combination of books and baseball, the only two things I cared about.

As I grew older, I discovered more of Lansing. For two weeks one summer, I delivered newspapers for a friend who lived in a compact brick house near St. Casimir's Church, about a mile from downtown. In its early years, his neighborhood had been Polish, and the houses were workers' issue: a living room, kitchen, basement, and a few bedrooms packed under the roof. Some of the factories were within walking distance. As I lofted copies of the *State Journal* onto the square concrete porches, I heard the iron hammering of the Lindell Drop Forge and smelled the oven-warm bread from Shafer's Bakery, an odor that made the humid air of summer taste lighter. The neighborhood was like an ethnic enclave of Chicago, although roomier, with bungalows and yards instead of row houses and stoops. The Catholic church was here, and so were the Polish Hall, the corner grocery stores (one fit to shop in, one run by a crazy widow who let food rot on the shelves), and the elementary school.

I came to love the city the way you would love a pond you had lived next to for years, or a forest you played in when you were a boy. Whenever I could, I walked or rode my bicycle around town, hoping to discover landmarks I hadn't seen before. Anything old, anything that suggested history, excited me: the brick arch in Durant Park, the plaque by the northside ice cream stand that marked the site of Lansing's first cabin. Sometimes, I even liked the greasy, rainbow-colored slick outside the Oldsmobile plant ("Old-smo-bile," I called the automaker's effluent.)

Lansing was a working town. Lansing—like Flint, Saginaw, or any other city of industry—takes on unpleasant burdens, often for meager rewards, so that towns such as Ann Arbor and Grosse Pointe can remain little green jewelboxes unsmudged by factory exhaust. The factory workers live in my kind of town, the factory owners in the other. In the factory towns, a practical, almost grim attitude develops toward The Job. Even white-collar Joes say, "A job doesn't have to be something you like." Our local work ethic is to be competent as all hell while appearing thoroughly irritated by your duties. A baseball player from Lansing would demand time and a half for an extra-inning game, hit the winning home run, then have nothing to talk about when he got home except the traffic on the way back from the park.

At heart, I knew I would always be a white-collar kid: I edited the school paper, earned a letter in cross-country, played on the Quiz Bowl team, and made plans to go to the University of Michigan. But not all my friends did the same. Mitch Kolhoff, whom I had admired since he used the word *fart* in a poem in tenth-grade English class, was the brightest, most thoughtful guy I knew at Sexton. He was in the Honor Society, partly because he had earned straight A's in construction class. (He was one of the only students strong enough to handle the jackhammer.) Mitch introduced me to punk rock, playing a tape of "The Shah Sleeps in Lee Harvey's Grave" by the Butthole Surfers, while we built sets for the school play in the basement of the auditorium.

Mitch, though, was not going to college. His father, who stocked vending machines, could not afford the tuition, so Mitch never bothered to apply, or even to take the college-prep classes that might have qualified him for a scholarship. After we graduated from Sexton, I went to the University of Michigan in Ann Arbor, and Mitch stayed at home with his parents and got a job bussing tables at Kelly's, a downtown bar.

At college, my life was confined to a nine-by-twelve dorm room, my schedule defined by tests and term papers. I envied the freedom I imagined Mitch had. Compared to the uptight, career-mad preppies in Ann Arbor, he lived like a bohemian. On weekends, when I was home from school, we drove around in his sports car, holding forty-ounce bottles of beer on our laps, looking for an empty park to get drunk in. (Mitch, bald at eighteen, could buy at the less-discriminating liquor stores.) While the car stereo blasted Steppenwolf or Flipper, Mitch talked about his latest hobby. He was, depending on the week, a painter, a musician, a devotee of Taoism, or a student of karate. He read Carl Jung and Dostoevsky and took a class in Logic at Lansing Community College. He had no career plans but simply experienced whatever his mental appetites desired.

I felt aimless and alienated among the suburban-bred coffee achievers at the U of M, who thought my buzz cut and my Dead Kennedys records were stupid and didn't under-

stand why I never spent the weekend in the dorm. I was
homesick for the grubby city I'd been reared in, and after a
single semester in Ann Arbor's green groves of academe, I
dropped out and enrolled at Lansing Community College—
located in downtown Lansing, convenient to bus lines, six-
teen dollars a credit, buy your books across the street at
Chiwocha's Mini-Mart.

My motto became "Bloom where you were planted."
Eventually, I landed at Michigan State, in East Lansing,
which had been my collegiate ambition all along. At the
campus newspaper, I was the Lansing reporter, writing features glorifying the city's eccentrics: a man who wanted to
light the Capitol dome red, white, and blue, a city council
candidate who claimed a fortune-teller had predicted she
would win (wrongly, as you can guess). On Saturdays, I
wrote and photocopied "97 Blocks," an underground dope
sheet on Lansing politics, which I distributed at record
stores and food co-ops all over town. The University of
Michigan had made me feel depressed and mopish, but
Michigan State invigorated me. There, I had a cause, which
I attacked with preacherly zeal: telling MSU students the
good news about the wonderful, colorful town that lay
alongside their campus.

Most MSU students lived in fear of Lansing. They saw it
as a Little Detroit, a menacing collection of blacks and red-
necks that combined the worst elements of a hick town and
a slum. Most had seen nothing but East Michigan Avenue,
the seedy main strip that ran from the campus to the Capitol, and from its adult book stores and soup kitchens concluded that the entire city was unwholesome.

I carried on my mission in my circle of college friends.
"Lansing is a good place to live," I told anyone I thought
would believe me. "It's the best place." My girlfriend told
me I had a "Lansing fetish."

The summer before I graduated from Michigan State, I
worked as a stringer for the *State Journal,* and a few weeks
before diploma time, I got a phone call: come to work as a
part-time reporter, $240 a week, nights, the police beat. It
was the only job I'd ever wanted, in the only town I wanted
to live in.

That winter should have been the happiest and most satisfying of my life. I had the job I had worked for all my youth. I rented a big house on the river, from which I planned to launch canoe trips once spring came. At Christmas, I was still enthralled with the city. We had a blizzard that night, and I trudged through the empty streets to watch snow swirl around a street lamp, the flakes glowing in the circle of waxy light. Then I walked down the river, to listen to the music of the cold water as it burbled downstream, the only sound in all the still, snowy night. But that winter, I was assailed by feelings of boredom and an urge for adventure that could no longer be satisfied in Lansing.

By the time the sharp blue skies of December had been covered by the dingy, down-in-the-mouth clouds of January, I needed to leave. During those months when the days are gray and the nights long and black, I began to feel I was rotting. The paper gave me three days off each week, and I had trouble filling them: I read *Dr. Jekyll and Mr. Hyde,* I trained for a marathon, I took up cross-country skiing. When I was really desperate for stimulation, I shuffled up to the Vietnamese grocery and bought a Little Debbie jelly roll. In Michigan, wintertime is Miller time, all the time, and the shelves at my house began to fill with empty bottles, drained in front of the TV set. So what had happened? How had I slid from excitement to ennui in just a few months?

Well, first of all, I had graduated from college at the beginning of the winter. During my final term as a Michigan State Spartan, I had been consumed by my new job at the newspaper and a slate of esoteric humanities classes: Chaucer, English History, Philosophy of Language, and Christianity. Once I was handed my diploma, the entire structure of my life collapsed. For the first time, I had nothing to look ahead to. Four days a week, I wrote and reported for the *Lansing State Journal,* and every Thursday they gave me a check that took care of all my needs. What I did with my time off and my money was up to me. Not marching ahead, not tethered to an institution, I began to feel I was living a sort of weightless existence. Lansing had excited me because it was a place to grow. Now, I had acquired the marks of a grown-up—a diploma, a job—and I wondered: What happens next?

I wrote to my younger brother in St. Louis and described my restlessness.

"I don't know anyone who loves Lansing more than you," he wrote back, "but I think you've gotten all you can out of the town."

At the *State Journal,* the man I considered my mentor was a cranky, old-school newsman who still believed that all reporters should have bar tabs. He shunned all exercise except smoking and hoisting his belt up over his thirty-eight inch waist. He hated Lansing. He called all Michiganders "Mittenheads," after the shape of the state, and vowed to commit suicide before his two-year anniversary at the *State Journal.* The very first time I asked him for career advice, he said, "Get the hell out of this state."

So I did. It shocked my editors, whom I'd harangued endlessly with my hometown patriotism, but I announced I was quitting my job and moving to Albuquerque, New Mexico, a city I knew from having spent the night there during a spring-break trip the year before. What was I looking for? An unfamiliar city to explore, a job in which I could work forty hours a week, a bigger sky, and freedom. What was I giving up in Lansing? A part-time job with no benefits and take-home pay of $9,500 a year. Nothing, or so I thought.

I blitzed every daily newspaper in New Mexico with my résumé, and three days before I was scheduled to leave town, I got a call from *The Albuquerque Tribune,* which I considered the most colorfully written newspaper in America. *The Albuquerque Tribune* wanted to interview me! I had never been so excited.

I traveled to New Mexico in a Ford Econoline van driven by my friend Jason Portier, who was lured to California by dreams of rock and roll fame. We arrived in New Mexico at sunrise on a Monday morning, after an all-night drive across the Texas desert. At the state line, I pulled the van to the side of the highway, leapt from the driver's seat, and danced in the sand by the roadside, celebrating my arrival in my new home state.

I was in Albuquerque twelve days. During my interview,

I was promised a job as the *Tribune*'s University of New Mexico correspondent, but the next week, I got a phone call from an editor. There had been a budget cut. Perhaps I would like to try back in a couple of months. So a few weeks after I had left Lansing, bearing my hopes like a personal banner, this message appeared on computer screens at the *Lansing State Journal*: "Ted Kleine is back in town and looking for work." No luck.

The city was so dismal that in November I left again, to seek my fortune in San Francisco. But though I had left Lansing again, I could not escape my memories of it. At night, after coming home from my job as a record-store clerk, I wrote short stories about a fictional city called Grand Banks, which was, in almost every way, a double for Lansing. Eventually, I began to believe in this romanticized version myself, and to want to go home to it. At the library, I checked out books on midwestern history, and I began to feel in myself the flame of a mission: I would go back home and write a book about what I called the "modern folkways" of the Upper Midwest: deer hunting, hockey, and oaczki, those lardy jelly doughnuts Detroit's Poles eat before Lent. San Francisco had plenty of writers, I figured, and Michigan didn't have enough.

I returned on a muggy Saturday morning in July of 1991, with four damp dollars in my pocket, and none in the bank. My car had broken down as I tried to cross the Sierra Nevada mountains, so I abandoned it and took a Greyhound bus across the country. After the bus let me off, I took a walk through downtown, which, after the taxi horns and monumental towers of San Francisco, seemed quieter and sparser than I remembered it. Then I phoned Mitch to ask for a ride to my mom's house.

My first job was cleaning out the parking lot of a laundromat. I chopped the weeds that had grown through the fence around the lot and picked up broken bottles, candy wrappers, and used condoms. The ice-cream truck drove by every noon, and one day I bought popsicles for three children whose mother was washing clothes. The oldest boy asked to try my shovel, then inquired, "Do you have a real job?"

I only got a little way on my great book. I decided to write a chapter on "Hilbillies in the North," so for the last two months of the summer, I made several trips to Flint to interview southerners who had come north in the fifties and sixties, when Michigan was still a land of promise, to work in the auto factories.

Talking with the southern migrants, I began to realize what a bounty Michigan had once offered, and how far we had fallen. Most of the men got jobs in the factories within days, even hours, of arriving from Tennessee or Missouri. Nowadays, not even the canniest, string-pullingest scion of a three-generation Yoo-A-Dubya family can get a work boot in the door of an auto plant. The day after my class graduated, in 1985, the line of would-be autoworkers outside Fisher Body's personnel office looked like the ticket queue for a Van Halen concert. My guess is that most of those guys ended up working on landscape crews for four dollars an hour.

Industrial labor was once a young man's game, but now the average UAW auto worker is forty-six, an age that used to mean retirement time. Eventually, the middle-aged workers will retire and give way to a new generation of welders, tool-and-die makers, and quality-control inspectors, but young people graduating from high school in the eighties and nineties will probably never get a chance at a lucrative shop job. And I do mean lucrative: an average of $16.75 an hour after the first ninety days. That's how much you make in a day on a half-time, minimum-wage job at an auto-parts store or a lumberyard, places you might find young men who were born too late to be autoworkers.

Today, if you're from a blue-collar family, and you're bright, you go to a community college or a small-town State U like Ferris State or Saginaw Valley State. There, you take a vocational program, something practical, like computer-assisted drafting. That enables you to get a seventeen-thousand-dollar-a-year job at an engineering company. Lots of people try this, but few seem to succeed. Lansing Community College, alias "Last Chance College," bills itself as "A Great Place to Start," but legion are the high-school grads who begin "taking some classes" there, then drift away after a year or two and spend the rest of their young adulthood talking about how they're "thinking about going back to school." Those junior-college dropouts once would have had the factory to fall back on, but now it looks as though they're on the low road to postindustrial oblivion—a job in a warehouse, a room at Mom's, and a crappy Chevy with a worn-out tranny and a heater that blasts cold air.

It wasn't just the auto plants. You couldn't buy a good job anywhere in Michigan. By fall, I was broke, and I needed a regular job. I found one in a video rental store, where, I will freely admit, I was the worst employee ever. My lack of motivation might have had something to do with the wages: $4.25 an hour, no raises. I filed the tapes at an arthritic pace and fantasized about ways to make the company go bankrupt. When the boss visited, I sneaked outside to spit on his Buick.

A year before, the video-store manager would have looked at my résumé (Michigan State University, *Lansing State Journal*) and asked, "Why would someone like you want a job like this?" But this was the fall of 1991, the pits of the recession, and it was understood that these were desperate times. And desperate men were ready to shelve copies of *Dumbo* for the minimum wage.

One day, as my dad and I ran along the riverfront, I went into my harangue about work. He told me that my friends and I had been born at the wrong time to find good jobs. Because he'd come of age in the sixties, during the biggest employment boom since the building of the pyramids, he'd been lucky in the job market. Sorry, son, better luck next life. What was I supposed to have done? Kicked out a Morse code message against Mom's womb: "MICHIGAN HEADED FOR FINANCIAL, ECONOMIC DISASTER. NO JOBS IN 25 YEARS. GO BACK TO MARYLAND." I blew up at my dad, falsely assuming he was being smug. Renting out copies of *T2* and *The Doors* had made me surly and cranky.

Throughout 1992, I searched for a real job, all the while working just enough to keep my belly above the starvation level. "Well, I guess these are my Ramen years," I sighed whenever I dropped a brick of pasta into a pot of boiling water. My unemployment and poverty were my own damn fault, after all, I'd had a good job with the newspaper, and I'd quit. But I could still tell family friends, "There are no jobs out there" and receive a sympathetic reply.

If I had tried that dodge in 1967, I would have heard "(Fill in any business in the Yellow Pages) is hiring. Go down there and help build the Great Society." In the sixties, it seemed, there was so much work that the hippies had to construct an alternative system of morality to justify their indolence: "I'm not going to work to support a system that's carrying on an immoral war in Vietnam and pigs blah blah blah Mao blah blah blah." It was intellectually rigorous being too lazy to work back in the hippie days.

As a minimum-wage jerk-of-all-trades, one of my jobs involved going door-to-door, taking down names for the city directory. After a tiring, discouraging day during which I had a door slammed in my face ("I don't want to be in your directory!"), I was seized by regret over the dumb choices that had led me to that line of work.

It was becoming clear that Lansing had no use for me anymore. It hurt to find that out, because I wanted to stay in my hometown. I still wanted to write something that would define the "heart of Lansing." As a newsman, I hadn't been able to figure out what that was. Now I knew: at the heart of the Lansing experience was failure.

One concrete cold day in February, I was running up Michigan Avenue when I saw an old friend standing at a bus stop, head down, bundled into a thrift-shop tweed overcoat, a scarf, and a wool cap. Tam was not supposed to be at that bus stop. She was supposed to be in Chicago, working in a coffee shop.

I broke stride and called her name. She lifted her chin out of the warm bundle of wool around her neck, and her face opened in surprise when she saw me. I wasn't supposed to be on this street, either. I was supposed to be in San Francisco.

We both had complicated excuses for meeting at that Michigan Avenue bus stop. Tam had been fired from her waitressing job at about the same time her musician boyfriend was declaring his homesickness for Lansing. She read the tea leaves, decided the sojourn to Chicago was a bust, and emptied the apartment into her boyfriend's car for the four-hour drive back to Square One.

In Lansing, she was managing a small suburban restaurant called the Travelers Club and Tuba Museum, earning less money than she had in Chicago. Now she was saying, with some regret, that she probably could have found another job if she had held on in Chicago.

Tam and I were both part of the same pathetic picture: having chucked our big-city dreams, we were reunited on this frozen, still-life afternoon in our small city. Being a washout meant having plenty of peers and commiserants. The rents were cheap—five people could crowd into a house for $125 apiece—and the pressure to achieve something was nonexistent. In Tam's circle, postcollegiate slackers smoked pot, drank coffee in restaurants, watched videos late into the night, and listened to their friends' grunge bands play in cement basements.

In a myth, the hero travels to a distant place and returns with a gift that enriches his people. The story of Lansing was an antimyth. Young men and women ventured to a big city, like Chicago or Los Angeles, and returned, diminished and defeated. All my friends had made the round trip: Mitch had tried San Francisco, lasting three weeks. Even Jason Portier, my ride to New Mexico, came home for a while, to start a band. But after a few months, he realized that Lansing musicians play nowhere but three-dollar-cover college bars, and he drove back to L.A.

"This town is the Black Hole of Ambition," I carped. Young people came limping back into town with lame excuses like "I didn't know anyone in Los Angeles," or "I wanted to come back and get a band together," or "It was too expensive." I kept thinking of that R.E.M. song that runs: "Don't go back to Rockville/Waste another year." Those Georgia boys could have been singing about Lansing, Michigan.

Lansing was never a Horatio Alger town. If you wanted to be rich or famous, this was not the place. But it was once a city of promise. In the Factory Days, a Lansing life was simple and secure: a $20,000 job as an engineer for Oldsmobile. A new ranch house on Belaire Drive, walking distance from Frances Park and the Elks Club. A pew in St. Casimir's Church, your name on the list of donors to the building fund. A summer cottage on Duck Lake, where the Saturday air carried cool winds off the water. Each May, you hitched your sailboat to the tail of your Olds Delta 88 and drove the boat to the lake for the summer. That was the old Lansing Dream.

Young people can still find assembly work in Michigan, but it usually has nothing to do with cars. During my minimum-wage summer, I answered a newspaper ad for "assemblers" and ended up putting together Easter fruit baskets for Meijer, a local supermarket chain. Some of my coworkers had serious experience working on the line. My supervisor had been laid off from a factory and was building fruit baskets because "it beats watching soap operas." The guy who wrapped the baskets in cellophane was an ex-Oldsmobile shoprat who had lost his job when he refused a transfer to GM's Saturn plant in Tennessee. "In Lansing, they give you just enough to get by," said a friend of mine who was a forklift driver. "Enough to live on, but not enough to save and move on to something better."

That summer, I finally began to plot an escape. This time I was going to do what every slacker in Lansing and East Lansing fantasized about: I was going to ditch the city for good. I refused to endure another dirty winter of waking up at 6:30 A.M. to warm up my pickup truck for a drive through the slush to a $4.50-an-hour temp job at a warehouse. That's what my life in this romantic city had come down to, and I finally came to the conclusion that eventually strikes every son of a dying town: life is elsewhere.

I should have realized that the first time I left when, shining with optimism, I quit the *State Journal* and ran away to New Mexico. After that, to expect to be welcomed home with hugs, kisses, and a full-time job was foolish. When I wrote to the *State Journal,* asking for another shot at journalism, my old employers didn't answer, not even with a rejection letter. After my year of low-wage jobs and low-rent living, I finally accepted that it was all over between me and Lansing.

And so I said the hell with Lansing, and I began working, diligently, to find a new home. Nearly every day, I set my manual typewriter on my bed and tapped out letters to companies all over the country, asking for a job. But job or no job, money or no money, prospects or no prospects, I was getting out of there. If my job search failed, I was going to move to Florida, where my grandmother owned a condominium. I'd heard there were good jobs in that state, even some newspapers starting up. Had I made the move, I would have helped close an ironic circle in Michigan history. In the fifties and sixties the southerners moved north to escape worn-out hometowns. In the eighties and nineties the northerners migrated south, for the very same reason.

I didn't go to Florida, though. Instead, I had some luck. A magazine in Washington, D.C., chose me as an intern ($5.25 an hour? Thank You, Thank You, THANK YOU). During three months in the capital, I issued even more résumés and letters and found my first real job, at a newspaper in Illinois.

Lansing has produced other refugees, young people who realize there is no profit in living in Lansing and are working to stay away for good. Jason Portier is in Atlanta, where he is the bassist for a blues-rock band. They have a recording contract, or so I hear. Tam lives in Chicago again and swears that "my every action is motivated by a desire to stay out of Lansing." Wherever we are, we have one thing in common. We are living the new Lansing Dream, which is to say, we're not living in Lansing anymore.

FLIRTING WITH COURTSHIP

Karen Lehrman

I was brought up to like sex. Not by my parents, surely; the subject never made it past clinical descriptions. Somehow, though, enough feminist zeitgeist penetrated suburban Philadelphia during the seventies to convince me that not only was I allowed to like sex as much as a man, but I was also supposed to act as though I did.

Being good feminists, my high-school friends and I also shunned provocative clothing, makeup, and fashion magazines. We tried to refrain from flirting, teasing, and other overtly feminine mannerisms and behaviors. All forms of courtship and chivalry were viewed as tools of the patriarchy, used to reinforce women's subjugation. Instead, we believed it crucial to call guys, ask them out, pay our own way. If we found ourselves longing for traditional customs we convinced ourselves that we just had more gender conditioning to overcome.

These social goals, which were to be pursued with the same relentless dedication as our career goals, were shared with our young male friends, who in turn gleefully anticipated many years of little effort in the social arena and much satisfaction.

Today, my female friends and I run around in miniskirts and heels and flirt shamelessly. We rarely call guys and ask them out; we like men who help us on with our coats and buy us flowers; and we have begun to say no when we want to say yes. Our male friends, meanwhile, are showing symptoms of confusion.

Now, before conservatives get too excited about this and before feminists start yelling "backlash," I think it should be made clear at the outset: this is progress, not regression. I don't want to generalize, but at least the women I know are not returning to traditional notions of femininity and courtship; what we seem to be doing is redefining—individualizing—the terms. And we're able to do this because our professional success has finally turned into sexual power—real sexual power, not of the manipulative variety. I think we've begun to recognize that, in the commendable effort to bring equality to the private sphere, we lost much of what was special about relations between the sexes—namely, the fact that we're different.

The first step was realizing that working women other than prostitutes could have sexual identities. Off went the dress-for-success suits, the billowy peasant skirts, the baggy overalls. On came the fishnets, the bustiers, the lipstick. Personally, it was when I found myself relaxing with fashion magazines just for the pictures that I knew some orthodox feminist line had permanently been crossed. Feminist theorists tend to believe that the fashion industry forces women to wear sexy or feminine clothing so that they'll remain empty-headed sex kittens, and presumably buy more clothes. Same with the beauty industry and makeup. Women like myself and my friends are believed to be now living in a state of false consciousness: we're wearing tighter dresses or nail polish because we feel we have to in order to be successful with jobs or men.

If only. Some men can be as bad as many feminists on this issue. Several years ago, I went to a party wearing one of those body-hugging cat suits that were all the rage for a fashion nanosecond. The next day, when my then-boyfriend inadvertently discovered this fact, he was horrified. How could I be seen like that? His dismay did not stem from any rigid notion of propriety (he had stopped by on his way to work and was wearing his usual ripped jeans, shoulder-length locks, and earring). Rather, he couldn't understand how I could degrade myself by wearing something so (theoretically) provocative. To him, an outfit that emphasized my body, my femininity, undermined my ability to be taken seriously as a writer and editor—my feminism—despite the fact that I was nowhere near a computer.

Other men, especially in a repressed town like Washington, view sexy clothing as personal invitations to, at the very least, offer their aesthetic appraisal. Women can be even worse. One friend told me that after *Backlash* came out, which doesn't have kind words to say about miniskirts, she would get disapproving glances and remarks from her more sartorially correct friends whenever she happened to put one on. A lawyer-type woman on a bus once eyed my fishnets and called me a "tramp."

As far as having to spend endless hours beautifying ourselves for our jobs, my friends complain of not having enough time even to get their hair cut. Actually, contrary to all these conspiracy theories, I think women have more control now over our bodies and our sexual identities than we've ever had, for the simple reason that we're stronger, more confident, and financially independent: we no longer have to rely on our sexuality for our livelihood. Perhaps more important, we no longer measure our own worth solely on the basis of our physical attributes.

Feminists were always concerned that a woman's sexuality negated her individuality. Today it's a woman's individuality that makes her sexy. Some of us are more ambitious, some more nurturing; in individualizing "femininity," we've allowed ourselves many female natures, many beauty ideals, and no rules. Each of us chooses to follow certain beauty rites and rituals and not others, and we don't feel demeaned by them. Feminist no-nos such as leg shaving aren't even discussed anymore, let alone considered political issues.

Of course, there are still women who try to have it both ways, who try to use their sexuality as a ploy in their work lives. One young female journalist is known for getting great stories via low-cut dresses, flattery, and fluttering her eyelashes. And there are still women who have, for example, Ph.D.'s in nuclear physics and who turn into naive, adoring little girls whenever they're in the company of men. One woman I know, very bright and quite successful in her career, has also mastered the vacuous doe eyes, sweet little nothing of a voice, irrepressible giggles. Guys—the same types of guys, by the way, who complain that women aren't developing themselves enough—fall all over her.

Let this not be confused with flirting, a game of great skill, sophistication, and pleasure that women are finally able to engage in on a level playing field. The great myth of feminism is that women want a completely gender-blind society, or even a completely gender-blind workplace; what we really want is men to admire our brains and lust after our bodies—exactly what we do to them. The problem, of course, is when this interferes with our ability to do work, and that's why flirting is so crucial to office efficiency: it not only relieves excess sexual tension, it also works to hide one's true feelings, thus protecting fragile (male) egos. The creators of those bloated sexual-harassment policies also don't seem to understand how dreary work life would be without flirting.

Or life in general. I flirt with my old boyfriends, my grandfather, my podiatrist. A friend enjoys dressing herself up, going to a bar, and flirting with every man who walks through the door. She teases them with her eyes, her smile, her sarcasm, her crossed legs. Sure she's "objectifying" herself and seeking "external affirmation." So? She likes men. She also likes guitars; playing with one can be equally satisfying, nonaddictive, and harmless.

Moreover, women have always objectified men just as much as they objectify us. We give them a critical once-over, checking out their legs, their rears, their chests. We prefer when they wear some clothes and not others and fantasize about them when they're not around. We even keep pictures of them in various states of undress near our beds. And we do all this only with men we find attractive. Is this also "looksist"? You bet. That's the funny thing about sexual chemistry: it doesn't respond well to political ideology (and I'd like to know how many opponents of "looksism" are involved with people they don't find attractive).

Another very practical use of flirting is to mask true feelings between friends. Since the lines between friends and lovers are not so distinct anymore—couples tend to go from being friends to lovers to friends, often in one evening—flirting has been a crucial defense against unrequited sexual desire, as well as a crucial tool in testing the waters.

My parents have never understood any of this. In fact, they still can't figure out how some of my best friends can be male; how I can spend so much time with a man—even sleep in his bed—and not be anything more than friends. Sometimes it isn't easy. But when the platonic feelings are mutual, friends of the opposite sex can make much better companions than either friends of the same sex or lovers. With male friends, you don't have to look your best, feel your best, or act your best; they're rarely jealous, possessive, or competitive; and you owe them nothing. They're also educational: women learn from their male friends just how much intimacy men are capable of, and men learn the same about women and independence.

In the past, having many of our relationships emerge fully formed out of these friendships relieved us of all the bourgeois and messy details of dating, which also fit in nicely with our feminist consciousness. Today it can still be very convenient and comfortable: familiarity breeds familiarity; you already know each other's addictions. As long as you get safely past The (preaffair) Conversation.

Unfortunately, I think I've spent half my social life having The Conversation. It always starts out with something about "valuing our friendship" and then painfully wends its way to something about "dreaming about you every night." The Conversation always ends awkwardly, even when the sexual attraction is mutual. When it's not, The Conversation can take on a life of its own, conspicuously making its presence felt at the most inopportune times and forever altering the friendship. Some people are good at The Conversation; others can allow it to drag on for years. You know you've fallen into Conversation Hell when you start to question your judgment ("well, he is *objectively* attractive") or worry about dying alone.

The Conversation's alter ego is the postaffair Pronouncement: "I think we should just be friends." My parents also ended affairs using this device. But in their day people didn't mean it. When a man stopped liking my mother, she never had to see him again. I'm expected to make him dinner once a month.

The Conversation can be avoided, of course, with a dose of unthinking romanticism. A stolen kiss under the moonlight after a game of miniature golf is far more efficient and effective than a tortured passive/aggressive confessional. But in the past that was considered uncool. Moreover, it would have denied us our need to overintellectualize and verbalize everything. And thus developed one of the more pathetic contracts in the history of sexual relations: our friends/lovers made it easy for women to be good feminists, and we made it easy for them to be unromantic. There were no heartrending love chants under our windows, no worshipful poems, no magical candlelit dinners, not even an occasional crummy rose. We mocked anything sweet or sentimental, acting as though we were one sex until we got into bed.

And that happened quickly. The slow discovery of another person, enhanced by anticipation and fantasy, was not fashionable for putatively liberated women. Indeed, the ideal sexual encounter envisioned by many women I know went far beyond sex with friends. Inspired by Isadora's notion of the "zipless fuck" in *Fear of Flying,* we looked forward to having affairs in which no feelings, phone numbers, not even names were exchanged; long train rides were considered perfect. No matter that Isadora eventually falls in love with her supposedly perfect zipless fuck, that she ends up with her tedious husband in the end. Being able to have sex ziplessly was considered proof that a woman didn't need a man. Our images of living passionately consisted of going from lover to lover—at least two a day—though most of us became content with the occasional well-planned one-night stand.

Fortunately, my friends and I seem to have discovered the limitations of this forced sexual freedom. (AIDS did a good job of hastening the process.) About the only thing we proved is that the more "casual" the sex, the less motivation men have to figure out how to please a woman. Moreover, many men—men who grew up with women as buddies, men who have full respect for women's brains—still seem to follow some very traditional rules regarding sexual relations, namely, dividing women into Madonnas and whores and not showing a whole lot of respect for the latter. These guys have taken full advantage of women's new attitudes and behaviors without trying out some new ones of their own.

But what men have been doing or not doing is really beside the point. Conservatives have always feigned confusion over why women would want to dispense with the old sexual mores, seeing chastity as such a great source of power. As they're well aware, that "power" was based on manipulation, not strength, and it didn't exactly get women very far. Now that women's sexual choices and desires reflect our tastes, not our financial conditions, we have the very real power of writing our own rules. And just as some of us like to wear miniskirts and lipstick, some of us want to revive a few of the rites and rituals of courtship.

For one, many women I know have stopped viewing male sexual behavior—eroticism without intimacy—as an ideal to aspire to. That's not to say we've stopped having flings or stopped sleeping with men on the first date. It's just that we've stopped feeling as though we had to do it in order to be fully liberated. (To be fair, there were some feminist theorists who warned us of this trap, but we never listened.) So now some of us act like a Madonna with some men, a whore with others, or a creative combination of the two; double standards only exist if women care about them.

And contrary to Republican theorizing on the subject, women are capable of being just as horny as men, just as frequently. But my friends and I also seem to be rediscovering the added value of anticipation and fantasy, of allowing enough tension to build so that someone's mere touch on your arm makes you tremble, of allowing kissing its rightful supremacy.

Thus, to an even greater extent than in the past, "no" doesn't always mean "no." Women sometimes use it to mean: "Not quite yet, but please try again in fifteen minutes / a day / a week." Ironically, the overheated anti-date-rape propaganda undermines women's burgeoning sexual power, by implying not only that we have very little control over sexual encounters but also that we can like just one kind of sex and it doesn't involve submission. Yeah, right.

The new courtship by choice has also inspired a revival of dating. While the optimal state of social sanity is still considered involvement in a monogamous, semiserious "relationship," between these we now go out with more than one person at a time, a concept considered rather gauche just a few years ago. And we tend to allow these minirelationships to evolve slowly. This is not always easy since we still mostly go out with people we already know. But there seems to be more of a desire on the part of both men and women to make these outings special.

For instance, we now try to look good on a date. I don't mean we wear our finest, but we now seem to acknowledge a degree of effort in our appearance. Plans are made beforehand. Overtly romantic ventures, such as candlelit dinners, are no longer instantly dismissed or pursued only for their ironic value. Men ring women's doorbells (we used to meet them on street corners). Sometimes, they bring us flowers; we accept graciously. The day after, men call us, send us chocolates; I once received a lovely note by fax. (No one I know has yet been serenaded, but we remain optimistic.)

On these dates women are now inclined to allow men to treat us like women. Notice I didn't say bimbos. We don't follow men around adoringly, speaking only when spoken to, giggling at all other times. What I mean is that there is an awareness that we are different, not unequal, just different, and a respect and appreciation for that difference.

On the most superficial level, this respect for difference has showed up in the revival of chivalry. Men increasingly open doors for us, help us on with our coats, pull out our chairs. And we like it. Armed with our ostensible equality, this momentary passivity doesn't feel demeaning. Rather, it adds a certain quaint yet charming formality to the evening—to life—that makes everyone feel better about themselves.

Courtship, of course, can go both ways, and my friends and I have reciprocated in kind, sending men flowers, making them meals, buying them assorted novelty items, which best remain nameless. What we have shown resistance to is switching the roles of pursuer and pursuee. In fact, it seems as though we call guys and ask them out even less than before, which was never all that much. It's horribly schizophrenic. At work we're bulldozers, fearlessly asserting our opinions and ordering about our underlings. But socially we hesitate, allowing men to make the first (and often the second and third) move. It's often more comfortable and fun this way. Is that so wrong? Moreover, while guys always say they want women to call and ask them out, they have this funny habit of running whenever they're pursued.

Regardless, the upturn in dating may make us all a lot less picky. I don't mean we should (heaven forbid) lower our standards. But maybe we need to lower our expectations. To a large degree because of our male/female friendships, we each have these long lists of requirements stretching from "intellectually engaging" to "good in bed." (Actually, only women seem to mention the latter.) It must have been so much easier when all you had to look for was "financially stable" and "cute."

My female friends complain that in addition to having trouble finding a man who's discovered his emotions, it's nearly impossible to find one who is secure enough to support them in their careers. (I sometimes think there's an inverse relationship between a man's professed desire to do good in the world and his ability to have an egalitarian relationship.) A few friends have resigned themselves to finding men who at least don't mock their goals. Part of the problem seems to be that, while women have done a great job redefining femininity so that it encompasses both ambition and high heels, we still aren't sure what we want masculinity to mean. Men appear to be even less sure.

Meanwhile, some of my male friends complain that they can't find women, especially attractive women, who have "developed" themselves sufficiently. They joke that they should put a moratorium on dating pretty women until they learn how to have intelligent conversations.

It's a brilliant idea. Unfortunately, these particular guys would never do it; since their tastes haven't expanded much beyond Barbie the cheerleader or Buffy the sorority sister, they would be sitting home a few too many Saturday nights.

It sometimes seems that the moratorium is on intelligent women—not dating them until they learn not to threaten guys so much.

My male friends also complain that women's emotional independence hasn't kept pace with our economic independence, that women can still become quite clingy rather quickly. Unfortunately, here they have a point. Despite our high-powered careers, far too many women still make finding and keeping a man the centerpiece of our lives, still feel incomplete without aligning with a male identity. Of course, romantic myths of love and courtship in the past always included this kind of desperate need and longing for another person, of searching for one's other half. But no one was exactly happy about it; these myths also involved a lot of heartbroken stupors and suicides.

Ironically, the new, more autonomous modes of dating may force women to spend more time by ourselves, to learn to make ourselves happy, to complete ourselves. This doesn't mean we still can't dream of being swept off our feet, of "falling" in love, of merging souls and spirits. It just means that the most romantic line of all—"I can't live without you"—won't be so true.

The best thing about being part of the transitional generation, of being feminism's guinea pigs, is that we get to pick and choose which aspects of which eras we want to test out. The process is often grueling and not a whole lot of fun, and it's far from over. But we're hardly in an interminable "gender war," and no one appears to be begging for a reinstitution of the old marriage contract. Much has changed in relations between the sexes; we still have a long way to go. Yet maybe the most important thing we've discovered is that some things are not going to change—and that we wouldn't want them to anyway.

A CHINAMAN'S CHANCE: REFLECTIONS ON THE AMERICAN DREAM

Eric Liu

A lot of people my age seem to think that the American Dream is dead. I think they're dead wrong.

Or at least only partly right. It is true that for those of us in our twenties and early thirties, job opportunities are scarce. There looms a real threat that we will be the first American generation to have a lower standard of living than our parents.

But what is it that we mean when we invoke the American Dream?

In the past, the American Dream was something that held people of all races, religions, and identities together. As James Comer has written, it represented a shared aspiration among all Americans—black, white, or any other color— "to provide well for themselves and their families as valued members of a democratic society." Now, all too often, it seems the American Dream means merely some guarantee of affluence, a birthright of wealth.

At a basic level, of course, the American Dream is about prosperity and the pursuit of material happiness. But to me, its meaning extends beyond such concerns. To me, the dream is not just about buying a bigger house than the one I grew up in or having shinier stuff now than I had as a kid. It also represents a sense of opportunity that binds generations together in commitment, so that the young inherit not only property but also perseverance, not only money but also a mission to make good on the strivings of their parents and grandparents.

The poet Robert Browning once wrote that "a man's reach must exceed his grasp—else what's a heaven for?" So it is in America. Every generation will strive, and often fail. Every generation will reach for success, and often miss the mark. But Americans rely as much on the next generation as on the next life to prove that such struggles and frustrations are not in vain. There may be temporary setbacks, cutbacks, recessions, depressions. But this is a nation of second chances. So long as there are young Americans who do not take what they have—or what they can do—for granted, progress is always possible.

My conception of the American Dream does not take progress for granted. But it does demand the *opportunity* to achieve progress—and values the opportunity as much as the achievement. I come at this question as the son of immigrants. I see just as clearly as anyone else the cracks in the idealist vision of fulfillment for all. But because my parents came here with virtually nothing, because they did build something, I see the enormous potential inherent in the ideal.

I happen still to believe in our national creed: freedom and opportunity, and our common responsibility to uphold them. This creed is what makes America unique. More than any demographic statistic or economic indicator, it animates the American Dream. It infuses our mundane struggles—to plan a career, do good work, get ahead—with purpose and possibility. It makes America the only country that could produce heroes like Colin Powell—heroes who rise from nothing, who overcome the odds.

I think of the sacrifices made by my own parents. I appreciate the hardship of the long road traveled by my father—one of whose first jobs in America was painting the yellow line down a South Dakota interstate—and by my mother—whose first job here was filing pay stubs for a New York restaurant. From such beginnings, they were able to build a comfortable life and provide me with a breadth of resources—through arts, travel, and an Ivy League education. It was an unspoken obligation for them to do so.

I think of my boss in my first job after college, on Capitol Hill. George is a smart, feisty, cigar-chomping, take-no-shit Greek-American. He is about fifteen years older than I, has different interests, a very different personality. But like me, he is the son of immigrants, and he would joke with me that the Greek-Chinese mafia was going to take over one day. He was only half joking. We'd worked harder, our parents doubly harder, than almost anyone else we knew. To people like George, talk of the withering of the American Dream seems foreign.

It's undeniable that principles like freedom and opportunity, no matter how dearly held, are not enough. They can inspire a multiracial March on Washington, but they can not bring black salaries in alignment with white salaries. They can draw wave after wave of immigrants here, but they can not provide them the means to get out of our ghettos and barrios and Chinatowns. They are not sufficient for fulfillment of the American Dream.

But they are necessary. They are vital. And not just to the children of immigrants. These ideals form the durable thread that weaves us all in union. Put another way, they are one of the few things that keep America from disintegrating into a loose confederation of zip codes and walled-in communities.

What alarms me is how many people my age look at our nation's ideals with a rising sense of irony. What good is such a creed if you are working for hourly wages in a dead-end job? What value do such platitudes have if you live in an urban war zone? When the only apparent link between homeboys and housepainters and bike messengers and investment bankers is pop culture—MTV, the NBA, movies, dance music—then the social fabric is flimsy indeed.

My generation has come of age at a time when the country is fighting off bouts of defeatism and self-doubt, at a time when racism and social inequities seem not only persistent but intractable. At a time like this, the retreat to one's own kind is seen by more and more of my peers as an advance. And that retreat has given rise again to the notion that there are essential and irreconcilable differences among the races—a notion that was supposed to have disappeared from American discourse by the time my peers and I were born in the sixties.

Not long ago, for instance, my sister called me a "banana."

I was needling her about her passion for rap and hip-hop music. Every time I saw her, it seemed, she was jumping and twisting to Arrested Development or Chubb Rock or some other funky group. She joked that despite being the daughter of Chinese immigrants, she was indeed "black at heart." And then she added, lightheartedly, "You, on the other hand—well, you're basically a banana." Yellow on the outside, but white inside.

I protested, denied her charge vehemently. But it was too late. She was back to dancing. And I stood accused.

Ever since then, I have wondered what it means to be black, or white, or Asian "at heart"—particularly for my generation. Growing up, when other kids would ask whether I was Chinese or Korean or Japanese, I would reply, a little petulantly, "American." Assimilation can still be a sensitive subject. I recall reading about a Korean-born Congressman who had gone out of his way to say that Asian-Americans should expect nothing special from him. He added that he was taking speech lessons "to get rid of this accent." I winced at his palpable self-hate. But then it hit me: Is this how my sister sees me?

There is no doubt that minorities like me can draw strength from our communities. But in today's environment, anything other than ostentatious tribal fealty is taken in some communities as a sign of moral weakness, a disappointing dilution of character. In times that demand ever-clearer thinking, it has become too easy for people to shut off their brains: "It's a black/Asian/Latino/white thing," says the variable T-shirt. "You wouldn't understand." Increasingly, we don't.

The civil-rights triumphs of the sixties and the cultural revolutions that followed made it possible for minorities to celebrate our diverse heritages. I can appreciate that. But I know, too, that the sixties—or at least, my generation's grainy, hazy vision of the decade—also bequeathed to young Americans a legacy of near-pathological race consciousness.

Today's culture of entitlement—and of race entitlement in particular—tells us plenty about what we get if we are black or white or female or male or old or young.

It is silent, though, on some other important issues. For instance: What do we "get" for being American? And just as importantly, What do we owe? These are questions around which young people like myself must tread carefully, since talk of common interests, civic culture, responsibility, and integration sounds a little too "white" for some people. To the new segregationists, the "American Dream" is like the old myth of the "Melting Pot": an oppressive fiction, an opiate for the unhappy colored masses.

How have we allowed our thinking about race to become so twisted? The formal obstacles and the hateful opposition to civil rights have long faded into memory. By most external measures, life for minorities is better than it was a quarter century ago. It would seem that the opportunities for tolerance and cooperation are commonplace. Why, then, are so many of my peers so cynical about our ability to get along with one another?

The reasons are frustratingly ambiguous. I got a glimpse of this when I was in college. It was late in my junior year, and as the editor of a campus magazine, I was sitting on a panel to discuss "The White Press at Yale: What Is to Be Done?" The assembly hall was packed, a diverse and noisy crowd. The air was heavy, nervously electric.

Why weren't there more stories about "minority issues" in the Yale *Daily News?* Why weren't there more stories on Africa in my magazine, the foreign affairs journal? How many "editors of color" served on the boards of each of the major publications? The questions were volleyed like artillery, one round after another, punctuated only by the applause of an audience spoiling for a fight. The questions were not at all unfair. But it seemed that no one—not even those of us on the panel who *were* people of color—could provide, in this context, satisfactory answers.

Toward the end of the discussion, I made a brief appeal

for reason and moderation. And afterward, as students milled around restlessly, I was attacked: for my narrow-mindedness—How dare you suggest that Yale is not a fundamentally prejudiced place!—for my simplemindedness—Have you, too, been co-opted?

And for my betrayal—Are you just white inside?

My eyes were opened that uncomfortably warm early summer evening. Not only to the cynical posturing and the combustible opportunism of campus racial politics. But more importantly, to the larger question of identity—my identity—in America. Never mind that the aim of many of the loudest critics was to generate headlines in the very publications they denounced. In spite of themselves—against, it would seem, their true intentions—they got me to think about who I am.

In our society today, and especially among people of my generation, we are congealing into clots of narrow commonality. We stick with racial and religious comrades. This tribal consciousness-raising can be empowering for some. But while America was conceived in liberty—the liberty, for instance, to associate with whomever we like—it was never designed to be a mere collection of subcultures. We forget that there is in fact such a thing as a unique American identity that transcends our sundry tribes, sets, gangs, and cliques.

I have grappled, wittingly or not, with these questions of identity and allegiance all my life. When I was in my early teens, I would invite my buddies overnight to watch movies, play video games, and beat one another up. Before too long, my dad would come downstairs and start hamming it up—telling stories, asking gently nosy questions, making corny jokes, all with his distinct Chinese accent. I would stand back, quietly gauging everyone's reaction. Of course, the guys loved it. But I would feel uneasy.

What was then cause for discomfort is now a source of strength. Looking back on such episodes, I take pride in my father's accented English; I feel awe at his courage to laugh loudly in a language not really his own.

It was around the same time that I decided that continued attendance at the community Chinese school on Sundays was uncool. There was no fanfare; I simply stopped going. As a child, I'd been too blissfully unaware to think of Chinese school as anything more than a weekly chore, with an annual festival (dumplings and spring rolls, games and prizes). But by the time I was a peer-pressured adolescent, Chinese school seemed like a badge of the woefully unassimilated. I turned my back on it.

Even as I write these words now, it feels as though I am revealing a long-held secret. I am proud that my ancestors— scholars, soldiers, farmers—came from one of the world's great civilizations. I am proud that my grandfather served in the Chinese Air Force. I am proud to speak even my clumsy brand of Mandarin, and I feel blessed to be able to think idiomatically in Chinese, a language so much richer in nuance and subtle poetry than English.

Belatedly, I appreciate the good fortune I've had to be the son of immigrants. As a kid, I could play Thomas Jefferson in the bicentennial school play one week and the next week play the poet Li Bai at the Chinese school festival. I could come home from an afternoon of teen slang at the mall and sit down to dinner for a rollicking conversation in our family's hybrid of Chinese and English. I understood, when I went over to visit friends, that my life was different. At the time, I just never fully appreciated how rich it was.

Yet I know that this pride in my heritage does not cross into prejudice against others. What it reflects is pride in what my country represents. That became clear to me when I went through Marine Corps Officer Candidates' School. During the summers after my sophomore and junior years of college, I volunteered for OCS, a grueling boot camp for potential officers in the swamps and foothills of Quantico, Virginia.

And once I arrived—standing 5'4", 135 pounds, bespectacled, a Chinese Ivy League Democrat—I was a target straight out of central casting. The wiry, raspy-voiced drill sergeant, though he was perhaps only an inch or two taller than I, called me "Little One" with as much venom as can be squeezed into such a moniker. He heaped verbal abuse on me, he laughed when I stumbled, he screamed when I hesitated. But he also never failed to remind me that just because I was a little shit didn't mean I shouldn't run farther, climb higher, think faster, hit harder than anyone else.

That was the funny thing about the Marine Corps. It is, ostensibly, one of the most conservative institutions in the United States. And yet, for those twelve weeks, it represented the kind of color-blind equality of opportunity that the rest of society struggles to match. I did not feel uncomfortable at OCS to be of Chinese descent. Indeed, I drew strength from it. My platoon was a veritable cross section of America: forty young men of all backgrounds, all regions, all races, all levels of intelligence and ability, displaced from our lives (if only for a few weeks) with nowhere else to go.

Going down the list of names—Courtemanche, Dougherty, Grella, Hunt, Liu, Reeves, Schwarzman, and so on— brought to mind a line from a World War II documentary I once saw, which went something like this: The reason why it seemed during the war that America was as good as the rest of the world put together was that America *was* the rest of the world put together.

Ultimately, I decided that the Marines was not what I wanted to do for four years and I did not accept the second lieutenant's commission. But I will never forget the day of the graduation parade: bright sunshine, brisk winds, the band playing Sousa as my company passed in review. As my mom and dad watched and photographed the parade from the rafters, I thought to myself: this is the American Dream in all its cheesy earnestness. I felt the thrill of truly being part of something larger and greater than myself.

I do know that American life is not all Sousa marches and flag-waving. I know that those with reactionary agendas often find it convenient to cloak their motives in the language of Americanism. The "American Party" was the name of a major nativist organization in the nineteenth century. "America First" is the siren song of the isolationists who would withdraw this country from the world and expel the world from this country. I know that our national immigration laws were once designed explicitly to cut off the influx from Asia.

I also know that discrimination is real. I am reminded of a gentle old man who, after Pearl Harbor, was stripped of his possessions without warning, taken from his home, and thrown into a Japanese internment camp. He survived, and by many measures has thrived, serving as a community leader and political activist. But I am reluctant to share with him my wide-eyed patriotism.

I know the bittersweet irony that my own father—a strong and optimistic man—would sometimes feel when he was alive. When he came across a comically lost cause—if the Yankees were behind 14–0 in the ninth, or if Dukakis was down ten points in the polls with a week left—he would often joke that the doomed party had "a Chinaman's chance" of success. It was one of those insensitive idioms of a generation ago, and it must have lodged in his impressionable young mind when he first came to America. It spoke of a perceived stacked deck.

I know, too, that for many other immigrants, the dream simply does not work out. Fae Myenne Ng, the author of *Bone,* writes about how her father ventured here from China under a false identity and arrived at Angel Island, the detention center outside the "Gold Mountain" of San Francisco. He got out, he labored, he struggled, and he suffered "a bitter no-luck life" in America. There was no glory. For him, Ng suggests, the journey was not worth it.

But it is precisely because I know these things that I want to prove that in the long run, over generations and across ethnicities, it *is* worth it. For the second-generation American, opportunity is obligation. I have seen and faced racism. I understand the dull pain of dreams deferred or unmet. But I believe still that there is so little stopping me from building the life that I want. I was given, through my parents' labors, the chance to bridge that gap between ideals and reality. Who am I to throw away that chance?

Plainly, I am subject to the criticism that I speak too much from my own experience. Not everyone can relate to the second-generation American story. When I have spoken like this with some friends, the issue has been my perspective. *What you say is fine for you. But unless you grew up where I did, unless you've had people avoid you because of the color of your skin, don't talk to me about common dreams.*

But are we then to be paralyzed? Is respect for different

experiences supposed to obviate the possibility of shared aspirations? Does the diversity of life in America doom us to a fractured understanding of one another? The question is basic: Should the failure of this nation thus far to fulfill its stated ideals incapacitate its young people, or motivate us?

Our country was built on, and remains glued by, the idea that everybody deserves a fair shot and that we must work together to guarantee that opportunity—the original American Dream. It was this idea, in some inchoate form, that drew every immigrant here. It was this idea, however sullied by slavery and racism, that motivated the civil-rights movement. To write this idea off—even when its execution is spotty—to let American life descend into squabbles among separatist tribes would not just be sad. It would be a total mishandling of a legacy, the squandering of a great historical inheritance.

Mine must not be the first generation of Americans to lose America. Just as so many of our parents journeyed here to find their version of the American Dream, so must young Americans today journey across boundaries of race and class to rediscover one another. We are the first American generation to be born into an integrated society, and we are accustomed to more race mixing than any generation before us. We started open-minded, and it's not too late for us to stay that way.

Time is of the essence. For in our national political culture today, the watchwords seem to be *decline* and *end*. Apocalyptic visions and dark millennial predictions abound. The end of history. The end of progress. The end of equality. Even something as ostensibly positive as the end of the Cold War has a bittersweet tinge, because for the life of us, no one in America can get a handle on the big question, "What Next?"

For my generation, this fixation on endings is particularly enervating. One's twenties are supposed to be a time of widening horizons, of bright possibilities. Instead, America seems to have entered an era of limits. Whether it is the difficulty of finding jobs from some place other than a temp agency, or the mountains of debt that darken our future, the message to my peers is often that this nation's time has come and gone; let's bow out with grace and dignity.

A friend once observed that while the Chinese seek to adapt to nature and yield to circumstance, Americans seek to conquer both. She meant that as a criticism of America. But I interpreted her remark differently. I *do* believe that America is exceptional. And I believe it is up to my generation to revive that spirit, that sense that we do in fact have control over our own destiny—as individuals and as a nation.

If we are to reclaim a common destiny, we must also reach out to other generations for help. It was Franklin Roosevelt who said that while America can't always build the future for its youth, it can—and must—build its youth for the future. That commitment across generations is as central to the American Dream as any I have enunciated. We are linked, black and white, old and young, one and inseparable.

I know how my words sound. I am old enough to perceive my own naïveté but young enough still to cherish it. I realize that I am coming of age just as the American Dream is showing its age. Yet I still have faith in this country's unique destiny—to create generation after generation of hyphenates like me, to channel this new blood, this resilience and energy into an ever more vibrant future for *all* Americans.

And I want to prove—for my sake, for my father's sake, and for my country's sake—that a Chinaman's chance is as good as anyone else's.

GENERATION MEX

Lalo Lopez

GLOSSARY OF POCHISMO

This is for those of you who have yet to encounter Pochismo in your life. For those of you that don't speak or read Spanish or Spanglish—LEARN.

Aztlan (*ahst-lawn*) 1) Original homeland of the Aztecs. 2) Land stolen from Mexico in 1848 by the U.S. The U.S. Southwest—i.e. Arizona, California, Colorado, Nevada, New Mexico, Texas, and Utah (you can keep that one). *"Even though there're a lot of Mexicans in Chicago, it's still in the Outer Territories, not in Aztlan."* 3) Homeland of the Chicanos and the Pochos. *"Welcome to Aztlan. Now go home."*

Chicano, Chicana (*Chee-kah-noh*) A Mexican-American who knows what's up and it really pisses him or her off. *"Victoria is a hard-core Chicana."*

cholo (*cho-low*) 1) Chicano street warrior. 2) Gang member. 3) Run!

chones (*choe-nehs or chonees*) Underwear. *"Just a minute, keep your chones on."*

coconut (*koo-koo-for-koko-puffs*) Brown on the outside, white on the inside. *"Assimilationist writer Richard Rodriguez is America's leading coconut."*

frijol (*free-whole*) Bean, as in *"How you bean?"*

frontera (*front-era*) Literally the frontier but really the Mexico/U.S. border. *"Living on the frontera is hard, especially in Tijuana and San Diego because of those racist INS agents."*

gringo (*green-go*) Affectionate term for Anglo, Whitey. *"Kill the Gringo!"*

Hispanic (*hissssssss*) 1) A phony Eurocentric label created by the Nixon administration intended to lump all Latinos into one mushy ball of Wonder Bread dough. *"I'm not a dirty Mexican, I'm a Hispanic!"* 2) A money-hungry Latino businessperson. *"Look at the suit he wears. What a Hispanic!"* 3) Sellout. *"She used to say she was into helping the community, but now she's working for the CIA. What a Hispanic!"*

Latino (*lah-teen-oh*) General term for Spanish-surnamed peoples in the western hemisphere but still not specific enough for some of us. A remnant of French colonization.

loco (*loh-koh*) Crazy. *"Down, deep inside I really think Bill Clinton is a loco hillbilly!"*

MEChA (*you-betcha*) Acronym for el Movimiento Estudiantil Chicano de Aztlan, a Chicano student organization common in colleges and high schools. *"She's become so militant since she became a Mechista!"*

Mex (*mecks*) Jeez, do I have to explain everything? Short for Mexican. Pro golfer Lee Treviño is known as Super Mex. "Mex to the Max" is the slogan for a certain bland gringo-made salsa.

mijo (*mee-ho*) From *mi hijo* or "my son." Also *mija*, my daughter. Affectionate term for younger relative or child.

mocoso (*moh-koh-soh*) Snot-nosed youngster. *"Who does Lalo think he is, disrespecting the sixties Chicanos? What a mocoso!"*

nalgas (*nawl-goss*) Your butt. *Get off your nalgas and do something for La Raza!*

papas (*paw-paws*)   Potatoes. Also "shit," as in "talking shit." *Don't talk papas to the L.A.P.D. 'cuz they'll Rodney King your ass.*

pedo (*peh-doh*)   Literally, fart. Commonly a fight, or a big stink. *"That iconoclastic Pocho Magazine is always stirring up pedo."*

pendejo (*pen-deh-ho*)   Idiot, jerk, a stupid person. Literally "pubic hair." *"At one time, Dan Quayle was this country's highest ranking pendejo."*

pochismo (*poh-cheez-moh*)   An action or situation created by Pochos. *"That Linda Rondstadt can sure sing in Spanish, but she can't even speak it. What shameless pochismo!"*

Pocho (*pocho*)   From Pochteca, traveling merchant class of the Aztecs 1) A culturally inept Mexican-American *"That Pocho cannot even pronounce his own Spanish surname."* 2) Literally, a stubby bean.

Raza (*rah-rah-rah-sah*)   The Mexican race, a mixture of indigenous and European, the Cosmic Race. *"Viva La Raza!"*

respeto (*res-peh-toe*)   Respect. *"I demand respeto por my favorite musical group, Banda Machos!"*

vendido (*ven-dee-doh*)   Sell out, see **Hispanic**. *"Lalo wrote that essay for that gringo book. What a vendido!"*

GENERATION MEX

I am a *Pocho*. I'm not just Mexican-American, not a fifty-fifty split, but a mixed-up Mex living and toiling in the US of A for an artist's minimum wage. I ride between two vastly different cultures and end up splitting the difference. Mexican culture urges civility, family, and honor. American culture requires vast amounts of money (I mean, if you really wanna do it right). Born on the fence, not on the Fourth of July, I represent the new generation son-of-an-immigrant that just doesn't give a flying *frijol* what the whacked-out gringo's got to say. Never before has a generation been so overarmed with well-earned wit and education to confront the weakening White Establishment. We diss the mainstream just as much as we offend our elders. Generation X? *'Stas Loco!* As a proud member of the under-thirty Chicano population, I loudly proclaim Generation MEX!

I'm so busy punching around American notions of ethnic identity that I rarely have time to see what "hot, new, and improved" Gringo label is being affixed to my age group. Everything is "universal" when it comes from the Gringos, but when we do something it's "ethnic specific" and nobody wants to understand it. For the Gringorder, there's gotta be baby boomers and thirtysomethings, Generation Xers and slackers. I'd like to be a slacker, but my family would kick my ass. A poor Mexican worrying about esoteric emotions like angst? Get a job, *mijo*.

I just read the funniest cover page for a full-color (all-white) Sunday Gen X article. It read, "Generation ANGST. The twentysomething generation is mad as hell." Mad at what? Mad because they're not rich? Or is it that they can't exploit others as successfully as the generation before them? They're probably not mad at the photographer, because she made them look adorably chic. There's two "90210" white boys in their twentyteens with baseball caps on, one wearing a leather jacket bedecked with pins and buttons (one a happy face!?). Both flank a thrift-store-blouse-wearing, thick-framed eyeglasses-sporting young madwoman. They look as though like they actually believe the copy. Of course they don't seem to realize that they're angry young white people in an angry brown world.

A really funny part of this article recounted an Xer's bewilderment at the boomers' obviously selfish reluctance to "move over." He felt the editor of *Rolling Stone* was not playing fair because, being in his forties, he wasn't quite ready to leave his desirable position to make room for the twentysomethings—namely him. No shit, SherloX. That's how I feel every day—it's called the Glass Ceiling. That happens to him once, and he wants to justify a movement with it.

My movement is the Pocho Movement. The motley mixture of Mexican, Chicano, working-class, TV, and American cultures creates a vibrant indigenous patchwork. Unadulter-

ated displays of Pochismo are helping to define a new generation of Chicanos. We are hunters and gatherers of culture;
we make do with what we find. The Pocho enjoys a peanut-
butter-and-jelly tortilla, eats Crispurritos, Enchurritos, and
Double Cheeseburgerritos regularly at Hell Taco and loves
it. Pocho's failure to master the Spanish tongue and inability
to eat spicy Mexican cuisine doom him to a life of inbe-
tweenness.

While the older *Raza* called themselves Mexican-American, the sixties and seventies rads were *Chicanos,* a term that
made the older generations recoil in disgust. *Chicano* once
identified the lowest, tackiest, most uncultured border-
crossin' Mexican; its meaning approaches cuss-word status
the farther back you go generationally. In the sixties, our
Chicano elders changed it to a term of pride and defiance.

We in turn declare its successor, the once-loathed term
of *Pocho,* to be the righteous cultural and political force that
will shape the "New World Border." Pochismo is Chicanismo with a sick sense of humor.

My first *Pocho* trip was in a yellow cab which brought my
laboring mom into the U.S., to her obstetrician in San
Diego. I was a resident of the Mexican frontier town of Tijuana, Baja California, both as a fetus and after becoming a
newborn. For a four-dollar cab ride I became a U.S. citizen
in a scene replayed up and down the *frontera* for a hundred
years (and hundreds to come). That makes me a typical
first-generation Chicano, hopping international borders at a
single bound.

I had to cross socioeconomic borders just to go to high
school. Hooray for the Helix Highlanders. Yeah, I went to
a high school whose mascot was named Bagpipe Billy or
something snidely Scottish. All the buildings had clan
names painted on them so that we could be reminded of
our rich Scottish heritage. No wonder all my fellow *Pochos*
dropped out or got their asses kicked out of Helix by the
time I graduated in 1982. Everyone who wasn't six feet
under had either three kids or five to ten years.

I survived thanks to the strength of my tribal life at home.
Mexico and things Mexican were the rule, even though I
watched something like eighty hours a week of American

TV. My father was a stern man who had immigrated to the U.S. to escape the foul air of the silver mines in which he worked in his native Zacatecas, Mexico. His dislike for the Gringo was something that kept me from becoming one of those mindless bleached-hair, blue-contact-wearin' Latinos. He worked his way up to the front office at a plant nursery but was stopped by the English-language barrier. Mom was also perplexed by *Inglés* but could laugh it off easier than pissed-off Pop. "Why do Americans name their kids after animals?" she asked me about my fourth-grade classmate Doug Williams. "No, Ma, *se llama* DOUG, not DOG!"

Even in death, my father cemented my beliefs about Gringos. On Saturdays, he and I would go and clean white people's lawns. After his death, I had the unpleasant job of notifying his clients about his untimely passing. I called one lady, a certain Mrs. Vegetable—I'm not making this up—who lived in a nice suburban place with lots of potted plants in the back. I told her my dad wouldn't be coming in the following Saturday. She mechanically said she was sorry to hear he had died, and did I get her a replacement yet to clean her yard? Quite a load for a thirteen-year-old. I told her, "No, that's my father," and hung up. I had been told they were cruel, and that cold-hearted Gringa was proof positive.

The only way I was going to escape my destiny as a landscaper's assistant was through education. Having an artistic streak actually paid off one summer. When I was sweet fifteen I worked in a "Keep the *Cholos* off the Streets" program at my high school, doing janitorial maintenance type stuff like painting columns "Highlander green" and other mind-bending physical tasks. We usually got stoned in the bushes we were supposed to be clearing. I got pulled out of the group when Coach Ash, our summer warden, found out I could reproduce things on walls. They needed a sign-painting *cholo* to illuminate school mascots in the girls' gym. I figured this could be my only chance to get in that room, so I did it. Painting indoors and getting paid while the homeboys burned in the summer heat was just too much to ignore. This led me to vocational graphic-arts tracking at that high school which, ironically, got me lots of A's. These grades helped me make it into an art school, despite my other subject grades.

As a first-generation poor California Chicano that went to college, I was supposed to study a field with ripe career opportunities such as counseling, sociology, or criminal justice (probation is cool but not the PD!), or something easily portable back to the community. Art is also an honorable Chicano profession—witness the countless murals in barrios all over—but try to fill that line in the pragmatic Mexican family monthly budget. Above love of country (Aztlan) or destruction of the Gringo system, pulling your family out of poverty was the primary stated ideal of the Chicano student in the eighties. Unfortunately (as my mother so often reminds me), by taking the Barrio Bohemian route, I haven't quite yet pulled anyone out of anything.

On paper, I possess the finest militant Chicano college student credentials—active poster-making member of MEChA at both San Diego State University and UC Berkeley, the top Chicano finishing school in Aztlan. In a decade of rousing actions, protests, and speeches, we fought our clear-cut evil racist opponents in the sheltered college world. The fight to instill the United Farm Workers' Grape Boycott was a typical college Chicano battle. Despite Hispanic urgings to "Get beige—drop the rage," I was on the tail end of a generation that still believed fervently in sixties and seventies Chicano ideals.

A big *pedo* stink arose in MEChA one year between students who glorified the past and those who were ready to move on. In 1984 playwright Luis Valdez was speaking at UC San Diego where he was heckled and questioned accusingly by militant Chicano students. Luis had basically created Chicano theater and comedy, a feat I am drawing upon even today, but was starting to move away from his militant Chicano stance of the sixties. The hecklers were jibing him for what appeared to be his compromising position with Hollywood, not to mention his touchy-feely Mayan pop philosophy.

I didn't know the whole story; I just knew that people were talking *papas* about a great Chicano, so I joined the conservative camp in MEChA. Our argument was "There are certain people here who haven't done as much for the Movimiento as Luis Valdez, so SHUT UP!" Pretty airtight, eh? Well he was a role model dammit and you just don't fuck with role models. We had so few of them as it was, we even counted the college professors that guided us through the unfamiliar terrain of higher learning.

At the university we listened eagerly to our Chicano professors as they taught us our Chicanismo. We learned to reexamine American history as it had been taught to us as far back as elementary school. Remember The Alamo? *We* won! Cortez wasn't a great Spanish explorer—he was just as much a rapist as that other Euro-monster, Columbus! We ate up new info on old unsung Chicano heroes like Reyes Tijerina, who had actually taken up arms in a land struggle in New Mexico.

But as I got past the typical college student naïveté, I realized that our profs were stagnating, doing obscure academic research on subjects like migrant worker eating patterns in 1920s Arizona. The only time these tigers showed their teeth was when it came to protesting their denied tenures. Most of these teachers were former student activists straight out of the sixties and seventies, but they weren't crazed nationalists anymore. One professor I had was a respected Chicano Studies researcher but was best known in the Anglo ivory towers as an expert on the history of the Wizard of Oz. Not Aztlan, or even Oz-tlan, but Oz. In their eagerness to be validated by the academic system, they came to school with their briefcases, their coats and ties, to teach us about the old revolution but not to encourage any new ones. I yearned for someone young, brown, and angry to lead the way, but all our leaders had to report to work the next day.

The Creation of Chicano Secret Service, *Pocho Magazine*, and L.A. Cucaracha

Even though I had never seen so muchos Mexicanos in one place, not everything was well with the students at Berkeley. This is where I had my first contact with the Chicano middle class. And speaking of contacts, lots of these Chicanos were into green and blue contact lenses, orange hair, and calling Mexican immigrants "wetbacks." The doors had finally opened to the universities, but not many poor Chicano/ Chicanas—those most likely to be ANGRY—were getting in. These comfortable kids didn't know much cultural history and were more likely to be concerned with fashion than fascism. It became obvious that something needed to be done, not only to school these kids, but also to present Chicano culture and politics in media and on stage, because it was not being represented fairly anywhere else.

These students, whether they liked it or not, were on a voyage of self-discovery, and I wanted to be right there to give them a kick in the *nalgas*. The Chicano movement of the past had lost its steam, and one of the reasons was its inability to be honestly self-critical. It seemed to me that the natural and *Pocho*-perfect remedy was to learn to laugh at ourselves, to take ourselves less seriously. So, in the raucous political atmosphere of Berkeley in 1988, my friend Elias Serna and I created the comedy group Chicano Secret Service. In 1990 we drafted San Francisco State graduate Student Tomas Carrasco into C/S/S. Unlike those before us, we had the confidence in ourselves and our culture to spoof our own shortcomings as a community. During one show, we created a spoof of a racist radio commercial for a Mexican restaurant in L.A. that claims to have more than "Just Tacos." It goes like thees, *señor!*:

[*Goofy Mexican stereotype spokesmodel enters wearing a purple mariachi sombrero and a bloody apron*]

MEX: [*To audience*] At Just Tacos Mexican Restaurant, that's all we have—JUST TACOS!

[*He whips out plastic toy in the shape of a fast-food taco; then he speaks to drive-thru client who is at the offstage mike*]

            Si, señor! May I help you!?
CLIENT: Yes, uh . . . can I get an enchurrito?
MEX: No, JUST TACOS!
CLIENT: Well, how about an enchilada—hold the chile?

MEX: *[Shocked]* Hold your own *chile!* (penis). JUST
             TACOS!
CLIENT: Give me a burrito.
MEX: *[Angry] Mira*—no enchiladas, no enchurritos—
             whatever the fuck that is—no burritos, JUST
             TACOS!!
CLIENT: Do you have any BRAINS!?
MEX: No! JUST TACOS!!!
CLIENT: They must be paying you a lot of money to act
             like a stupid Mexican!
MEX: *[Sad realization of his own exploitation]*
             No . . . just tacos. . . .

*[Then in a moment of pure Pocho silliness he puts the rubber
taco up to the mike and squeezes it, making a squeaking noise
much to the delight of the audience]*

An older gentleman wanted to make a point during our
Q&A session after the show. "I fought so hard in the sixties
to rid us of the sombrero-wearing lazy-Mexican stereotypes,
yet I see your show and here they are again." Talk about not
getting it! Unfortunately, the *señor* could not understand
that we employed a Mexican stereotype to crush that very
misrepresentation. I asked him, "Would you like to see a
chorus line of His-panic attorneys and CEOs dancing up
here? That's the image you would rather we promote?" He
didn't reply. I guess we'll just have to write a new show
called *Latin Lawyer Follies*.

Our honorable ancestors wanted us to believe that they
had already taken care of all the problems we face. Although
C/S/S owed much to its forerunners, especially to aforemen-
tioned frolicking Mayan Luis Valdez, the elders took themselves so god-damn seriously, and that bugged the hell out
of me.

Distraught over the failings of the Movimiento, and out
of severe thirst, I spent the summer after grad school roam-
ing the streets of Berkeley drinking beer with one of the
natives, Esteban Zul. Out of that drunkenness came *Pocho
Magazine,* a rudely written graphic publication that converts

our anger into satirical drive-bys over white (and brown) picket fences. We realized that we had to knock down some Chicano icons to see if they could get back up by themselves—and that Anglo icons had to be toppled and DESTROYED. When we write, we utilize a *Pocho*-speak that is a combination of militant Chicano political speech of the sixties and a Monty Pythonesque silliness. Here's a sample, from the Editor's Statement of *Pocho* #3, EVERYTHING'S GONNA BE ALL-RIOT:

You are now in the greasy grip of POCHO #3, the ALL-RIOT ISSUE. We at POCHO MAGAZINE wholeheartedly supported and participated in the uprisings all over Los Angeles and Aztlan. We hope that you are all sporting new footwear, clothing, and/or home entertainment devices. And just remember, everything's gonna be All-Riot. Throughout Aztlan, Pochos find comfort in knowing that they have a magazine they can call their own. Our rivals, the so-called "Hispanic Magazine," have looked down their long Spanish noses at us and have constantly pooh-poohed our every move to promote Pochismo to Pochos one and all. We could give a mestizo's moco about what those surly unbathed Spaniards have to say about our publication. We stand by to represent the needs, desires, and particular fetishes of Pochos everywhere (Chato Boys included). Hear our rousing cry! Awaken to the righteousness of TRUE POCHISMO! As Pochos and citizens of Aztlan we demand and will not rest until we receive the following:

Free medical care from the *Curandero* of our choice
Free cable to include an All-*Pocho* channel
Weekly car wash privileges at the Montebello Car Wash
A King Taco fax machine
Annual subscription to *Pocho Magazine*
24-hour Kmart service, with free delivery

The leading Chicano scholar of Aztlan, Dr. Rudy Acuña, author of the Chicano Studies bible, *Occupied America,* has pronounced *Pocho Magazine* and Chicano Secret Service (and me) "on the fringe." I guess that means we've made it! Being public *Pocho* pushers, we also get wild letters from dubious public figures.

CARTAS TO THE EDITOR

Dirtbag Chicanos,
I heard about your plans to imprison me when you *Pochos* take over Mazatlan. It is my pleasure to inform you that I hail proudly from the heart of Spain—New Mexico, you dirty lettuce-picking heathens. While you were clearing a place in the brush to sleep, I was building my glorious Spanish empire. Using professional right-wing semantics and crafty breeding choices—my men are heavy on the mayo, if you know what I mean—I intend to destroy your pathetic *Pocho* parade of incorrect grammar, poor sanitation, and loud banda music. **Don't fuck with me** or I'll crush you as easily as I crush a can of Coors on my forehead after I've sucked down every last drop.
Linda Chavez
Destroyer

Dear Silly Chicanos,
Why do you continue to attack my wonderfully apologetic book, *Days of Constipation: An Argument with My Mexican Plumber?* In this book I show a certain maturity of political thought and a rethinking of my antiminority viewpoint. Also I am trying to rehabilitate myself in the eyes of the Latino book-buying public. You childish Chicanos, you pimply *Pochos,* you are so racially stunted! You merely embarrass yourselves even further when you mock my wacky racial views. Why don't you follow my daring example? I am not a mere Mexican, nor a simple Spaniard—I am a world citizen! I am a veritable racial smorgasbord! When I eat sushi, I *am* Chinese! When I smell a putrid *pupusa,* I *am* that masculine Irish nun that shaped my world view and *nalgas!* I am the world, I am RAZA-RABID!
Look for my new exercise video, *Days of Perspiration—An Argument With My Mexican Pansa.*
Richard Rodriguez
Brooding Latino Coconut

Pocho Housing Committee,
I'm personally writing to notify you that your application for the purchase of the Alamo fort in San Antonio, Texas, has been soundly rejected by the Secretary of Housing and Urban Development, namely me. The Alamo is a nationally protected landmark and cannot be converted into a drive-in theater showing

only Mexican action movies. Your "Water Slides on the Border" proposal is still under consideration. However, simply invoking the name of Mexican wrestling star "El Santo" does not qualify you for tax-free Church status. And please stop calling me "Hank 'Sizzlin' ' Cisneros" in print.

Hank "Sizzlin' " Cisneros
HUD Secretary and High-Ranking *Pocho*

I was photocopying *Pocho Magazine* at a copy store where I have a special *Pocho* "Help Yourself" discount, when a small older woman about forty-five approached me to see if she could talk me out of my machine (she couldn't). She looked at the page from *Pocho* #4 which contained the blaring headline—CHICANOS WITH GUNS. She asked if I was an artist. I said yes. "A Chicano artist?" *"Simon,"* I replied. "Well, I'm Chicana, too." In the course of small talk, I dug into my Magic Bag of Pochismo to see what propaganda I could hand out to her: a finished *Pocho,* a Chicano Secret Service promo pack. She got the fat package of press clippings. "Oh, I've heard of you guys," she said as she studied our photo images on the cover. I told her we have a new show on the Westside of L.A. She proceeded to tell me she was into show business—a former censor at ABC. I invited the censor to our show.

She said she was too busy, as she was going to law school at Loyola or something. But she started to tell me that we would do good by talking to her because she "knows so much more" than my partners and I. I told her politely that we would give her a run for her learning money. She said, "Oh no. I know so much more than you because I went to protests and rallies—I was an Activist." This was a scene straight from "Bad Chicano Playhouse." "Well, I'm an activist, too—I went to rallies and protests at San Diego State and at Berkeley, too!" I was about to tell her that the only thing she had on us was age. Comparing levels of activism? Even young snot Mechistas don't do that.

One is not supposed to say bad things about other Latinos in front of Gringos. Benjamin Hernandez, editor of *Q-Vo* magazine, a lowriding type of Chicano magazine that spouts political self-determination for Chicanos yet litters its glossy sheets with denigrating Chicana soft-porn cheesecake shots, says, "I don't like the word *Pocho*—It's a bad word." He didn't appreciate my use of my hero Emiliano Zapata in a cartoon in my comic strip, "L.A. Cucaracha." I show land liberator Emiliano sitting down in an easy chair, holding his sombrero in one hand and the remote control in another. He is staring zombielike into a TV just the way most of the people in our community do every night after their hard day at work, or after their "stimulating" day at college. My point was to show that activism needs to get up off the couch and turn that tube off. Their argument is that we shouldn't abuse the few symbols we have.

According to a fable, Latinos, but specifically Mexicans, behave like crabs in a tub. The story goes *asi:* There's a fishing dock. A tourist walks by a fisherman guarding some tubs full of crabs. This fisherman, in covering one of his tubs, has obscured the identity of the crustaceans inside. "Excuse me, what do you have in this covered tub?" asks the visitor. "Why, those are Korean crabs," responds the fisherman, "and I must keep them covered up because they climb up on top of each other and help one another escape." "What about this tub?" says the tourist pointing to an uncovered tub. "Those? Those are Mexican crabs! I don't have to cover those because when one climbs up to the top to escape, the rest pull him down."

This fishy story is used to keep the lid on dissenters in our community. "Don't pull the rest down by criticizing them." As usual, the crabs, those little individualistic bottom-dwellers, get the blame for their own misfortune. No one ever questions whether the crabs asked to be in the tub in the first place. Or why the fisherman controls the tubs, or why this tyrannical Ahab is such a racist asshole. The moral of this story is that there must be no dissent because AS EVERYONE KNOWS, Mexicans are so full of *envidia,* or envy, that whatever problems we experience as a people must be our own fault.

I want Chicanos to appreciate what I do. Some don't understand my raucous art, saying that by working with stereotypes we are like the crabs, pulling our *Raza* down. Down from where? As a community, we still aren't doing so great. Many of us still live in poverty, our kids drop out of school at high rates. We have a long way to go to get out of the tub and into the promised Aztlan. We must allow for self-scrutiny and criticism. It's not the sixties anymore and the struggle does not call for us to be overly dogmatic, strident, or stingy with our *frijoles*.

Many older Chicanos can't understand that their successes have freed us from the narrow definitions that once constrained them. Because we *Pochos* grew up more confident in our "Chicanoness," we can espouse not only that culture but all the cultures that influence us. We give our Chicano culture a flexibility it has never had before—we can bend it, fold it, slice it, and dice it.

Pochismo is informed by the icons that my generation grew up with. The *Pocho* attacks problems from a more sardonic perspective than the Chicano, but the goals are the same. I'm just as alienated and repulsed by mainstream culture as those browns before me. We want to build up our community, we want education, we want to give our people the freedom to dine on authentic Mexican cuisine or microwave burritos or burgers con jalapeños.

There is still a big task ahead of us. Anti-immigrant hysteria has gripped the United States. Establishment pollsters bombard us with America's low opinions of mostly Latino undocumented immigrants, and particularly with the negative views that middle-class Latinos hold of the undocumented. This trend must be reversed if we are ever to rise as a community. The *Pocho* is the perfect candidate to cross that rickety bridge over the Rio Grande between the immigrant and the fourth-generation, middle-class Mexican-American.

All comers should beware! *Pochismo* will one day rule the earth as the mutt rules the streets! The surgeon general of Aztlan declares: WARNING—DO NOT TRY TO UNDERSTAND *POCHISMO*. IT IS A RIDDLE WRAPPED IN AN ENIGMA WRAPPED IN AN ENCHILADA. Or, as white male CBS head anchor Dan Rather once said, "If it's not the whole enchilada, then it is a very large taco."

HOW DIRTY PICTURES CHANGED MY LIFE

Lisa Palac

Burn it," I said. The words clinked together like ice cubes. "Burn every last bit of it. Or it's over."

I pointed at the stockpile of hard-core porn that had just slid out of the closet like an avalanche. If looks could kill, my boyfriend would have dropped dead. How could he, Mr. Sensitive Guy, enjoy looking at such disgusting trash? Oh, I was livid. I paced around his tiny one-room apartment, spitting venom, devising his punishment. "Either all this sleazy shit goes or I go."

He looked at me as if he were about to cry; his fingers nervously picked at the edges of his flannel shirt. "I'll get rid of it all, I promise," he whispered. Silence fell around the room like a metal drape. "But first will you watch one—just one—video with me?" The nerve. Here I am threatening to walk, and he's got the audacity to ask me to watch a fuck film before I go. He prattled on about how he just wanted a chance to show me why this stuff turned him on and that it didn't mean he didn't love me and if I didn't like it he would, as agreed, torch everything in a purging bonfire. I crossed my arms and chewed on the inside of my lip for a minute. If I was going to make him destroy his life's collection of porno, I guess I could allow him one last fling. So that evening we watched *Sleepless Nights*. It was the first dirty movie I ever saw. A seminal film.

I saw that movie when I was twenty years old, and now I'm twenty-nine. Since then I've watched hundreds of X-rated videos, patronized plenty of erotic theaters, put money down for live sex shows, and even run up a few phone sex bills. Today, I make my living making porn. I edit an erotic magazine titled *Future Sex* and recently produced the virtual-reality-based sex CD, *Cyborgasm*. I've always been a firm believer that if you want something done right, you've got to do it yourself.

Until I sat down and watched an adult film, the only thing I knew about porn was that I shouldn't be looking at it. Growing up female, I quickly learned that girls don't get to look at girlie magazines. Sure, you could take your clothes off for the camera (becoming, of course, a total slut and disgracing your family), but the pleasure is for *his* eyes only. The message to us girls was, stay a virgin until you get married, procreate, and don't bother finding your clitoris. Whatever you do, stay away from porn because it's a man's world, honey. Ironically, certain strains of feminism gave a similar sermon: Pornography can only exploit, oppress, and degrade you. It will destroy any female in its path, unless you can destroy it first. And if you don't believe this, you've obviously been brainwashed by The Patriarchy.

If the truth be known, the forbidden aspect of pornography made me a little curious. However, I wasn't about to be caught renting a porn video. So when Greg challenged me to watch an X-rated movie, I decided to see for myself what all the fuss was about.

At the time, I thought of myself as an antiporn feminist. Before that, I had identified as a rock-and-roll chick from Chicago. I grew up on the northwest side of the the city, not too far from Wrigley Field: the last in a line of four Polish Catholic middle-class kids. My childhood was carved out of a loaf of Wonder bread: I went to church on Sundays, was Cinderella in the kindergarten play, got gold stars in spelling and math, took tap and ballet lessons, forged my troop leader's signature to get extra Girl Scout badges, read all the Judy Blume books (starting with the menstrual manifesto of

the sixth grade: *Are You There, God? It's Me, Margaret*),
scarfed down Swanson dinners while watching every episode of "The Brady Bunch," cried when I got caught shoplifting a Bonne Bell Lipsmacker, played doctor with the
kids in the neighborhood, and asked my older brothers why
they didn't wipe when they peed. It was like, you know,
normal.

"But how did you get so interested in sex?" I always get
asked. I interpret this question to mean, "What terrible
trauma did you experience as a child that made you so perverted?" The answer: I was a corrupted papist.

Catholic school was twelve long years of wool-plaid pen-
ance, confessing to empty boxfuls of sin and silently debat-
ing whether Mary stayed a virgin even after Jesus was born.
I'd stare up at the crucifix and wonder how much it must
have hurt. Then I'd wonder what Jesus looked like naked.
Because of my profane thoughts, I always had a fear that I'd
become a nun—seriously. That would straighten me out but
good. On Career Day, joining the convent was always presented as a fine choice. "But not everyone is chosen to do
the Lord's work," the sisters would say and go on to tell us
how one day they just "got the calling" and that was that.
"Please don't pick me," I would whisper to myself over and
over, bowing my head. "Oh please, oh please, oh PLEASE!
Don't make me go!" Needless to say, I never got *that* calling.
I chalked it up to the fact that God would never pick someone who mentally undressed his only Son.

Or perhaps I simply inherited a kinky gene. My brothers
read *Playboy*. My dad read *Hustler*. I know that because I
used to steal peeks at it every time I had the chance. Whenever I'd start to feel bored and like there was nothing to do,
I'd find myself thinking, "Maybe I should go look at that
Hustler magazine again." My father had a couple of them
hidden with his fishing tackle in the basement. On hot summer days when my mom was out mowing the lawn, I'd go
downstairs, lie down on the cool concrete floor, and look at
those bizarre, naked pictures. The one I remember most was
of an Asian woman smoking a cigarette out of her pussy. It
was the weirdest thing I ever saw. These magazines fascinated me for a long time, and then one day, they weren't

there anymore. I think my mother found them and threw them out. I didn't look at any more sex magazines until I got to college.

I moved to Minneapolis in the early eighties and enrolled at the University of Minnesota. I really wanted to go to Berkeley, but the family leash would only stretch as far as the land of ten thousand lakes. My career choice: midwife. I applied to the school of nursing. I'd already completed one year of premed at Loyola University in Chicago, but I had to escape from the Jesuits—and my prosaic little existence. In our house, if you were smart you picked a career that showed it in dollars and cents. Dad looked at college as one long training seminar for the occupation of your choice: business, medicine, or law—the trinity of success. After all, I had to recoup all that college tuition, so forget about majoring in psychology or getting some crummy art degree. If I didn't land a high-paying job when I graduated, I might as well flush my diploma down the toilet. This was the philosophy of the survivors of Operation Bootstrap, the camp that made my dad. I solemnly vowed to rise above my Hallmark card life and get to know the edges of the world.

Most of my sophomore year was spent either studying, getting wasted, or undergoing some kind of mutation. I went from heavy metal chick to New Wave punk (albeit about four years late), squeezing into leopard-skin leggings and low-cut sweaters trimmed with ostrich feathers. I spiked my hot pink hair up with gobs of gel and swam all night in hot pink heels. I turned on to Joy Division and said "gnarly" a lot. I went to gallery openings. Ronald Reagan bored me and Patti Smith thrilled me. The way things were going, I could handle the tough science it took to get a nursing degree, but I couldn't handle the outfits. White slacks and a tasteful perm were unconscionable. I dropped out and went to art school.

I came out as a film major. My roommate came out as a lesbian. She was the first dyke I ever knew. Suzie was from California and was totally rad. I met her when I was at the U and we escaped dorm hell together. Together we ate our first mouthfuls of feminism.

I had never heard the word *feminist* before. My mother

wasn't a feminist, my older sister didn't call herself a feminist. Yet feminism gave me the words to describe my own experience. I quickly learned that being treated with less respect simply because I was female was called sexism, and it was not okay. Feminism illuminated the offenses that I'd chalked up to being a girl: enduring public comments on the size of my breasts, being paid less for the same work than my male counterparts, putting up with shoddy contraception. This knowledge was power: the power to take control of my life and make my own choices about everything I did.

Armed with our new feminist thinking, Suzie and I resolved to be women, not girls. We tromped on every bit of sexism in pop culture. We marched for Pro-Choice. We resented having to be constantly on guard against the threat of rape. We mourned the plight of women all across the globe who lived in squalid cages. We turned into pink sticks of dynamite, the crackle and spit of our fast-burning fuse getting louder all the time.

Pornography, of course, was the big bang. At that time, Minneapolis was a hotbed of radical antiporn politics. Catharine MacKinnon and Andrea Dworkin were teaching a class on porn at the U of M, and they drafted the very first feminist-inspired antipornography law, defining pornography as a form of sex discrimination. The *Story of O* was picketed on campus, with flyers denouncing S/M as just another bourgeois word for violence. *Not a Love Story,* a documentary about one woman's adverse experience in the adult business, became a Women's Studies classic. One woman set herself on fire in Shinder's Bookstore on Hennepin Avenue, a martyr for the right to a porn-free society. The message was clear: this battle was as important as ending the Vietnam war.

Meanwhile the Meese Commission was in full swing, bringing *Deep Throat* star Linda "Lovelace" Marchiano's disturbing testimony of coercion into the living rooms of America and alleging a link between pornography and violence. Women Against Pornography toured the heartland with their slide show, featuring the infamous *Hustler* cover of a woman being fed through a meat grinder. The tenet seemed to be this: Get rid of porn and get rid of all injustice against women. All the battles feminists were fighting could be won, by winning the war on porn. So I enlisted.

I didn't have any firsthand experience with porn. I had never watched an adult film, bought an explicit sex magazine, or known anyone who did. Aside from a few stolen glances at my father's collection, the only pornography I saw was in the classroom. This carefully selected group of pornographic images didn't appear very liberating: she's tied up and gagged with clothespins biting down on her nipples; she's spreading her legs wide open showing pink, his come squirting all over her face. These images were described as inherently degrading and oppressive. No other interpretation was offered. I looked at these images (which were supposedly representative of all porn), added my own experience of being sized up as a piece of ass, and agreed that pornography was the reason women were oppressed. Pornography bred sexism. Like Justice Potter Stewart, I knew pornography when I saw it and I'd seen enough to swallow the rally cries of the antiporn movement. I chanted and marched and applauded the spray painting of LIES ABOUT WOMEN over Virginia Slims ads and across the fronts of XXX black-veiled bookstores. I learned the slogans like "Porn is the theory and rape is the practice" from older feminists like Robin Morgan.

But soon I began to wonder how it all fit in with what I was doing in my bedroom. I still liked men, even if I didn't like all their piggish behavior. And I liked sleeping with them even more. Since I was fifteen, I used my feminine charms to lure them in. They used their virility to seduce me. Did this constitute sexual objectification? I wasn't sure. I questioned the definition of pornography I'd been handed. Yes, the images I'd seen offended me, but surely there were sexual images that weren't sexist. Where were the erotic alternatives? If the bottom line here was that looking at images of people having sex was wrong, then I hadn't come very far from Catholic school after all. Plus, lumping all men under the heading Sexist Patriarchy seemed a little unfair. The guys I hung out with were caring, respectful, and intelligent—but could they suddenly turn into psychopathic rapists if I waved a porn mag in front of their faces? Under-neath it all, I had a lot of questions. And then my boyfriend's porn came tumbling out of the closet.

"**R**eady?" he said, looking at me with dark eyes full of some corrupt knowledge I didn't yet have. We were both nervous; he was afraid I was going to hate it, leaving him with a mound of prurient ashes and a dead relationship. My fear was more tangled.

"Yeah," my voice cracked like a dry twig. Greg slipped *Sleepless Nights* into the VCR.

Sitting on the floor in the TV room, my mind began churning up shame-filled scenarios: What if my roommate walked in and caught us watching this dirty movie? Or worse, what if I am so turned on by this hideous smut that I became a full-blown porno addict? I could hear the voice: *What a disgusting girl. No one's gonna want you once they find out about this.* Or what if I laugh?

My initial reaction was, boy is this stupid. Everything was bad, bad bad: lame script, lousy acting, garish lighting, crip-pled disco soundtracks, anachronistic garter belts, and repulsive leading men. As a film student, I was appalled that the director of this cheap thing didn't even bother with the basics of good filmmaking. The plot was forgettable. I vaguely remember a contrived sex scene on a pool table. I was waiting for the violent rape scene, which never hap-pened. "Is that all?" I asked when it was over. I expected my porno research to yield some kind of groundbreaking vision, the same way that my first glimpses of feminism did.

It's hard to remember exactly what made me want to watch another one. Part of it was like social anthropology, peeling back the layers to see what I could see. And the unladylike act of watching porn was piquantly rebellious. But as we watched other X-rated films, I noticed they suf-fered from the same plague of filmic badness. I spent my early viewing hours counting the pimples on performers' asses and mimicking the orgasmic fakery of the starlets. Some of the actors looked bored out of their minds; others looked painfully luckless. They fucked in unnatural positions for the sake of the camera. Sometimes they were so unemotional they reminded me of Spock. Some were so skinny and so young, I felt like shouting "Get out of porn and run for your lives!" I imagined myself in their place; I imagined what my father would think if I did such a thing. Wouldn't all these women rather be doing something else but just don't have the skill or means?

A paradox emerged that I didn't understand. Sometimes I'd see an image of a woman on all fours begging for his cock and think, how humiliating. Other times during scenes like that, the actress's eyes filled up with fire so genuine, and he stroked her hair so tenderly while she sucked him off . . . it seemed romantic, like an unfiltered moment of pleasure. I began separating the images, recognizing that all of them weren't the same. I began to have flashes of lust.

But I wanted to have what Greg was having. He was getting something out of these movies that I wasn't. The movies didn't turn me off, but they didn't completely turn me on either—he did; his sexual excitement. He was sharing a very intimate part of himself with me and trusting me not to reject him. I wanted to know the side of him he'd so painstakingly hidden from me. Watching him watch the screen, I got turned on by the fact that he was turned on. But this Pavlovian eroticism worried me. While he slipped into erotic wonderland, I stood outside, waiting.

Then I made an important decision: I decided I needed to be alone with pornography. I wondered what might turn me on—if anything. God only knows what could happen to a girl who got turned on by thinking of a naked Jesus. I wanted to perform an experiment, to watch it by myself without him, without talking. I could no longer scrutinize these images from an intellectual distance. I had to get a little dirty.

I made a date with an "all-lesbian" action feature called *Aerobisex Girls*. I tried not to care about the plot. I didn't wonder about the performers' family histories. I didn't think about anything. The movie featured an oiled-up orgy where the women shook with the fury of real, uncontrollable orgasms. I could feel the heat between my legs. As if my erotic imagination was being mapped to the screen, I fingered myself in sync with the women in the film. I opened and closed my eyes, imagining I was part of their scene, replaying certain close-ups over and over. Then my mind began moving back and forth between the real-time video and the frozen frames of cherished erotic memories. I fed the screen with my own fantasies, splicing together an erotic sequence that played only in my head. When I came, it was intense.

Now I knew firsthand what most women don't think about: what men do with all those sex magazines. Guys don't buy *Playboy,* turn to the centerfold and think "I'd like to marry her," then turn the page and go grab a burger. No, they masturbate to it. They jerk off. Masturbation is such a big part of every man's life, and to a much lesser extent every woman's, but nobody talks about it. Men do it and don't talk about it, while women don't talk about it and don't *do* it. This is a fact. Studies like *The Kinsey Report* and *The Hite Report* have documented the high percentage of women who do not masturbate. This statistic is further mirrored in our language: we don't even have the words to describe female self-stimulation. If there is any jerking, wanking, or beating off to be done it involves a penis, not a clitoris. It's a testimony to how cut off women are from their sexuality, both physically and psychologically.

Despite the fact that seventies feminist liberation honored the female flower and encouraged women to talk more openly about sex, masturbation still remains a taboo. In addition, women still aren't given any social encouragement to use erotic pictures to stimulate their sexual imagination. So when it comes to understanding how to use porn, they're in the dark. They don't get what it's for. Men, on the other hand, are very familiar with the concept of stroking and since they've always had such easy access to sexual material, they can't understand why it's such a big deal for a woman to get off on porn. "So you masturbated to some porno, big deal," they say. "I did that when I was thirteen."

The truth is, I didn't masturbate until I was nearly twenty years old and a vibrator hit me on the head—literally. I was cleaning out a closet in my new apartment, when a battery-operator vibrator fell off a high shelf and bonked me. As if I were a cartoon character, a light bulb went off inside my brain and I decided to give myself a buzz. It was the first time I had an orgasm. Strange but true, I never really thought much about touching myself until then. Try to imagine a guy who doesn't masturbate until an appliance hits him on the head at the age of twenty.

Until this point, I never felt in charge of my own pleasure. I was taught that sexual satisfaction was something I lay back and waited for. An orgasm was something my boy-friend gave to me—only he didn't. Although I'd been having penis-in-vagina sex since I was fifteen, I hadn't come from it. I heard plenty about the Big O, but clearly never had the feelings they described in *Cosmo*. I remember one time when an old lover asked me the inevitable question after sex: Did you come? Embarrassingly, I said I didn't—ever. "Don't you masturbate to come?" he asked. I was bewildered.

At the beginning of my porn adventures, I was also con-fused. I was looking for a political theory instead of a sexual experience, and that's why it hadn't been working. Now I had the carnal knowledge that so few women possessed: how to use porn and come. What's important about this isn't just that I learned how to get physically aroused by pornography, but that I became sexually autonomous. I was now in complete control of my own erotic destiny. My expe-rience was sexual liberation in action. I now knew how to use my mind to turn a two-dimensional image into a flesh-and-blood erotic response and explore sexual fantasies.

Before I watched porn, my erotic imagination was groggy. I didn't know what a sexual fantasy was; I hadn't really had them. Even when I masturbated I didn't think about any-thing, except the physical sensations. When I had sex with my lovers, my thoughts were filled only with them, the way they were touching me, the immediacy of the act. And that was good. But there were all these other thoughts that I hadn't explored yet. Pornography dangled sexual fantasy in front of me. It made me aware that my sexual imagination wasn't limited to the heat of the moment or a sensual remi-niscence. I could think about *anything*. I could use *any-*

thing—books, magazines, videos—for erotic inspiration.

One of my most formative sources of inspiration was a journal titled *Caught Looking.* Written by a group of East Coast feminist activists, this book combined academic refutations of the antiporn argument with hard-core sex pictures. As its title implied, it gave women the rare opportunity to look at a wide variety of pornographic images. *Caught Looking* confirmed what I had been living: the censorship of pornography is unfeminist. The book represented a whole new breed of women who were reclaiming the power of female sexuality. I felt very much a part of that breed.

Soon I was reading *On Our Backs,* a lesbian sex magazine edited by a woman named Susie Bright. This was pornography created by women for women—how revolutionary! It not only challenged countless stereotypes about lesbian sex being boring and vanilla, but it also defied the myth that women weren't interested in erotic pictures. The magazine ripped apart the notion that porn was only for men. I uncovered Candida Royalle's series of feminist porn videos, *Femme,* and watched every one with fervent camaraderie. Other books like Nancy Friday's *My Secret Garden,* which detailed women's wide-ranging sexual fantasies, and *Coming to Power,* edited by the lesbian S/M group Samois, further validated my position that female sexuality was a powerful force that could not be politically pigeonholed.

My newfound sexual freedom was sweet, but finding the pornography that waved it along was rare. Wading through the swamp of split beavers and raging hard-ons, I felt by turns critical, angry, depressed, pensive, embarrassed and bored. I began a relentless search for the right stuff. Often, I was surprised at the things that made me wet; things that would no doubt be labeled "male oriented," and "degrading" by any number of good feminist soldiers. But these "good parts" were so few and far between, I spent more time fingering the fast-forward button than anything else. I wanted lots of images that reflected my erotic desires and depicted authentic female sexuality. I scanned for cute guys with long hair, punk butchy women, plots with lots of psycho-sexual tension, come shots where he doesn't pull out and most of all, genuine female orgasms—most of the actresses' orgasms were so fake they were laughable.

It seemed the biggest problem with pornography wasn't that it was evil smelling and immoral—it was artificial and predictable. But despite my exhaustive search through all the local dirty bookstores, I came up rather empty-handed. Finally I realized I couldn't wait around any longer for somebody else to give me what I wanted. I had to create it myself.

In 1986 during my senior year in college, I created a two-page erotic fanzine called *Magnet School: A Sexographic Magazine*. I felt strongly that the problem with porn wasn't that it was inherently degrading but that it was, for the most part, an erotically retarded genre that needed to get real. I wanted to create something that aroused people sexually and intellectually, where the complexity of human sexuality had a voice. Because I so badly wanted to produce something different, I called it something different. In my first editorial column titled "Yeow!" I did away with those loaded language guns *erotica* and *pornography* and put *sexography* in their place.

Sexography was alternative sexual expression in all its lush and lusty glory. In Issue One, I defined sexography as "absolutely no writing about harlots, no getting off with big orchids, no high heels in bed, no masturbating to Lionel Ritchie, and no split beavers." (Okay, so I've changed my mind a bit since then.) There were other contenders for a newer, blue title—cliterature, lustography, climaxerox, and even Ovaria—but they didn't have the right egalitarian ring.

Although the Macintosh computer had already made its debut, this 'zine was still a cut-and-paste production. I hammered the first issue out on my typewriter, reprinting text from a Throwing Muses album, daring my best girlfriend to pen a porn story and pirating any decent hard-core images I could find. I xeroxed it for free during the middle of the night at the twenty-four-hour copy center, since I'd made friends with the anarchist punks who worked there. I handed it out in cafes and bars, and of course made distribution rounds to every dirty bookstore in town, telling every dildo clerk about the coming erotic revolution. It was very grassroots.

At the same time I was publishing *Magnet School,* I was completing my senior thesis at art school: a sixteen-millimeter color erotic film called *What You Want.* It was a dark and abstract narrative that dealt with issues of female sexuality, control, and erotic relationships. Basically, it was my life turned porn drama with me as the star in a long red wig since no one else auditioned. Greg and I got naked in a bathtub, toyed with oral sex, and even fabricated a nipple-piercing scene. I had intended deep introspection, but my unpolished direction made it corny. I was disappointed that my best intentions had turned camp because I was trying to make a very important point: sexual images can be profoundly liberating, rather than oppressive.

During the making of this film, we had student critiques in the screening room. Everyone in my class was always very opinionated until I showed *my* work in progress. Then there was dead silence, followed by, "God; what are your parents going to think?" Well, I wasn't making this film for my parents. I was making it for my peers, and I wanted to know what they thought. At first, they were sort of . . . shocked. They didn't know what to say. The silence was uncomfortable and sometimes hurt me. But outside the classroom, my colleagues had a lot to say.

Much to my relief, my female friends were extremely supportive. They related to my journey from antiporn feminism to sex-positive feminism, because many of them were on the same trip. They, too, were fed up with everyone shouting "Don't look!" when it came to porn. The wanted to see it and they wanted me to show it to them. My friend Bitsy even asked me to invite all the girls over for pizza and porno night.

As we talked, I realized that learning how to use porn is an option most women are never aware of. Too many women only react to pornography as a political debate. Pornography, erotica, sexography, whatever you choose to call it, is a tangled genre with a few razor-sharp sides. This complexity is a reflection of the mystery and depth of our own sexuality, where erotic conflict often makes for excitement. My investigation into the erotic world has resulted in a few mixed feelings. There were images that troubled me, and there still are. But I believe my initial knee-jerk reaction against porn was a result of my own misunderstanding and lack of sensitivity to erotic images.

Pornography as a whole is usually described as offensive. Yet I found that much of what is offensive about porn has to do with interpretations, not sexual acts. Take the controversial example of a woman sucking a man's cock until he comes all over her face. This image can be presented in a very crass and repellent way, or it can be depicted as sensuous and kind. To me, the act itself isn't degrading; feeling my lover come all over me can be the most intimate gift. But no matter how artfully presented this image is, it is almost always interpreted as crass and repellent because people refuse to believe there can be other interpretations.

The words *degrading* and *oppressive* are often presented as absolute, objective terms. I found them to be vague and subjective. Was the very act of a woman spreading her legs and wanting sex degrading? Were photographs of her genitals outright demeaning? Why is the image of a woman's sexual appetite seen as oppressive rather than liberating? If we're going to talk about oppressive images of women, we'd better include laundry soap commercials. The depiction of women as vapid Stepford wives, valued only for their stain-removing talents is, to me, completely oppressive.

Another thing that really surprised me as I explored this erotic underworld was the lack of violent porn. I was taught to believe that all porn was violent. However, my own exploration quickly revealed that the majority of commercial porn is rather peacefully formulaic. No knives, no blood, no rape scenes. Instead, there was a lick-suck-fuck formula that ended in orgasm, not murder.

Ultimately, I felt the antiporn feminists viewed women as being without sexual self-awareness. Their arguments for the elimination of porn were shaky and flawed. Their claims denied women independence by refusing to acknowledge that women had rich sexual fantasies, powerful libidos, and the power to choose.

I chose to discuss sex in a way my older sister probably never did, particularly with my women friends. We traded vibrator tips, talked about our erotic fantasies—or the lack of them—and shared the secrets of our guilt-ridden, latent masturbatory experiences. We didn't waste time dissing men—we mainly focused on ourselves and figuring out how to power up our own orgasms—although we did agree that the general lack of male nudity was lame. Tits and ass flood our culture, but his bare body is nowhere in sight. We also found it interesting how pornography is usually discussed as the sexual depiction of women, although almost all heterosexual porn features women *and* men. We felt that if porn was going to come of age, not only would the images of women have to change, so would the images of men. Paunchy guys with overgrown mustaches who had little to offer except their big dicks weren't our idea of sexy. We wanted bad boys with angel faces who understood the meaning of seduction. We also wanted them to be a little, well . . . vulnerable.

Although what we said was significant, how we said it was also important. These conversations didn't take place behind closed doors, but in public. At parties, in cafes, and in living rooms across Minneapolis we talked about what turned us on. We didn't care who heard us. We had so many questions and we felt so powerful being able to ask them out loud.

Men, on the other hand, were less sure how to act. They were intrigued by my bold sexual independence. It struck a chord with them—they saw their own masculinity reflected in me. In other words, they admired my balls. At the same time, they were a bit confused by my overt sexuality. It conflicted with their understanding of feminism. A lot of men my age were raised to believe that if you respected women, you didn't look at naked pictures of them. So if I was a feminist, how could I like pornography? To them, the concept of a loudmouthed, sexually self-governing woman was exciting, challenging, and sometimes a bit scary.

Surprisingly, or maybe not, I was never directly attacked by any antiporn feminists. People often expect me to tell horrifying tales of how I was branded a traitor and was run out of Wimmin's town on a rail. But the truth is, the response to my work has always been overwhelmingly positive. I believe it's because more and more women are realizing that erotic images have a necessary place in their lives. Sexual freedom is an integral part of freedom and justice for all. If the basic tenet of feminism is giving women the freedom to choose, then it includes making choices about what we do sexually.

This freedom to go for the erotic gusto, however, exists because of the tremendous gains founding feminists have made. If it wasn't for social and economic battles won during the last few decades, female sexuality would still be chained up in ignorance and silence. The sexual revolution of the late sixties and early seventies paved the way for my generation's erotic liberation.

As a card-carrying feminist, I chose to pursue a career as a pornographer. With eight issues of my homegrown zine *Magnet School* completed, I gave in to my crush on California and headed west to San Francisco—Sin City. For two years, I worked with my mentor Susie Bright, as a senior editor at *On Our Backs* and as a freelance journalist.

In 1991 I was hired to edit *Future Sex,* a magazine for women and men that explores the intersection of sex, technology, and culture. I had written about so many aspects of sex, but not this one. What was the link between sex and technology anyway? Was it virtual reality sex? Digital porn? Fucking robots? While these concepts were certainly futuristic, I hoped they weren't the only things the future of sex had to offer.

The fact that today's young women are able to think more critically about pornography is due, in part, to technology. The VCR brought a female audience to porn and gave them the unprecedented opportunity to see exactly what it is. Video porn allows both women and men to investigate sexual imagery in a more independent way. Moving X-rated images out of public, often unclean theaters and into the privacy and comfort of the bedroom gave women safe and direct access to this previously off-limits material. In fact, women now represent the fastest-growing group of erotic consumers.

I now realize that technology may be this generation's key to taking control of our sexual identities. While computer technology may seem isolating rather than unifying at first, personal computers, modems, camcorders, and a host of other tools offer the potential for unparalleled communication, including erotic communication. In many ways high technology puts the means of production back in everyone's hands. We no longer have to depend on someone else's mass-produced idea of eroticism; we can create our own— easily, cost-effectively, often instantly. Moreover, digital technology gives us the chance to transmit our ideas globally, not just locally.

Today, we must also contend with something no other generation had to: AIDS. Since this devastating plague sends the message that sex can equal death, it forces us to talk publicly about sex in a straightforward way in order to save lives. Latex is vogue. Jerking off is in. Safe sex is hot. AIDS is a catalyst for rethinking our relationship to erotica. And the stigma of pornography is slowly being chipped away.

But this new-world pornography will suffer the same pitfalls of the old world if we don't take advantage of the possibilities. A naked babe on a computer screen is just the same old babe, unless we add change. Technology doesn't magically transform—or even replace—erotic traditions. People do. The depth of both female and male sexuality can't be explored if we don't break the mold of prefabricated turnons. We've got the power to turn the tired, piston-driven porn formula into a fluid reflection of modern erotic culture. What's hot isn't limited to high heels and big cocks. Genderbending, multiracial eroticism, bisexuality, and a range of other polymorphous departures from the standard are all a part of the erotic spectrum, but we rarely see them presented as such. That's why the genesis of this new erotic entertainment must be influenced by people with more diverse points of view. And I intend to be influential right from the very start.

Since I watched *Sleepless Nights* almost nine years ago, I've learned a lot about myself and the power of being female. I've learned that the erotic impulse is a part of being human, that it can't be controlled through political warfare or replaced by a silicon chip. I've learned that pornography is a mirror reflecting our rosiest desires, our blackest fears. It catches us looking. And these days I like some of what I see—especially when I've created it.

DAUGHTERS OF THE REVOLUTION

Robin Pogrebin

People frequently ask me what it's like to be the daughter of a leader of the women's movement. I have always given the same answer: it is the only way of life I've ever known, and I wouldn't trade it for any other. Only recently, in my late twenties, have I come to see it not only as a privilege but also as a burden. Not simply because, as someone who seems to "have it all," my mother is a tough act to follow. But because, as the daughter of a feminist pioneer, I fear that I am squandering her legacy.

And I am not alone. Many young women like me, we so-called daughters of the women's movement—who were raised with a feminist conciousness, if not by feminists themselves—sense that we are falling down on the job. Not only aren't we out there fighting for progressive causes, but many of us are also embracing the very old-fashioned ideals our foremothers fought so hard to leave behind. Where they struggled to declare their independence, many of us are pre-occupied with finding husbands and starting families. Where they fought to give women a wide breadth of options and a strong sense of self-worth, we feel inhibited by self-doubt. And where they broke into professions once closed to women, many of us are merely enjoying the fruits of their labors, rather than actively seeking to advance women's progress in the work force.

It is embarrassing to admit such apparent failings. More-over, it all seems sadly illogical: according to the natural order of things, we ought to have taken their strides several steps further. We should be more courageous than they, more committed, more confident. Instead, we seem conser-vative and they look like the radicals. We're supposed to be adventurous young women looking forward to the future. Instead we seem to be the pragmatists and they look like the dreamers.

Why this disparity? Why aren't we soldiering on where they left off, emboldened by their example? Why aren't we determined to pave the trail they blazed for us? Largely, I suspect, it is because we are part of a decade that has become defined by disillusionment rather than hope. The nineties have been all about confronting our limitations as a country; the sixties symbolized an age of infinite possibility. While we grew up taking certain options for granted, eco-nomic and social hard times have conspired to make the future seem newly precarious. Now, a college degree and a stable upbringing no longer guarantee professional success or financial security. Gone are the days when college seniors plucked plentiful job listings off the bulletin boards of career offices. The job market is the poorest since World War II and getting worse.

This pessimism has taken a particular toll on young women of my generation. Our uncertainty about the future has exacerbated the uncertainty so many women often already feel about themselves. It has clouded the lessons handed down by feminist leaders. And it may be holding us back. Externally, we are the very model of liberated modern women. We hold jobs, we live on our own, we have come a long way. But while decisive, feminism's victories still feel somewhat fragile. We are the first generation to inhabit this brave new world for women. So we are not entirely comfort-able staking a claim or taking the floor.

We are still well aware of the battles to be won—the scar-city of women in boardrooms and public office, the persis-tence of sexual harassment. We are still hindered by the insecurities that our mothers tried to overcome. We agonize over whether to stay home after we have children or to continue working. We still waste too much time and energy worrying about our appearance.

When I confess frailties such as these, my mother marvels at me incredulously. "You look terrific," she says. "What are you worried about?" Or: "You're so smart and accomplished, why don't you feel great about yourself?" If only it were so clear-cut. Intellectually, I know I should shut up and count my blessings and be more self-assured. But instinctively, I cannot stanch this undercurrent of inadequacy. Making a difference seems like an abstract and overwhelming prospect. The kind of high-minded objectives that my mother and her contemporaries pursued seem risky and remote. I am afraid that I might fail in trying to achieve such goals.

To complicate matters, just when we young women are trying to embrace our hard-won autonomy, along comes the recession to undermine our economic self-sufficiency. Along come the pundits predicting that our generation will never approximate—much less surpass—our parents' standard of living and declaring the nation to be in a state of psychological depression. In light of such doomsaying, it's hard to feel that there is a lot to look forward to. Consumed with pinning things down, we become cautious about shaking things up.

Rather than chance that our activist efforts may come to naught, some of us take cover in conservative short-term goals: building a career, making a home, having enough money to make it through the month. Shoring up these essentials gives me a sense of accomplishment, however superficial. When I graduated from college, some six years ago, the nuclear family was considered a sellout. Now I find myself envying my college roommate who lives in a big suburban house with her husband, their new baby, and two cars. She seems more like a crusader than a cliché. She's all set. Although I still resist such picket-fence aspirations, they have grown increasingly attractive. No wonder we twentysomethings used to gather to worship at the television altar of "thirtysomething." To us, watching married couples juggle jobs and children in suburbia was as compelling as "Beverly Hills 90210" now is to teenagers.

Although, as liberated women, we're not supposed to worry about being single, we also don't want to face the future alone. If the journey ahead is going to be hard, we want to have someone struggling along with us—an ally, a cheerleader, a soulmate. As a result, people my age are caught up in a dating scene that some describe as desperate. Single women are wondering if they should have stayed in past relationships, no matter how flawed, as if to settle for someone less than perfect might be better than winding up with no one at all. Listening to the anxieties of these friends, I find myself not only grateful to be happily married but relieved to be married, period. At least I have surmounted one hurdle: finding a husband. Some feminist.

If I can just get the everyday things in place, I tell myself, that's when I'll turn my attention to more profound pursuits. I've heard friends say the same. We seem to have reconciled ourselves to the postponement of ideals; oblivious to the incongruity of young voices talking wistfully about "someday," we are playing it safe now so we can afford to take risks later. Of course, we are only heading for the notorious trap that so many middle-aged people wish they had avoided: deferring dreams only to be full of regrets later. And this kind of self-denial is sadly premature. There will be plenty of time for such trade-offs. We are young. We're supposed to be impulsive, spontaneous, even cocky. This is reputedly a time for experimentation, when mistakes are not only permissible but valuable. We have a whole life ahead of us to worry about supermarket bills and mortgage payments and college tuition for the kids.

Right now, however, such parochial concerns seem imperative, and activism—even feminism—seems like a luxury. A feeling of inefficacy may explain the lack of enthusiasm among some women my age about making commitments that are intrinsically hopeful. Friends of mine who have tried volunteer activities have often abandoned such efforts after finding them to be a mere drop in the bucket.

After exploring several volunteering possibilities, I recently became a mentor to an inner-city teenager—her name is Ieasha—and committed myself to helping her through four years of high school. Ieasha and I get together about twice a month to go to the movies, or roller skate, or walk a street fair, and we speak regularly on the telephone. I believe my presence in her life has helped her to know that there is someone out there besides her family who cares about her future. But there are days when I wonder if I am making any impact on her life. I cannot force her to concentrate in math so that she won't fail the course. I cannot make her crowded Bronx apartment any bigger to accommodate her siblings better. I cannot make her neighborhood safer or her family closer. And I feel isolated by the solitary quality of my involvement.

Where are my comrades? Why is there no groundswell of social or political reform? Somehow, activism seems to have lost its cachet. In the sixties everyone was getting into the act. These days, do-gooders are often dismissed as touchy-feely types who are out of synch with reality. And those few who continue to speak out in the name of political principles are often chided as anachronistic rather than visionary. There is a scarcity of insurgent voices. People my age seem silenced. I too find myself hesitant to venture ideas that might be controversial or to expose feelings that might make me seem vulnerable. I don't feel comfortable shouting about something, let alone hearing my own voice for very long.

My mother tells me I am being too hard on myself. Just because I'm not out there marching in the streets, she says, doesn't mean I'm not breaking any ground. We daughters have a different role to play in the revolution, she assures me: to make what our mothers started stick. We are living proof of their progress, she reminds me. We have seized the professional opportunities they opened up to us and, by performing well, demonstrated that we deserve them. We have given younger women role models to emulate. We are building our female version of the old-boy network that will someday help give women the same leg up that has eased the way for so many men. We are the next stage—the Third

Wave, as a group of young feminists now call themselves. While we may not be boldly taking on the powers that be, my mother insists, we are making inroads merely by bringing an ingrained feminist consciousness into the mainstream.

There is certainly truth to this logic. In my work as a reporter, I find that my feminist sensibility informs what stories I choose to cover and the way I go about writing them. On several occasions in my career, I have steered articles—both my own and those of my colleagues—away from the sexist proclivities that threatened to perpetuate stereotypes. I have made sure that a newsworthy conflict between two women doesn't come off looking like a trivial catfight. I have eliminated physical descriptions of women in stories where they are not relevant. At one job, I confronted a male editor when his sexual overtures made me uncomfortable. At another job, I made a female editor aware of the fact that she consistently called on me last in our otherwise all-male story meetings. After that, she almost always called on me first.

Yet, while I can see how I may be doing my share in some subtle way, sometimes I yearn to be part of something larger, more defiant and less decorous. I wonder what will define my generation of women if we fail to join forces for a greater good. And I crave the camaraderie, the sense of belonging, and the collective identity that come with enlisting in a common cause.

My mother's activism has given her that sense of purpose and sisterhood. As a result, she seems consciously to keep it alive in her life. There have been plenty of opportunities for her to take a break. But she is not content to sit back and coast on her accomplishments. So after years as a founding editor of Ms. magazine and writing and lecturing on feminism, she turned her energies toward achieving peace in the Middle East. She locates herself in the world by fighting for something.

I don't know how I will locate myself in the world. I am still unsure of what I want my life to be because I am constantly worrying about what it ought to be. Should I have children before I'm thirty so I can be a young and active parent? Or should I wait to have children until after I'm thirty so that I can secure my career? Should my husband and I buy a two-bedroom apartment before we can really afford it because the real estate market is good and we're going to need one when we have a family? Or should we move out of New York because I've never lived anywhere else? And so on. The worst question someone can ask me— and people ask it all the time—is where I want to be in five years. Or ten years. I haven't yet been able to come up with an answer.

My ambivalence is particularly acute in comparison to those women who seem to know exactly what they want and go after it without regard to the practical ramifications. They are the writers, painters, and actors who press on in their work despite the daunting odds against critical success or financial reward. They are the fresh voices who speak without screening what they say and state their views aggressively, without the usual maddening female question marks or disclaimers.

I have sought the company of these women, in the hope that their confidence might rub off on me. When I'm with them, I feel challenged and inspired. I have easily found such people in my mother's circles, such as the Seder Sisters who created a feminist Passover ritual about eighteen years ago. At this annual all-women's event, which supplements the two nights of regular family seders, we sit in a circle on the floor, read from a feminist haggadah written by one of the seder's founders, and honor women in the Bible who are typically slighted by traditional ceremonies. What has made these evenings most memorable is the ritual of going around the room and having each woman speak about the year's chosen theme, such as political struggle or personal plagues.

Last year, we younger participants broke off and started a Seder Daughters ceremony of our own. We who organized it each invited several friends, all of whom gathered at my home for the ceremony. We adopted some of the same rituals from the original feminist seder—sat on the floor, introduced ourselves by giving our matrilineage—and invented new ones. We asked each woman there to talk about what she was looking for in a feminist seder. Almost without exception, each one spoke of wanting to fill a certain void. Like me, they felt that this kind of community of women was missing in their lives. They didn't know where to find it and felt at a loss to create it. The religious aspect of the gathering was clearly secondary. It was the femaleness of the event that was most important to the people there.

We came away from that evening proud of ourselves for establishing such a tradition and committed to its continuation. But seders are only once a year. Three years ago, I became part of a discussion group made up of about eight women in their late twenties and early thirties. We meet on the first Sunday of every month at a different member's home, order in Chinese food or pizza, and discuss what is pivotal in our lives at the moment. Sometimes we choose themes, such as "mothers," "sexuality," or "anger." Mostly we just take turns talking about ourselves. I value this group as one of the few places where I can analyze my life out loud with the support of women I trust. It has made me realize that there are women out there like me—well educated and accomplished—who often share my confusion.

Although we didn't all grow up as daughters of activists, each of us is grappling with our own version of what Harold Bloom calls the "anxiety of influence"—in this case, trying to free ourselves from the pressure to emulate or satisfy our mothers. Although we were raised with a sense of entitlement, each of us still has difficulty exercising it—whether it be demanding a pay raise or asking a husband to pull his weight in household chores, or letting friends know when we're angry.

But while I feel comforted by the affirmation I find in these communities of women, something still troubles me. Unlike our mothers' band of revolutionaries, our women's groups seem to grow out of weakness rather than strength. The support we draw on from one another is important. But is our echoing of one another's experience empowering or debilitating? Does validating one another's needs prevent us from fulfilling them? I worry that, by dwelling on what is holding us back, we may be delaying our ability to move forward.

In social settings—strange as it sounds—I think women

could benefit from being a little more like men. When women get together, they tend to talk about their feelings, particularly regarding relationships. When men congregate, they tend to talk business—if not sports. Women connect. Men network.

Some young women seem to have recognized the need to move beyond commiserating to coalition building. This year, Naomi Wolf and other young feminists formed a group called Culture Babes—the name has been the topic of some debate—made up of women in the media. It was founded not so that we could sit around bemoaning the underrepresentation of female editors at major newspapers or the rarity of quotes from female experts in news stories, but so that we could do something about these problems.

Culture Babes's monthly gatherings offer its members the opportunity to get to know other women in various fields, to alert one another to job openings, and to tap into a pool of collaborators for future projects. Among the group's specific goals is the assembly of a "Goddess Rolodex" featuring female authorities on various subjects so that the mainstream media can reach beyond its standard roster of male talking heads. Culture Babes also plans to reach out to female college graduates who are interested in the media, to help them make job contacts and communicate with potential mentors.

It is in this group that I have begun to glimpse the future face of women's activism. And it looks promising. Its principles are reminiscent of the impassioned 1960s. But its style and implementation are emblematic of the practical 1990s. There will probably always be a part of me that equates progress with ferment and mutiny. I will probably always feel somewhat nostalgic for crusades like those that swept up my mother's generation of rebels. But we need to find our own approach, to honor our progressive heritage, but also to interpret and apply it in ways that feel authentic. There may be no marches, no banners or bullhorns. But there can be significant moments of triumph.

So my mother may be right, after all. While we are not necessarily brazen change-makers, we can still make change. We are less the revolution than the evolution. And the greatest relief comes in realizing that my mother's generation of activists is not disappointed in us. We haven't let those women down. In fact, we have even made them proud. They didn't work so hard only to have us duplicate their dreams and deeds. They struggled so that we could someday determine our own.

TRASH THAT BABY BOOM

Ian Williams

. . . clean your baby room, trash that baby boom. . .

—*The Replacements, "Bastards of Young"*

If you are a self-confessed twentysomethinger with any sort
of clue, you have no doubt winced every time some news-
weekly made our ain't-we-kids-got-angst generation their
pet topic of the month. Admittedly, it's a damn sight better
than cover stories about Liz Taylor or the trouble those
kooky "Diff'rent Strokes" kids keep getting into, but more
often than not, the article falls way short of giving us any
more identity than we had when we started. Usually penned
by some hastily recruited twenty-eight-year-old with just
the right sort of disenchanted panache, the article will bitch
about how they will be paying off their share of the national
debt at Taco Joe's until they're sixty, or how no one came to
their campus Rock the Vote Dry Toga Party, or how having
sex these days is as spontaneous as the Brezhnev funeral.
Worse yet, they might be complaining about all the other
abortive attempts to define our generation by fellow twentysomething artisans. Whichever route they take, the article
usually ends with a call-to-arms to generational buddies, for
us to get off our rectae and *do* something about it all. The
problem is, these articles are written by the wrong people.

I call it the "MTV Video Fight" Syndrome. A few years
ago, MTV would play a couple of videos and give you a 900
number to call, so you could vote for the one you liked best.
Naturally, the most mind-bendingly moronic song you'd
heard since "Boogie Oogie Oogie" always won, and why?

Because only true idiots with *way* too much free time bothered to call, thus giving MTV (along with the rest of the Free
World) a devastatingly warped cross section of its audience's
true feelings.

Armed with that theory, you can see the problem with
these Generation X articles. The only people willing to burn
the calories to bitch in public about the perils of being direc-
tionless and apathetic possess far too much direction and
gumption to come close to representing the kind they call
their own. If you want a reliable, realistic representation of
our generation, you will have to find someone who won't
dare tell his true feelings, share his meditations, or have anything particularly coherent to say to today's media—a little
like trying to see if the light really does shut off when you
close the refrigerator door.

Why anyone should listen to me, then, is anybody's
guess. Generalizations infuriate me as much as the next
crotchety young American, especially the ones that are
about me. I can make this generalization, though, without a
stutter: those of us in our twenties and early thirties feel a
distinct and undeniable alienation from the culture that has
been coming at us for the last few decades. And the reason
we are like this, so sullen and unresponsive, private, confusing, and completely non-user-friendly, is largely tied up in
the generation just before us. We are like this because of the
baby boomers.

"Every generation / blames the one before" proclaimed a
rather anesthetized hit from Mike and the Mechanics in the
late eighties, and this one is turning out to be no exception.
Our gripes with the baby boom, until now, have been
muted and unspecific: "the boomers are selfish and hypo-
critical, man . . . all those hippies put on suits and sold
out . . ." Like a small child, aware but not conscious of
something unsettling, we couldn't get the right words out
until recently. It's no coincidence that our public dissatisfac-
tion with our place in history happened right around the
time that a few of us could put pen to paper without feeling
as though we were absolutely full of shit. Even then, we
have to deal with holier-than-thou goggleboxes who claim
all this self-pitying generational angst is no different from

any other in history, and how outrageous it is to make crass generalizations about millions of strangers. They have a point, but the fact is that we wouldn't think generationally (or place blame, for that matter) if the boomers weren't so wrapped up in the concept of The Generation themselves.

To really understand, though, how we have come to begrudge boomers so much, one has to look at how we grew up with them. I was born in 1967. Time's "Man of the Year" that year was "People Under 25," and though technically I, too, counted as a people under twenty-five, they were referring to the bright-eyed idealists that haunted college campuses. I was actually released the same week as "Sgt. Pepper" and rode home from the hospital concurrently with *Rosemary's Baby*. I have early, damp-pants memories of college kids in my professor dad's university having a crazy old time; nothing tangible, but there was a definite spirit in the air that something big and wonderful was happening.

When the seventies came around, this feeling of wonder and excitement was being replaced by a vague sense of doom, as though our elders were all exhausted and a little bored. I recall huge cars, gas lines, bad music, silly haircuts. In first grade, I remember being dragged from the tetherball court to see the president resign on TV. A few years later, I often watched "Saturday Night Live" when my parents were out to dinner and sat quizzically through jokes about drugs and boobs. My friends and I bought tickets to the "PG" version of *Saturday Night Fever* and then sneaked into the "R" version playing next door; there we marveled at all the incredible wanton fun those guys and girls fifteen years older were having on the dance floor and in the backseats of cars.

In the early 1980s, my friends and I went through the rites of passage typical of adolescents throughout history, passing judgment on our parents, hanging out at the mall, and developing the tightly knit cliques that sheltered us from the rest of the world. In high school, we heard all kinds of conflicting evidence; we were either a blessed or cursed group of people. The dwindling number of workers in the American labor force meant that we would have no problem getting all kinds of jobs; at the same time, every government agency also said that we couldn't find St. Louis on a map to save our lives. While we were scraping up enough money to buy the "Rio" single from Duran Duran, the media told us that folks in their thirties were buying up the planet and bringing pasta makers home to their clean, disinfected apartments. Later on, as we hit college and the boomers hit middle age (both events happening rather sourly) we were forced to relive boomer exploits from twenty years before, through anniversary specials and reunion tours featuring lots of acoustic guitars and distended bellies.

Nothing, though, could have prepared us for the generational onslaught we have faced this decade. When we started leaving school with boundless energy, many of us encountered a double whammy; not only had our elders gobbled up every job north of custodial work, but they began an incessant whine about turning back to what they quaintly termed the "simple life." Lifestyle magazines have fiddled a pastoral tune on cue, putting a hearty and rustic pair of boots by a country staircase on one cover, while annoying pseudo-soothsayers like Faith Popcorn decree that we are going to spend our twenties in an America that is busy "cocooning." While most of us younger folks walk around, passionate and wild-eyed with unchecked testosterone and estrogen levels, aching to endure meaningful contact with the other gender, we have to endure brittle, desiccated articles with titles like "Sex in the Snoring '90s." In late 1992, as I thought about what to do with my twenty-fifth year, *Newsweek* actually had the poetic sense of closure to put on its cover "Oh God . . . I'm Really Turning 50! The New Middle Age." Then, of course, Clinton and Gore turned the presidential election into a two for one at the Baby Boomer-o-Rama.

It's impossible, without sounding whiny and hypersensitive, to explain why folks my age eventually find this stuff unbearable. The most practical and pressing reason for our jealousy is, as expected, financial. Boomers have the job market in a full nelson, asphyxiating any hope we have of approaching their collective wealth anytime before the year 2050. They can't be directly blamed for this; they just had the luck to be born at the beginning of the largest industrial boom in any nation's history.

This historical argument, however, doesn't sit well in the heart of a twenty-four-year-old college graduate who is sweating cyanide at Kinko's at four in the morning for five bucks an hour as he hurriedly prepares coursepaks for a self-righteous forty-year-old Speech professor. Nor for a bicycle messenger with an M.A. dodging cars to deliver portfolios to folks infinitely more important than he. Nor especially for the legions of men and women in their twenties working in the food-service industry, bussing tables and washing dishes throughout Washington, D.C., Atlanta, New York, and San Francisco so that they can make rent by the fifth of the month. For most of these bright and energetic people, the very notion of being their own boss and running their own show is a pipe dream in an enchanted forest so far away that most of them have given up thinking about it. That's not to say they aren't happy and don't have a hell of a lot of fun; it's just that average men and women in their twenties, even those with a decent education, approach their future with a fatalism that would put most bomber pilots to shame.

And always, *always,* there is the supervisor, a slightly balding boomer who needs the bicyclist's message by ten or it's *his ass,* or demands that all the coursepaks be done again on both sides of the paper. Always, there seems to be someone stupider than we are, getting paid a lot more. This is an unfortunate stereotype, since boomers, with their history of revolution and authority thwarting, should make wonderful bosses—instead we are stuck with a gaggle of impatient forty-year-olds who can't seem to find a kind word in their hearts for the twenty-year-olds who replenish their tea. Our career aspirations are one thing, but the overbearing thought of the baby boom fermenting above us in the job market for the rest of our lives is indeed harrowing and real, and the fact that most of us don't feel particularly appreciated only cements our sourness.

Another element of the boomer groupthink that drives us nuts is their hypocrisy, which is, by now, legendary. Their philosophical track record is laughably inept; these guys all seemed (to us, anyway) to change their entire life theory the nanosecond something cooler came along. This "intellectual weathervane" way of thinking manifested itself everywhere, but the most obvious examples I can think of come from pop culture.

Take disco. Heralded in 1976 as the New Thing that would lift the Top 40 out of its coma, folks danced for about three years until it was declared not only defunct but completely ridiculous. Meanwhile, we kids around the ages of five to fifteen were left at the Kmart Picture Pose Center still wearing our miniature leisure suits and forced smiles. Much the same could be said of the by-now clichéd greedy eighties aftermath: the minute we started seeking our own fortune, the boomers turned around and declared the pursuit of money and material goods as inherently evil, even as they continued to flaunt the Cuisinarts they leveraged our future to buy.

It's not that they were especially hedonistic or mean-spirited about the way they molded the last few decades; it just seems as if they lacked any kind of permanent conviction or historical perspective. Any generation with the motto "Never trust anybody over thirty" obviously has the foresight of a fruit fly. No wonder their parents couldn't stand them—I would have hidden the car keys from them, too.

"So what?" a legion of elders could say. "So we aren't exactly the same people we were in the sixties—so you're not happy with your work situation. Deal with it!" And deal with it we could were it not for one huge, final roadblock: the baby boom refuses to shut the fuck up.

At no time in the history of communication has one demographical lump of people tried meticulously to document every whim it ever inflicted on the world—if a boomer had written the Rosetta Stone, he would have signed it. From conservative to hippie, from "we" to "me," from Pet Rocks to salad shooters, wherever went boomers, so went the lot of us, even if we were too young to know what was going on. Most of us even have proof: another dark secret of every "baby buster" is that ubiquitous Polaroid in the family album of each of us in the tiny disco outfit, or perhaps even a Nehru jacket, smiling uncomfortably at the cameraman, longing to put our cruddy little flannel Garanimals back on again.

This leads to the most devious pop culture terrorism I can think of, best explained with another phenomenon: the Bryan Adams "Summer of '69" Syndrome. In 1985, when "Summer of '69" was a hit, I remember reading a magazine review of the album. They gave it the perfunctory nod for being a commercial success but went on to dismiss its core as being soulless and inconsequential. Not only that, they said, but "Summer of '69" was downright dishonest, if you look at the lyrics: "I bought my first real six-string at the corner at the five and dime / played until my fingers bled— it was the summer of '69 . . ." The problem is, Bryan Adams would have been a ripe seven years old that summer and therefore unlikely to begin banging on a Strat, let alone till it got all bloody. Later I read that he was originally going to call the song "Summer of '75," but the folks at the record company didn't think it quite had that "take me home" feel to it. So he buckled. I was furious, because the mere thought of any *year* being considered more marketable than another seemed ludicrous, especially when the original one was a year I could actually remember.

Now whether this story is apocryphal or not, it still shows the mentality of a population so self-aggrandizing that it eschews the mention of a time it is not collectively proud of. Nineteen seventy-five, with its Carter campaign, Tony Orlando & Dawn, and "Jive Talkin'," doesn't measure up to 1969, with its youth movement, "Abbey Road," and Wood-stock. So instead of opting for Bryan Adams's adolescence, the boomer mentality grafted their own onto the song, and the pop culture had another hostage. I don't think I would have made the cut either; I bought my first real six-string in the autumn of '81, when Olivia Newton-John's "Physical" was at number one for ten weeks.

For most young people this selective rehashing of the past is just frustrating, as it only seems to highlight how anemic and desolate our current pop culture is, without giv-ing us a fighting chance to concoct anything better. Weaned on the classic rock that still tirelessly spews out of car radios, many of us would rather hear "Layla" for the 45,000th time than try something new, mostly because we've been taught that rock music as a genre died right around the same time Janis and Jimi did.

Boomer attitudes affect everybody differently, but the net result is the same—we are made to feel as though we were young and we will be getting old, both at the wrong time. It's as if we showed up late for school on the first day of class, cold and uncomfortable, without having done the summer reading. Sad? That is what the authors of these "lost generation" articles would have you believe, but they let their metaphors get away from them. The truth is, our culture is just as diverse, fun, and exciting as anything the boomers dreamed up, and to tell the truth, so are we.

No one can make me laugh the way my friends can: we possess a language of humor that is intelligent, silly, and distinctly our own. Any TV sitcom based on our wonderful conversations, though, would languish at the bottom of the Nielsens, because our way of relating to one another can't be translated to any medium other than the moment. To onlookers, especially to those who are a bit older, our dinner conversation must seem like a strange mélange of sarcastic inside jokes, misused clichés, and completely unrelated movie quotes. We don't talk like this to alienate our guests, we do it because we grew up surrounded by a maelstrom of video input, and, for most of us, family dissolution. The grand ideas in life—everything from the presidency to our own parents' marriage—were exposed long ago to us as dubious conventions at best. It turned more than a few of us into philosophical nomads, believing very little of what we hear and giving us a "bullshit alarm" more sensitive than any seismograph. When we spout off about something stupid that raises our ire ("Jesus, Bon Jovi can't write a song to save his dad's life!") or remain strangely quiet when a situation arises for us to take a stand ("I guess I'm prochoice, but I don't see how that means anything . . ."), we think we're behaving normally, but we give our elders the impression that we are an unsavory combination of stupid and cynical.

The only test I have ever used to define the difference between our generation and the baby boomers is to ask a simple question: Have you ever lived in a time when you felt America was on the right path, heading in the right direction, with a wonderful future? With little exception, anyone born after 1960 cannot. Even the brief moment of national hubris that erupted when Reagan took office seems like a good dinner date that went awry. We have lived our entire lives in this country without a blueprint for national sanity, whereas boomers grew up in an era with some sense of convention, potential, and stability. In simpler terms, we wouldn't know a truly wonderful world if it slapped us in the face.

This has led to our generation's greatest contribution to pop culture: the cultivation of the absurd. Nothing is black or white, right or wrong. We don't strive for high ideals and sweeping themes, and anyone caught trying to feed us any will be met with a devastatingly casual "yeah, whatever." We strive against boredom, our biggest foe, and do so by laughing—and what makes us laugh is the absurd.

Like a distant galaxy in a night sky, a generation is best seen looking slightly off center, and that is where you'll find our best, most forward-thinking artists. In music, that region has come to be known as the "alternative" scene (ostensibly an alternative from the idea morgue currently known as the Top 40) and although there have been sell-outs, wild speculation, and media implosion in that scene recently, it will always be the place where younger people turn to find the darker parts of themselves.

Instead of Joni Mitchell's "Woodstock" or Stephen Stills's "Love the One You're With," our world has "Suck My Kiss" by the X-rated rockers Red Hot Chili Peppers. On the charts of old, the Beatles sang, "Oooh I need your love, girl—guess you know it's true," in a lilting melody, while now Michael Stipe of R.E.M. rasps, "This one goes out to the one I love, a simple prop to occupy my time."

While Dylan and Lennon and others of the boomers' musical world crafted intensely personal and relevant lyrics, a lot of today's artists have given up trying, because, as David Byrne of the Talking Heads says, "Lyrics are just a trick to get you to listen to a song longer than you normally would." The messianic grunge band Nirvana gives up on their deeper thoughts halfway through a line: "I find it hard, it's hard to find—oh well, whatever, never mind." Techno dance bands and quirky rock groups like the B-52s simply repeat strange nonsensical sentences, and even a lush, beautiful, ethereal band like the Cocteau Twins bypasses words entirely, instead opting for unrelated syllables and Gaelic refrains. It's as if words themselves require a theme, and there isn't a theme left that hasn't been ruined or prostituted a hundred times over.

Boomers, looking askance at what we've created, combine this oral dysfunction with the two forms of music that they hate most—heavy metal and rap—and see nothing but a wasted, lobotomized generation with the most bankrupt culture since the Old Testament cities of sin. What they don't appreciate is that we know exactly how inane it all is, and that's precisely why we like it. When a rap artist yells that he's going to kill a dozen policemen and a metal guitarist screams kudos at the devil, we don't consider them guidance counselors—we laugh and then we dance.

One of the grossest miscalculations about our age group was made by Barry Williams (Greg, of course, from "The Brady Bunch"), who recently explained his sitcom's amazing longevity. He feels that we kids, wracked by divorce and other social pathologies, turn to "The Brady Bunch" because it offers a perfect family full of stability and compassion. Even the show's mastermind, Sherwood Schwartz, says that the Bradys will come back because "there's a subconscious longing in viewers for characters who genuinely love each other." While that may be .01 percent true, the fact is we all still watch the show continuously because it's so amazingly stupid.

Look at our movies: Whit Stillman's *Metropolitan* and Richard Linklater's *Slacker* both avoid happy resolutions and overarching themes at all cost, instead giving us a good helping of intelligent silliness. In *Boyz 'n the Hood,* John Singleton didn't think that the senseless murder of the football star was enough; he had to kill off another lead character in the final credits as well.

We have become masters of ironies, mockeries, and satires, unrelentingly cynical, drawn by the macabre and, of course, the absurd. This has led to the most devastating phenomenon of our age group: The Christa McAuliffe Spring Break Syndrome, which soberly states that "thou shalt treat all the great emotional moments in history with a callousness that defies description." There's no better way to see the difference between two generations than to look at their Defining Moments, and both we and the boomers have powerful ones. While most boomers were in grade school, they were told on the playground one day that their president had been shot in Dallas—this single act seemed to haunt many of them for the rest of their lives.

Twenty-three years later, when I was in Medieval European History class, the teacher from the lower school came running down the hallway yelling that all the kids in her third-grade class had just watched the space shuttle *Challenger* blow up live before their eyes. Some of the teachers actually started to cry, but what did we do? By the next day, most of us were trading our favorite "Christa McAuliffe Spring Break" jokes by the Coke machine. This syndrome has manifested itself everywhere from our reaction to the Berlin Wall falling down ("I guess that means Dresden gets Happy Meals now") to my own flippant response when I was told on the phone that my parents were getting divorced.

Are we that evil and devoid of grand emotions? Certainly not—that's just how we react to keep ourselves sane. We've been backed into this corner by years of being shown what happens when you put your faith in anything intangible. It is an unfortunate by-product of this cynicism, though, that we have paralyzed ourselves—suddenly all idealism is suspect, all action seems worthless. Environmental types are easily made fun of as granola-inhaling tree huggers with white guilt; standing in line to vote seems more like a pointless chore than an inalienable right worth dying for; every friend I have who cuts his hair to do scab temp work for IBM is a self-confessed and disappointed sell-out to "the Man"; we all avoid formerly benign words like *boyfriend* and *girlfriend,* preferring instead to file every relationship we have into an emotional purgatory that keeps us up at night wondering when it all starts to become real. The hardest thing about being young right now is being adrift, unable to let ourselves believe in anything. It may be fashionable and even humorous to be so full of acid (it certainly makes the dinner conversation more lively), but in our private moments this pessimism is deadly, and worse yet, we blame our elders for giving us a world that turned us into such dysfunctional creatures.

Maybe it's time, then, that the two generations seek a little group counseling to keep our uneasy relationship from imploding. First of all, the baby boomers could do the world a favor by releasing the chokehold they have on American culture. This asphyxiation has produced a delirious cadre of young Americans walking around stunned, half of us wistfully envious of the life they had, the other half silently furious about what we got.

Second, the boomers (along with their elders) should admit that as apathetic as we seem, they helped make us what we are today by being so hard to read. These big brothers and sisters, acting collectively, went through all their different lifestyles like a twister through a village—and then categorically called bullshit on every one of them. When we saw this, we surmised not only that grand, sweeping goals in life were not to be trusted but also that there probably wasn't a thought or idea we could propose that hadn't already been chewed and spat out by like-minded individuals years before. As Harry says in the movie *Pump Up the Volume*, "All the great themes have been made into theme parks."

In turn, perhaps my generation could stop being jealous and adopt a little of the naive optimism the boomers had when they were young. They may have been histrionic and goofy, but at least they *did* something. A lot of wonderful things came to fruition due to the fantastic groupthink of those who came just before us—and the only way we are going to evade boredom, low self-esteem, and these sad and lonely twentysomething articles is to cull a little of the boom's social energy before we get too old to bust down locked doors. Yes, we are a lucky group of Americans. We have what seems like inconsequential problems on a worldwide scale—we've never fought a world war or eaten potato soup through a great depression, never known a world that wasn't softened immeasurably by Nintendo, cruise control, and Easy Cheese. But we've got to do *something,* evade this unrelenting ironyfest that atrophies each of our souls, or else our grand question in life will be "You want fries with that?" clear into the twenty-first century.

Well, I did it. I couldn't resist the temptation to end with that call to arms, for all my fellow generational buddies to get off their butts, do something. I even tried to be coherent and show a little chutzpah—meaning, obviously, that I've succumbed the ol' MTV Video Fight Syndrome. All my friends will be so disappointed. I'll walk back into the room and conversation will stop; they will all be sitting on the couch eyeing me suspiciously as though I have relinquished a few of their secrets, talked too much, overanalyzed their private moments, and sold it back to them as entertainment. "It's okay," I'll say. "The whole essay's bullshit anyway," and with that, they'll relax and continue the discussion until the strongest fall asleep.

THE RITES OF SISTERHOOD

Naomi Wolf

EDITOR'S NOTE: This essay is adapted from a commencement speech delivered in 1992 by the author at Scripps College, a women's college in Claremont, California.

Guillotine joke:

Once there was a revolution. Three revolutionaries were charged with treason—two men and a woman. The first revolutionary was taken to the guillotine. He was asked, "Do you want to die facing up or down?" "I'll face down." The headsman pulls the string—nothing happens. The crowd says, "It's a miracle! Set him free!" The second man approaches the block and, given the same choice, he opts to face the ground. Again when the headsman pulls the string, nothing happens and the crowd cheers to set him free. The third revolutionary replies, "I'll face up." Headsman pulls string—nothing happens! She points upward and says, "I think I see what the problem is."

Even the best of revolutions can go awry when we begin to internalize the attitudes that we are fighting. During the past twenty years women have gained legal and reproductive rights as never before, have entered new jobs and professions. At the same time, anorexia and bulimia became epidemic; sexual assaults against women are at a record high, up 59 percent from last year; *Roe* v. *Wade* is about to be reconsidered in the Supreme Court; the weight of fashion models and Miss Americas plummeted, from 8 percent below the weight of the average American woman to 23 percent below. And the Blonde joke is enjoying a renaissance.

You are graduating in the midst of a violent backlash against the advances women have made over the last twenty years. This backlash is taking many forms, from the sudden relevance of quotes from *The Exorcist* in Senate hearing rooms to beer commercials with the Swedish bikini team. What I want to give you today is a survival kit for the backlash into which you are about to graduate, a sort of five-step program to keep the dragons from taking up residence inside your own heads.

First, let me tell you why it's so important for me to have been asked here today. My own graduation was the Commencement from Hell, an exercise in female disempowerment. I graduated eight years ago from Yale. The speaker was Dick Cavett, for little more reason than that he had been the college president's brother in an all-male secret society when they were both undergraduates. While the president was withdrawing college funds from South African investment, he was blind to the gender apartheid that he was endorsing on his own well-tended lawns.

Cavett took the microphone and seemed visibly to pale at the sight of two thousand female about-to-be Yale graduates. "When I was an undergraduate," he said, "there were no women here. The women went to Vassar. At Vassar," he said, "they had nude photographs taken of the women to check their posture in gym class. One year some of the photos were stolen, and they showed up for sale in New Haven's red-light district." His punch line? "The photos found no buyers."

I will never forget that moment. There were our parents and grandparents, many of whom had come long distances at great expense to be with us on our special day. There were we, silent in our black gowns, our tassels, our new shoes. We did not dare break the silence with boos or hisses, out of respect for our families who had given so much to make that day a success; and they in turn kept silent out of the same concern for us. Whether or not it was conscious, Cavett at that moment was using the beauty myth as it is often used in the backlash: whenever women get too close to masculine power, someone will draw critical attention to their bodies. Confronted with two thousand women who were about to become just as qualified as he himself was, his subtext was clear: you may be Elis, but you still wouldn't make pornography worth the buying.

That day, three thousand men were confirmed in the power of a powerful institution. But many of the two thousand women felt the shame of the powerless; the choking on silence, the complicity, the helplessness. We were orphaned from our institution at that moment—or rather, that moment laid bare the way in which the sons were truly sons all along, but the daughters were there on sufferance, intellectual and spiritual foster children whose membership in the family depended on self-effacement.

Commencement should be a rite of passage that makes you feel the opposite of how my graduation made me feel. My graduation did not celebrate in any way my wisdom and maturation as a woman; rather, it was a condescending pat on the head for having managed to "pass" for four years, in intellectual terms, as one of the boys.

So I want to give you the commencement talk I was denied. Since I'm only eight years older than you and still figuring things out myself, I don't feel comfortable using the second-person imperative in a way that would pretend that I have all the answers for your life. What I do when I say "you" is send a message back to my twenty-one-year-old self with the information I wish I had had then. As Gloria Steinem says, "we teach what we need to learn."

MESSAGE #1: The first message in your survival kit is to *cherish a new definition of what it means to "become a woman."* Today, you have ended your apprenticeship into the state of adult womanhood; today, you have "become women."

But that sounds terribly odd in ordinary usage, doesn't it? What is usually meant by the phrase "You're a real woman now"? Most connotations are biological: you "become a woman" when you menstruate for the first time, or when you lose your virginity, when you have a child. Sometimes people say "a real woman" to suggest decorativeness—a real woman wears a DD-cup bra—or a state of matrimony: a man can make a "real" or "honest" woman out of someone by marrying her.

These merely endocrinological definitions of becoming a woman are very different from how we say boys become men. Someone "becomes a man" when he undertakes responsibility or successfully completes a dangerous quest. Let us make a new definition of "becoming a woman" that includes the fact that you, too, no less and in some ways more than your brothers and male friends graduating today, have not moved from childhood to adulthood by biological maturation alone but through your own successful completion of a struggle with new responsibilities—a difficult, ultimately solitary quest for the adult self.

But we have no archetypes for the questing young woman, her separation from home and family, her trials by fire. We lack words for how you become a woman through the chrysalis of education, the difficult passage from one book, one idea, to the next. My commencement pitted my scholarship and my gender against each other. We need a definition of "becoming a woman" in which a scholar learns womanhood and a woman learns scholarship, each term informing the other; Plato and Hegel, Djuna Barnes and particle physics, mediated to their own enrichment through the eyes and brain of the female body with its wisdoms and its gifts.

When I say that you have already showed courage in earning your B.A.'s and passing through the forest, I am not talking about the demons of footnotes and poststructuralism. I'm talking about the extra lessons you had outside the classroom as well as in. Many of you graduate today in spite of the posttraumatic stress syndrome that follows acquaintance rape, which on campuses across America one-fourth of female undergraduates undergo. Many of you earned your credits while surviving on eight hundred calories a day, weak from ketosis and so faint from the anorexia that strikes one undergraduate woman in ten that it took every last ounce of your will to get your work in. Up to five times that number graduate today in spite of the crushing shame of bulimia, which consumes enormous energy and destroys

self-esteem. You managed to stay focused on political theory
and Greek while negotiating private lives through a mine-
field of new strains of VD, a 30 percent chlamydia rate
among U.S. undergraduates, and the ascending shadow of
HIV and AIDS. You had the force of imagination to believe
that Emily Dickinson and Jane Austen still had something
to say to you while your airwaves flickered with ever more
baroque and ingenious forms of glamorized violence
against women.

Not to mention the more mundane trials of undergraduate life. You fell in love, fell in love with the wrong person,
fell out of love, and survived love triangles, intrigues,
betrayals, and jealousies. You took false starts in finding
your life's work. Perhaps you questioned your religious
assumptions, lost spiritual faith, found it again in forms that
might alarm your grandparents, and lost it again to find it
elsewhere anew. You lived through cliques, gossip, friends
who borrowed your clothes and ruined them, dates from the
Black Lagoon, money worries, second jobs, college loans,
wardrobe angst, a Gulf war, earthquakes, and the way you
break out magically just when you have an important job
interview.

You made friends with people much richer or much
poorer than your own families, and I trust that made you
question how fairly this country distributes its wealth. You
made friends with people of other racial and religious backgrounds and sexual affiliations than yourself, which I trust
made you face the racism and homophobia that this culture
embeds in all of our subconsciouses.

In earning your B.A.'s while fighting these battles so often
labeled trivial, you have already proven that you are the tri-
umphant survivors you will continue to have to be as you
make your way through the backlash landscape outside this
community. You have "become women," and as women,
your commencement is not just a beginning but a confir-
mation of achievement. I applaud you.

MESSAGE #2 in your kit is the ultimate taboo subject for
women. It makes grown women blush and fidget, and no,
it's not sex. It's money. *Ask for money in your lives.* Expect it.

Own it. Learn to use it. One of the most disempowering
lessons we learn as little girls is the fear of money—that it's
not nice, or feminine, to ensure that we are paid fairly for
honest work. Meanwhile, women make fifty-nine cents for
every male dollar and half of marriages end in divorce, at
which point women's standard of living drops 43 percent.
To cling to ignorance about money is to be gender illiterate.

Of course you must never choose a profession for material or status reasons, unless you want to guarantee your
unhappiness. But, for God's sake, whatever field your heart
chooses, get the highest, most specialized training in it you
can and hold out hard for just compensation. You owe it to
your daughters to fight a system that is happy to assign you
to the class of highly competent, grossly underpaid women
who run the show while others get the cash and the credit.
Once you get your hands on every resource that is due to
you, organize with other women for a better deal for the
supports women need in the workplace—the parental leave
and child care that European women take for granted, and
that we need if we are to be what almost every man assumes
he can be: both a parent and a worker.

Get the highest salary you can not out of selfish greed
but so that you can tithe your income to women's political
organizations, shelters, crisis lines, cultural events, and universities. Ten percent is a good guideline that I use myself.
When you have equity, you have influence as sponsors,
shareholders, trustees, and alumnae to force institutions
into positive change. Male-dominated or racist institutions
won't give up power if we are sweet and patient; the only
language the status quo understands is money, votes, and
public embarrassment. Use your clout to open opportunities
to the women of all colors and classes who deserve the education and the training you had. As a women, your B.A. and
the income it represents don't belong to you alone, just as,
in the Native American tradition, the earth doesn't belong
to its present occupants alone. Your education was lent to
you by women of the past who made it possible for you to
have it; and it is your job to give some back to living
women, as well as to your unborn daughters seven generations from now.

MESSAGE #3: *Never cook for or sleep with anyone who routinely puts you down.*

MESSAGE #4: *Honor your foremothers,* literal and metaphorical. Ask your mom or grandmother about her own life story, her own quest as she defines it. Read biographies of women of the past that you admire. Knowing how hard women worked because they believed in you will remind you, in dark moments, just how precious your freedom—and hence you—really are.

MESSAGE #5: *Give yourself the gift of speech;* become goddesses of disobedience. Sixty years ago Virginia Woolf wrote that we need to slay the Angel in the House, the self-sacrificing, compliant impulse in our own minds. It's still true. Across America, I meet young women who tell me stories of profound injustice: rape cover-ups on campus, blatant sexism in the classroom, discriminatory hiring and admission policies. When I suggest proven strategies to confront the injustice—like holding a press conference about campus crimes if the administration is unwilling to listen—they freeze at the suggestion, paralyzed into niceness. Their eyes take on a distant look, half longing, half petrified. If only! They laugh nervously. They would, but . . . people would get mad at them, they'd be called aggressive, the dean would hate their guts, the trustees might disapprove.

We are taught that the very worst thing we can do is cause conflict, even in the service of doing what is right. Antigone, you will remember, is imprisoned; Joan of Arc burns at the stake; and someone might call us unfeminine! Outrage, which we would not hesitate to express on behalf of a child, we are terrified of showing on behalf of ourselves, or other women.

This fear of not being liked is a big dragon in my own life. I saw the depths of my own paralysis by niceness when I wrote a book that caused controversy. *The Beauty Myth* argues that rigid ideals of beauty are part of the backlash against feminism, designed to lower women's self-esteem for a political purpose. While I meant every word I said, and while enormous positive changes followed, from heightened awareness about eating disorders to an FDA crackdown on breast implants, all of that would dwindle into insignificance when someone yelled at me—as plastic surgeons, for instance, often did on television. I would sob on my boyfriend's shoulder, People are mad at me! (Of course they were mad; a three-hundred-million-dollar industry was at stake.)

Halfway through the slings and arrows, I read something by African-American poet Audre Lorde that set me free to speak truth to power without blaming myself when power got a little annoyed.

Lorde was diagnosed with breast cancer. "I was going to die," she wrote, "sooner or later, whether or not I had ever *spoken* myself. My silences had not protected me. Your silence will not protect you. But for every real word spoken, I had made contact with other women while we examined words to fit a world in which we all believed . . . What are the words you do not yet have? What are the tyrannies you swallow day by day and attempt to make your own, until you will sicken and die of them, still in silence? We have been socialized to respect fear more than our own need for language."

So I began to ask, at every skirmish: "What's the worst that could happen to me if I tell this truth?" The fact is that the backlash greatly exaggerates the consequences of our speaking. Unlike women in other countries, our breaking silence is unlikely to land us in jail and tortured, or beaten with firehoses, or "disappeared," or run off the road at midnight. Our speaking out will make some people irritated, disrupt some dinner parties (and doubtless make them livelier), get us called names and ridiculed. And then our speaking out will permit other women to speak, and others, until laws are changed and lives are saved and the world is altered forever.

So I wish upon you the ability to distinguish between silencings. Some are real: if you will lose your livelihood or get the life beat out of you. You will respect the necessity of the circumstance at that moment and then organize like hell so you are not faced with it again. But then there are the other 90 percent, the petty, day-to-day silencings, like when

THE RITES OF SISTERHOOD

you are being hassled by some drunken guests in a hotel and, rather than confronting them, the front desk tells you to lock yourself in your room. Or when your male classmates make sexist jokes. You know when you last swallowed your words.

Next time, ask yourself: What's the worst that will happen? So you might get called a bitch, or aggressive, or a slut, or the hostess will try to change the subject, or you might have to have a long talk with your male friends. Then, each time you are silenced, push yourself a little further than you think you dare to go. It will get easier and easier.

Then, once you are not immobilized with niceness, you know what? People *will* yell at you. They *will* interrupt, put you down, try to make you feel small, and suggest it's a personal problem. And the world won't end. And you will grow stronger by the day and find you have fallen in love with your own vision of the world, which you may never have known you had, because you were trying so hard not to know what you knew. And you will lose some friends and some lovers, and find you don't miss them; and new ones will find you. And you will still go dancing all night, still flirt and dress up and party, because as Emma Goldman said, "If I can't dance, it's not my revolution." And as time goes on you will know with surpassing certainty that there is only one thing more dangerous and frightening and harmful to your well-being than speaking your truth. And that is the certain psychic death of not speaking.

PARENTAL GUIDANCE SUGGESTED

Elizabeth Wurtzel

It is the spring of my junior year of college, I am lying in a near-catatonic state in a mental ward, I have just been given an industrial-strength antipsychotic—the kind they give to schizophrenics—because I have not been able to stop crying and shaking and wailing for hours, and the doctor is afraid that I might, quite literally, choke on my own tears. The pill they've given me—some variation on Thorazine—has knocked me into a silent state of submission that would be perfectly blissful if only the therapist on duty would stop trying to get me to talk to her. She wants to know what's wrong; she wants to know what I am experiencing that is so potent and profound that it takes a brain-draining drug to make it go away.

I don't know, is all I keep saying. I don't know, I don't know, I don't know.

What have you lost? she asks, trying a new approach.

I know I better come up with something. I better think of an answer before they start trying out other things on me—different drugs, electroconvulsive therapy (known in the vernacular as *shock*), whatever.

I think it's got something to do with summer camp, I say.

She looks at me blankly.

It's like this, I begin: I'm from New York City, my mom is Jewish and middle class, my dad is solidly white trash, they divorced when I was two, my mom was always unemployed or marginally employed and my dad was always uninvolved or marginally involved in raising me, there was never enough money for anything, we lived in state-subsidized housing, I went to private schools on scholar-ships, and my childhood, as I recall it, is one big flurry of application forms for financial aid or for special rates on this thing or that thing that my mother thought I should really have because she didn't want me to be deprived of anything.

My mom really did her best.

But then, as soon as I was old enough, my mother decided that I had to go to sleep-away camp for the sum-mers. She was overextended as a parent throughout the school year, my dad wasn't willing to take care of me, and there was nothing for a girl like me to do in New York City during the long hot summer except get into trouble with the neighborhood kids. So it was off to camp. That was that.

I went to camp for five years in a row—a different one each year, a different setup in a different rural town in the Poconos or the Catskills or the Berkshires or wherever I could enroll at a discount rate. And the funny thing is, I explain to the therapist, after my mother had sent me off to these places that I thought were so lonesome and horrible, instead of hating her for it, I just spent all summer missing her. All my waking and sleeping energy was devoted to missing this rather minimal and unstable home I came from. Starting on June 28, or whatever day it was that I got to camp, and never even achieving a brief reprieve until I'd come home on August 24 or so, I would devote myself fully to the task of getting back home. I'd spend hours each day writing my mom letters, calling her on the phone, just mak-ing sure that she'd know exactly where and when to pick me up at the bus when it was time to return. I would run to the camp's administrative offices to make sure that notices about the location of the return trip would be sent to my mother so that she'd know where to find me. I'd extract promises that she'd arrive there one or two hours early. I'd even call my dad and get him to promise to be there at least a half hour before the estimated time of arrival. I'd talk to the head counselor and express my concern that I might be put on a bus to New Jersey or Long Island and somehow end up in the wrong place and never find my way back home. I would ask other New Yorkers in my bunk if I could go home with them if my mother failed to materialize at the bus stop. I would call grandparents, aunts, uncles, and baby-sitters—always collect—to find out where they would be on August 24, just in case I had to go to one of their homes, in case my parents didn't show up to get me.

Instead of discovering the virtues of tennis and volleyball, or of braiding lanyards and weaving potholders, I would devote a full eight weeks of my summer to planning for a two-hour trip back home.

The therapist looks at me kind of strangely, as if this doesn't quite make sense, that summer camp was so long ago and I'll never have to go back again, so why is this still bothering me? There's no way, I realize, to ever make her understand that homesickness is just a state of mind for me, that I'm always missing someone or some place or something, I'm always trying to get back to some imaginary somewhere. My life has been one long longing.

And I'm sick of it. And I can't move. And I've a feeling, I tell the therapist, that I might as well lie here congealed to this hospital bed forever because there's no place in the world that's at all like a home to me and I'd rather be dead than spend another minute in this life as an emotional nomad.

A few days later, having lost all hope of anything else working, a psychiatrist gives me a prescription for a new, virtually untried antidepressant that she thinks might help. It's called fluoxetine hydrochloride, brand name Prozac. A few weeks later, I am better, much better, as I have been ever since.

But there's just one small problem. They can give me all sorts of drugs to stabilize my moods, to elevate the downs, to flatten the ups, to make me function in this world like any other normal, productive person who works, pays rent, has affairs, waters her own plants. They can make it all feel pretty much all right most of the time. But they can't do anything for the homesickness. There's no pill they can come up with that can cure the longing I feel to be in a place that feels like home. There's no cure for the strange estrangedness, and if there were, I am sure my body would resist it.

Since I first began taking Prozac, the pill has become one of the most commonly prescribed drugs in the country, with 650,000 orders filled each month. Back in 1990, the story of this wonder drug made the cover of periodicals like *Newsweek* and *New York,* while *Rolling Stone* deemed Prozac the "hot yuppie upper," and all the major network news-magazines and daytime talk shows began to do their Prozac-saved-my-life segments. While a backlash of reports linked Prozac with incidents of suicide and murder, the many people who it relieved from symptoms of depression had nothing but praise: Cheryl Wheeler, a Nashville folkie, even wrote a song called "Is It Peace or Is It Prozac?"

Yet this is not just about Prozac: it's about the mainstreaming of mental illness—it's about the way a state of mind that was once considered tragic has become completely commonplace. Talk of depression as the mental disease of our times has been very much in the air in the last few years, to the point where it has almost become a political issue: As Hillary Rodham Clinton campaigned on behalf of what she deemed "The Politics of Meaning," it was hard not to notice that her references to a "sleeping sickness of the soul," to "alienation and despair and hopelessness," to a "crisis of meaning," and to a "spiritual vacuum" seemed to imply that the country's problems have less to do with taxes and unemployment than with the simple fact that we were in one big collective bad mood. It is almost as if, perhaps, the next time half a million people gather for a protest march in Washington it will not be for abortion rights or gay liberation but because we're all just so bummed out.

Of course, one of the striking elements of this depression outbreak is the extent to which it has gotten such a strong hold on so many young people. The Valium addicts of the fifties and sixties, the housewives reaching for their mother's little helpers, the strung-out junkies and crackheads who litter the gutters of the Bowery or the streets of Harlem or the Skid Row of any town—all these people were stereotyped as wasted, dissipated, or middle-aged. What is fascinating about depression this time around is the extent to which it is affecting those who have so much to look forward to and to hope for, who are, as one might say of a bright young thing about to make her debut into the world, so full of promise.

Recently, I was reading a magazine on an airplane, and I chanced upon an article titled "The Plot Sickens," in which a college writing instructor sees the gruesome, pessimistic nature of the work that her students produce as an indication of a wave of youth malaise like none she'd ever noticed before in twenty-one years of teaching. "To read their work, you'd think they were a generation that was starved, beaten, raped, arrested, addicted, and war-torn. Inexplicable intrusions of random tragedy break up the otherwise good life of the characters," the author writes. "The figures in their fictions are victims of hideous violence by accident; they commit crimes, but only for the hell of it; they hate, not understanding why they hate; they are loved or abused or depressed, and don't know why . . . Randomness rules."

Perhaps for the author of that article, the nature of her students' work is surprising. For me, and for everyone I know my age, it just seems normal, peculiarly ordinary. I mean: Randomness *does* rule.

A few years ago, I wrote an article about my bout with depression for *Mademoiselle*. I was rather alarmed when the piece generated more mail than anything else they'd run in several years and was somewhat heartened but also terribly saddened to see that I had touched such a raw, exposed nerve in so many young women. Shortly after the article ran, I was on the phone with my editor, and she suddenly asked, "I wonder what Prozac would do for regular people—I mean, not clinical cases like you, but just the rest of us who are normally depressed."

Once again, that word *normally* seemed to be creeping up in a place where it oughtn't be. Since when is it *normal* to be depressed? What kind of world do we live in that someone can refer to depression as a *normal* state?

Christopher Ricks once wrote an essay about the difference between "disenchanted" and "unenchanted," the former describing someone sprung by reality from an
enchanted state, while the latter is a person who was never
enchanted to begin with. And that's me. And that's what
society's come to: the spate of depression that I have come
into contact with is not among people who've been disappointed by life—it's among those who have given up on it
before they've even given it a real go. So many of us who
are in our twenties now were born into homes that had
already fallen apart, fathers on the lam, mothers on the
floor, no sense of security and safety, no sense of home at
all. So we muddle through our adult lives wandering
around, kind of dazed, kind of wasted, looking like lost children who are still waiting to be claimed at the security office
of the shopping mall or amusement park or supermarket
where our parents last lost track of us. When Sonic Youth
titled its 1989 album *Daydream Nation,* I think they must
have been referring to this youth cadre of the walking
wounded, of people who spend so many of their waking
hours lost in thought, distraction, and abstraction, trying to
get a grip on the hopes—on the dreams—that they dare not
have in their conscious minds. Sleep is no relief because
they are always sort of asleep. All these young people are
homesick and in a reverie for an enchanted place they've
never known.

While I often get the sense that many older people look
back on their childhoods with a sense of sorrow that they
had to grow up and say good-bye to all that, most of my
friends could not wait to come of age and get out of the
house because the house was not a home. The lucky among
us had two active, participating parents and had to spend a
lot of time schlepping between two households, always lug-
ging an overnight bag or wondering whether the black-and-
white saddle shoes and box of Lego were at Mommy's or
Daddy's. In my case, only my mother really cared for me,
and she had a really hard time just making ends meet; she
seemed forever on the verge of a nervous breakdown, so I
spent much of my time just trying to keep her calm. My dad
used Valium and pretty much managed to sleep through my

whole childhood (when I was nine, we went to see *The Last
Waltz,* he fell asleep, and we ended up sitting through the
movie three times because I couldn't get him to wake up);
our Saturday-afternoon visits mostly involved his putting
me in front of the television set to watch "Star Trek" reruns
or college basketball while he dozed off.

But these are only the incidental, aftershock effects that
divorce has on children—far more terrifying is the violent
rupture it creates in any young person's life because any
sense of home is ripped asunder, any sense of a safe haven
in a cruel world is taken away. We did not learn about bitterness and hatred on the streets (the supposed source of all
terror)—we learned from watching our parents try to kill
each other. We didn't learn to break promises and (marriage) vows from big bad bullies at school—we learned from
watching our parents deny every word they once said to
each other. And we learned from them that it is not just
acceptable, but virtually normal, to realize that love does
not last forever. There are certainly plenty of kids whose
parents will stay together until death do they part and who
haven't experienced the symptoms I've just described. But
even they are affected by the divorce revolution because it
colors their worldview, too. They know that their own marriages might end in divorce. They know that the family unit
is not sacred, and this adds a degree of uncertainty to their
own plans.

But I don't want to get too down on divorce. It has
become all too facile a neoconservative impulse to blame
divorce or the decline of so-called family values for all the
ills of our society. Even more troubling is how easy it has
become for people in my age group to blame the lack of a
structured family life when they were growing up for all
their problems as adults. If I allowed myself to express the
full extent of the bitterness I feel toward my parents for not,
shall we say, having their shit together while they were
raising me, I fear that I might start to sound like an ally of
Dan Quayle. And I don't want to do that. The main reason:
it is precisely those family values that Dan Quayle referred
to in his famous anti–Murphy Brown speech that drove my
parents, and so many of my friends' parents, into marriages

they were not ready for and bearing children they were not capable of properly nurturing.

It was the family imperative, the sense that life happens in a simple series of steps (something like: adolescence-college-marriage-kids) that all sane and decent people must adhere to that got our parents in trouble to begin with. Remember, the progenitors of people in my age group are not, for the most part, those freewheeling, wild baby boomers who took it upon themselves to transform our society in the late sixties and early seventies. Our parents were, on the whole, a little too old for that, they are people who were done with college and had moved on to the work world by the early sixties—several years before the campus uprisings, the antiwar activities, and the emerging sex-drugs-rock-and-roll culture had become a pervasive force. By the time the radical sixties hit our home bases, we were already born, and our parents found themselves stuck between an entrenched belief that children needed to be raised in a traditional household and a new sense that anything was possible, that the alternative lifestyle was out there for the asking. A little too old to take full advantage of the cultural revolution of the sixties, our parents just got all the fallout. Instead of waiting later to get married, our parents got divorced; instead of becoming feminists, our mothers were left as displaced homemakers. A lot of already existent unhappy situations were dissolved by people who were not quite young or free (read: childless) enough to start again. And their discontent—their stuck-ness—was played out on their children.

My parents are a perfect case in point. Lord knows whatever possessed them to get married in the first place. It probably had something to do with the fact that my mom was raised with many of her first cousins, and all of them were getting married, so it seemed like the thing to do. And from her point of view, back in the early sixties, marriage was the only way she could get out of her parents' house. She'd gone to Cornell, wanting to be an architect, but her mother told her all she could be was an architect's *secretary*, so she majored in art history with that goal in mind. She'd spent a junior year abroad at the Sorbonne and did all the studiedly adventurous things a nice Jewish girl from Long Island can do in Paris—rented a moped, wore a black cape, dated some nobleman type—but once she got out of college, she moved back home and was expected to stay there until she moved into her husband's house. (Certainly there were many bolder women who defied this expectation, who took efficiencies and railroad flats with girlfriends in safe neighborhoods in the city, who worked and dated and went to theater openings and lectures—but my mom was not one of them.) She took a job in the executive training program at Macy's, and one day while she was riding the escalator up from the main floor to the mezzanine, she passed my father, who was riding down. They got married less than a year later, even though he hadn't gone to college, had no ambition, and was considered a step down for a girl like my mom.

My parents did weird things after they got married. My dad got a job at IBM and they moved to Poughkeepsie, New York, where my mom went nuts with boredom and bought herself a pet monkey named Percy. Eventually she got pregnant with me, decided a baby was better than a monkey, and she moved down to New York City because she could not bear another day in a town that was half Vassar College, half IBM. My father followed, I was born, they fought, they were miserable, he refused to get a college degree, they fought some more, and then one day I wouldn't stop crying. My mom called my dad at work to say that if he didn't come home immediately and figure out how to get me to calm down, she was going to defenestrate me. Whatever my father did when he got to the apartment must have worked, because I'm still alive today, but I think that moment marked the end of their marriage.

This was a marriage that could have peacefully ceased to be one fine day with an understanding that it was just a mistake, they were just two foolish kids playing house. Problem was, they had a child, and for many years after they split up, I became the battlefield on which they fought through all their ideological differences. This was New York City in the late sixties, Harlem had burned down, my mom was petrified about being a single mother with a deadbeat ex-husband, so she sent me to the synagogue nursery school, thinking this would provide me with some sense of community and stability. My dad would turn up to see me about once a week, and he would talk to me about atheism and insist I eat lobster and ham and other nonkosher foods that I was taught in school were not allowed. For years, my mom was tugging toward trying to give me a solid, middle-class, traditional upbringing, while my father would tell me that I should just be an artist or a poet or live off the land, or some such thing. She was desperate to keep at least a toehold in the bourgeoisie, and he was working overtime (or actually, not *gainfully* working at all) to stay the hell out of it. Back and forth this went for years, until it felt clear that all three of us were caught mostly in the confusing cross fire of changing times, and what little foundation my parents could possibly give me was shattered and scattered by conflict.

When I was ten or eleven, I really cracked up, started hiding in the locker room at school, crying for hours, or walking around the corridors saying, *Everything is plastic, we're all gonna die anyway, so why does anything matter?* I'd read this phrase in a picture of some graffiti in a magazine article about punk rock, which I decided was definitely a great invention. When I stopped talking, stopped eating, stopped going to school, and started spending my time cutting my legs up with razor blades while listening to dumb rock music like Foreigner on a little Panasonic tape recorder, my parents agreed I needed psychiatric help. To make a very long and complicated story short, my mom found a therapist for me, my dad didn't like him and kept trying to sneak me off to others, I never got terribly effective treatment, my father refused to file an insurance claim for the psychiatrist I was seeing, and the whole scenario concluded with me as messed up as ever, but with all the adults involved suing one another. My mom sued my dad for unpaid alimony and child support, my psychiatrist sued my dad for unpaid bills, and after years of lawyers everywhere, my father finally fled to Florida when I was fourteen years old and did not turn up in my life again until my freshman year at Harvard.

By the time I actually did grow up, I was so grateful to be out of my parents' firing range and not stuck in between them or torn apart like an overstretched rubber band they each tugged at for years that my depression actually began to lift. For me, growing up was not about coming face-to-face with the cruelties of the world; it was about relief.

Obviously, divorce is inevitable and at this point there is joint custody and divorce counseling and all sorts of other things to make the process less painful for the children and for the adults. Which might mean that things are better now, although I think things must be so much worse if divorce is being normalized—because let's face it, all these strangely pieced together families of half siblings and step-parents and all that are not natural. At one time, a kid got two parents who did their best to get it right, but now, taking stepparents into account, he can have twice as many guardians—along with nannies, therapists, tutors, and whatnot—but somehow, all these people put together can't seem to raise a child decently. It's like having ninety-two channels of cable and nothing to watch.

And that was pretty much the world I grew up in—a world where nothing seemed to matter because there was no strong parental force and no reasonable parental guidance (what paleolithic era were they thinking of when they invented the PG movie rating?). And that is why an album titled *Nevermind* by an unknown band called Nirvana became one of the most popular releases of recent years: nevermind is the code word of this life, nevermind is all we ever do—we never mind that we never mind that we never mind because there is nothing left to care about.

Critics complained that archetypal twentysomething movies like *Singles* or television shows like "Melrose Place" seemed to revolve around such mundane concerns that the characters were all wandering in a haze, looking for love and approbation in every person and every crevice of a person, looking for the next small fix to make the next few days bearable—above all, they complained that none of the Jennifers and Jasons seemed able to get out of their own heads long enough to take a look at the big picture. In a *Mirabella* essay titled "Twentysomething," Walter Kirn points out how cinematic young adults have been reduced to so little. "In this twentystuff soap opera, public causes exist to be gestured at ('Think Globally, Act Locally' reads a bumper sticker), but private life is all the life there is, the world's having shrunk to the cramped dimensions of one's wacky, sad, starter apartment with its sardonic, cheap, recycled furnishings," Kirn writes. Kirn is, of course, correct and astute in his observation, but like so many commentators he is unable to understand that getting by from day to day is all you can do when simple things like lovingkindness seem to be so scarce.

This fixation on private life and personal problems is constantly being assigned to twentysomethings as some sort of character flaw and one that seems especially flagrant when you consider that young people in the sixties were, at least in legend, in the throes of a belief that they could change the whole wide world. Of course, no one thinks that way any longer. These days, the first hard lesson you learn— most likely when you're too young to know that it's hard or that it's meant to be a lesson—is not to let it bother you too terribly much that Mommy and Daddy are trying to kill each other, that Mommy says Daddy's a jerk, and Daddy says Mommy is a hysterical bitch, or whatever. And the downward spiral of studied apathy just continues on from there: instead of learning to care about the world around us, we learn not to care about anybody. The possibility of mass movements that are antiwar or proecology are hard to organize in a country where on the simplest one-to-one level people have trouble making connections that last.

Let's translate this into more solid terms: let's consider the many things that *do* exist that we *should* care about— stuff like democracy, the environment, world peace, the future of our country. All these things are abstractions, pie-in-the-sky ideals, soft, slippery concepts that are hard to wrap your loving arms and loving legs around. That's not to say that no one my age cares about them—and heaven knows, when you throw us a concrete agenda like the right to abortion on demand, we can all get pretty worked up about it. But in order to have the personal strength and perseverance to see past your own most immediate needs and worry about the world as a whole, you must have a sense that your needs are being met.

Furthermore, the idea of growing up and assuming a responsible place in society is not a very happy thought to many children of divorce who have been taking care of other people since they were very young. We watched our parents get married not just twice but sometimes three or four times. And with our mothers and fathers out dating, breaking up and making up and discussing their affairs with us as if they were teenagers once again, the lines between who was the grown-up and who was the child were blurred. In an essay about *E.T.,* the sweetest, dreamiest movie of the eighties, John Podhoretz points out how this film is at its core a grim story of decaying family life. "Spielberg also touched a chord because his portrait of the demands placed upon Elliott and his friends by eighties America were starkly realistic," he writes. "These are children of divorce, saddled with incompetent parents and expected in some ways to rear themselves."

It is no wonder that there are certain rather regressive and infantilizing trends that are repeatedly pointed to in all the articles about people in their twenties: the first one is the habit that so many of us have of moving back in with Mom and Dad—or, more likely, Mom *or* Dad—after college graduation; the second is the creation of "slacker" culture, the tendency that some people with educations and prospects have to just get dumb jobs that pay the rent—waiting tables, working the counter of a video store—and give them plenty of time to sleep, read, watch TV, see movies, smoke pot, and to just, like, hang out in amenable extended-campus towns like Austin or Berkeley or Cambridge or Seattle. Usually, when either of these lifestyle choices is discussed, the trends tend to be attributed to simple economics, to the lack of available cheap housing and the lack of employment situations with a real future. I'm not saying that monetary concerns are not factors, but I really think that a lot of this is about wanting to be a kid a little while longer because so many of us were barely able to be children when we actually were children.

I can use myself as an example here. I don't live with either of my parents—in fact, I don't even know where my dad is—and for a long time I was the popular music critic for *The New Yorker*. But I was slacking off then and I still am now. If I wanted to, I could take many more magazine assignments than I do, but I'd rather sleep. When I was doing my pop music column, I'd pull myself together and get the necessary work done for a few days each month, and then I'd spend the other twenty-seven or so days just reading and going to movies and bumming around with friends. I did precisely what I needed to do to earn my living and not a single thing more. I would regularly accept magazine assignments and then just blow them off. At one point, my boyfriend asked me if I wasn't ruining my career with my laziness. All I could say was that I didn't know and didn't care. All through college I'd been a freelance writer to earn a living, and all through high school I had odd jobs and tons of schoolwork, and a lot of emotionally taxing entanglements and crazy parents to deal with, and now that I was old enough to choose, I just wanted to hang out. I wanted to be able to run for the hills on a sunny day; I wanted to be able to kick back in the sandbox at the local playground and toss frisbees with five-year-olds and do all sorts of fun, childish things I never got to do.

So I've got the whole life cycle backwards: all grown-up and running a household at ten and all set to jump on the seesaw and slip down the sliding pond at twenty-five. And I know I'm not the only person in this predicament. How many friends have I got who have already, in their mid-twenties, decided that they want to get off this hamster wheel to nowhere? There's the woman who was a year ahead of me at school who found her job as a stylist at *Harper's Bazaar* too taxing, so now she's a *maitresse d'* at a restaurant. There was the guy who worked as a magazine researcher but decided he'd much rather be a bike messenger (given the nature of most taxi drivers in New York City, to *want* to be a bike messenger here when you could be in a cushy

N E X T 210

office must surely constitute a new form of mental illness). There is my girlhood friend Jordana who decided she didn't want to be a social worker in the child-welfare department in the Bronx any longer, who concluded that all the idealism in the world wouldn't make a difference, and instead got married and decided to become a garlic farmer in upstate New York. There's Ben, a college classmate of mine who gave up the publishing fast track to work at a Mexican restaurant where his proudest accomplishment has been establishing a Jimi Hendrix brunch every Sunday.

And I know it is tempting to say this is just a bit of Ivy League lassitude, some form of slumming through our twenties before we get on an executive track in our thirties. But it's not just rich children of privilege who have surrendered the ticket before takeoff. There are working-class versions of the same phenomenon—in fact, I think it's become pretty clear that in every stratum there are some people on the fast track, many more on the slow track, and many many more on no track at all.

When I first got out of school, I lived in the far reaches of the East Village, which is supposed to be some kind of grungy epicenter of cool, but is really just a mess. Because I didn't ever have a normal work schedule, I'd spend a good deal of time in cafes or sitting in Tompkins Square Park, and I got to know a lot of my fellow Alphabet City residents who, no matter what the gentrification reports have claimed, were definitely not yuppies. Mostly they were a cohort of young people hanging on to the fringes of the Lower East Side, working as bartenders or waiters or in pet stores or in beauty salons to support a lifestyle with no apparent objectives. When I would meet them at the Life Cafe or Bandito's or King Tut's Wawa Hut, I discovered that the tacky-artsy kids with dyed black hair and do-rags and all sorts of body piercings are not, for the most part, aspiring artists—at best, some of the girls want to design oversize rhinestone earrings or clothing made with lots of leather and lamé. They've got the trappings—the untidy, unheated apartments, the *outré* dress code, the tendency to shoot heroin—of the previous generations of creative souls and Communists who lived in the Village, but they are not *committed* people. They've come to New York from the Everglades, the Appalachians, the Midwest, the Ozarks, the Black Hills, the small towns in Pennsylvania, and the suburbs outside of Chicago, but none of them seems to have gotten an education beyond high school, and none of them seems to be aspiring to anything more than living day-to-day. They don't think of themselves as bohemian and it's unclear whether they think at all. They don't read newspapers or watch CNN, they don't vote, they don't even *rock* the vote, and if anyone were to tell them that they are part of some twentysomething youth culture *thang,* they'd be truly amazed.

Don't get me wrong—in many ways I think it's just great that a visible group of young people is refusing to do things the normal, expected way. And I would never argue on behalf of conventional careerism—I don't think the nine-to-five world is good for many smart, creative people. Certainly, it is tempting to see the slacker culture as a boon compared to the go-go blind ambition of the eighties. But one thing that can be said in behalf of the investment bankers and corporate kids who made lots of money in the last decade; at least they had a certain spark, a desire, a dream— at least they approached life with faith and gusto and a plan to relish the benefits. These days, the slacker kids just draw a blank. And this abandoning of the straight-and-narrow path is not some sixties-style attempt at nonconformity, it is not about a search for greater spiritual truths, it is not about getting back to nature or basics or anything like that—in fact, as far as I can tell it's about one simple thing: fatigue.

How on earth are we ever going to run the world and behave like responsible adults when we're all just so tired?

Despite the exhaustion, I still think that adulthood has been a lot better for me than growing up was. And I believe the task of a lifetime for my generation will be to reinvent the family unit in a way that works and endures. Perhaps critics will say, *Those twentysomethings, all they ever worry about is their private lives,* but I for one believe our private lives deserve some thoughtful attention. If anyone had bothered to give our development as human beings some constructive thought while we were still young enough to receive the benefits passively, we wouldn't have to think about our personal lives so damn much now.

I have heard it said that in our modern world, twelve-step fellowships have become a substitute for family, that the rooms of alcoholics and junkies offering each other support in church basements and community centers is the closest thing anyone has to a familial setup. I have also heard that the neo-Nazi kids in modern Germany, the inner-city youth who join gangs in Los Angeles like the Bloods and the Crips, the homeboys hanging out on the corner—all these movements and loosely bound organizations are about young people trying to find a place in this world to call home, trying to find people in this world to call family. The interesting thing about the attraction of something like AA is that an organization like that involves such a large group of people—not just a few random friends but a big collection of helpful people. And I think we all need some version of that. In the worst moments of my depression, I used to wish I were a drug addict—I used to think it would be so nice if it were simply a matter of getting heroin or alcohol out of my life—because then I could walk into a meeting of fellow sufferers and feel that I'd arrived home at last.

But I'd hate to think that I'd have to become a junkie in order to find my place in this world. And I don't think that is the case. In fact, I think one of the ways many of us twentysomethings have come to deal with our rootlessness has been by turning friends into family. For those of us without addictions, those of us who are just run-of-the-mill parasites on society, our alliances are all that's left. For many of my friends, the world feels like one big orphanage—we're so far from our families, or without families at all, or without families that are able to serve a familial role, and here we get thrown into this lot of life together. Of course, some pundits make fun of us for turning friends and ex-lovers into pseudo-family members, but I believe this is an arrangement that actually works. (Besides, if anyone has a better idea, I'm glad to listen. Joining the Moonies, hooking up with the Branch Davidians, or running off to Esalen are *not* acceptable substitutes.)

And obviously, the theme of friends-as-family seems to resonate in the media a great deal: whether it's in the Banana Republic advertising campaign that pictures several versions of "Your Chosen Family," or it's in the United Colors of Benetton billboards and print ads that try to depict an international loving brotherhood of all races and nations. It's in MTV's attempt at *cinema vérité* with "The Real World," a series that shows a group of young people living in a loft together and puttering their way through the tribulations of everyday; and it's in the way the typical television drama or sitcom of today is likely to revolve around the odd connections and acquaintances made by single people or one-parent families in their apartment complex or subdivision, not on the freestanding biological family that was the center of almost every show thirty years ago. It's in all the press that surrounded the Clinton-Gore bus campaign that attempted to portray the two candidate couples—Al and Tipper and Bill and Hillary—as a little fun-loving family on a perpetual double date rolling its way across the country; and it was in Clinton's beckoning speech at the Democratic convention, in which he invited everyone out there to "join our family." All these examples just amount to a manipulation of Americans' simplest desire to imagine the possibility of home, and yet even as I know my emotions are being toyed with, I still appreciate all these public attempts to define family as something that's got nothing to do with blood.

All my friends, inadequately parented as we seem to have been, spend as much time looking after one another as we do just hanging out and having fun.

I recently spent a three-day weekend in Vermont with a man I was dating—who happens to be an alcoholic and going through a divorce—along with his father and his six-year-old daughter. As one can imagine, the pastoral promise of a few days in the country was frequently disturbed by his wife calling and the two of them having screaming fights for hours, or by his daughter getting hysterical because her parents were splitting up, or by his father not knowing how to handle the oddity of the four of us away together on this farm. The drama I experienced that weekend involved some terrain that was a little too familiar—this poor little girl reminded me so much of myself at her age—but on the whole it was a pleasant enough weekend.

Just the same, it was a great relief to walk into my living room on Monday night and see a bunch of my friends sitting on the sofas and wing chairs, waiting for me to return, wanting me to know that they were worried about me. I'm not kidding myself—I think they were mostly at my house to just kick back and watch the Knicks–Bulls game—but all of them seemed to know where I'd been, whom I'd been with, what the circumstances were, and I felt a comfort and security about myself and my world that I had never ever experienced the whole time I was growing up. I hate to think of what I'd do if I didn't have such patient and forbearing friends, if I didn't have people so willing to see me through years of crises, years of crying on the kitchen floor and running out of parties in tears and screaming for no apparent reason and calling in the middle of the night and everything else that comes with depression. Insofar as I'm now able to get work done, to make attempts at having relationships, to live a life that is fruitful and productive at all, I attribute it completely to the friends that I have turned into my family.

And if anyone finds that pathetic, I don't care. I don't want to spend another minute of my life supine and suffering in a hospital bed, praying to God for any form of relief he can give to a mind—not even a body—in terrible pain. I don't ever want to endure another morning of the orderlies coming in at 7:00 to take a blood sample and take my temperature because that is the routine in a health-care facility—even though the only thing that's wrong with me is in my head. I don't want to roam the streets at all hours of the day and night, feeling crazy from the heat in the middle of January, running like hell from the voices in my head. I don't want to live life as a sicko. And the friendships I have developed as an adult are probably the only thing standing between me and Bellevue. More to the point, they are the only thing standing between me and suicide. The hole in my heart that was left by a grievous lack of family connections has in some ways been patched over, if not altogether filled, by a sense of family I've found in the last few years.

But I must say, I'm sure my friends and I often seem like these sad lost people who are scared to grow up. I sometimes worry that the clinginess of our relationships is kind of a sorry thing, that we often seem to be holding on tight because of the depth of our desperation and need—and perhaps this just isn't healthy. We often spend time together in large groups of people, and I keep thinking we all really should be out on dates in couples, but it doesn't seem as though any of us is quite ready even to think about getting into deeply committed relationships. I have plenty of friends who have been going out with the same person for years, but none of them is showing signs of heading to the altar. We're all just much too frightened.

And it is this nervousness, this lack of trust, that makes this generation seem ineffectual to many older people on so many fronts.

But we are trying our best to take care of one another. And it is my hope that when we finally do have kids of our own, the sense of community we have created for ourselves will be passed along to them. I hope my children know that their father and I are not the only adults in their lives who can be counted on—I hope they feel that Christine, Jason, Mark, Larissa, Tom, Heather, Ronnie, and Sharon are as much a part of their family as they are part of mine. I hope my friends' children will play with my kids, and I hope they all grow up understanding that they too can choose families of their own. I hope they don't ever think that their world and their expectations are limited by two people who just happen to be their parents, and might do some really stupid, silly things along the way.

These days we all sit around, drinking Rolling Rock and smoking pot late into the night as if we were still in our college dormitory rooms, and sometimes we talk about how it will be to have kids someday. And we all say the same thing: we can't wait to bring children into the world and do everything right that our parents did wrong. Of course, I suspect that our parents had the same idea themselves, and look where it got them.

But still, I've got to believe I can do better. I've already brought up myself, so surely I ought to be able to raise someone else.

I think.

KEEPING WOMEN WEAK

Cathy Young

Not long ago, I attended a conference on women's research and activism in the nineties, attended by dozens of feminist academics, writers, and public figures. At the wrap-up session, a middle-aged history professor from the Midwest introduced a discordant note into the spirit of celebration. "The fact," she said, "is that young women just aren't interested in feminism or feminist ideas, even though they are leading feminist lives—planning to become lawyers, doctors, professionals. What is it about feminism, and about our approach, that puts young women off?"

In response, some blamed "the backlash," others "homophobia." One woman protested that there *were* young feminists out there, citing sexual harassment lawsuits filed by high-school girls—apparently a greater accomplishment than merely preparing for a career. Another declared that what feminist educators needed to give their students was "an understanding of the power dynamic," not "quote-unquote objectivity." (Could it be something about comments like these that turns female students off?) Missing from this picture was any serious discussion of what modern feminism has to offer modern young women.

Feminism meant a great deal to me when I came to the United States thirteen years ago, after a childhood spent in the Soviet Union. Indeed, one of the things that elated me the most about America was women's liberation.

The society in which I had grown up was one that offi-
cially proclaimed sexual equality and made it a point of
great pride yet stereotyped men and women in ways reminiscent of the American fifties. At school, we had mandatory
home economics for girls and shop for boys, a practice no
one thought of challenging. At the music school for the
gifted where my mother taught piano, to say that someone
played "like a girl"—pleasantly, neatly, and without substance—was a commonly used putdown; in literary reviews,
the highest compliment to be paid a woman writer or poet
was that she wrote like a man.

As I approached college age, I learned that there was tacit
but widely known discrimination against women in the
college-entrance exams, on the assumption that a less-
capable male would in the end be a more valuable asset
than a bright female, who would have boys and makeup
and marriage on her mind. And all too many smart, ambitious girls seemed to accept this injustice as inevitable,
assuming simply that they had to be twice as good as the
boys to prove themselves.

It was just as unquestioningly accepted that housework,
including the arduous task of Soviet shopping, was women's
work; when the problem of women's excessive double burden at home and on the job was mentioned at all, the pro-
posed solution was always for men to be paid more and for
women to spend more time at home, not for men to pitch
in with domestic chores. And although my parents' relationship was an uncommonly equal one, my father still quoted
to me the dictum (coming from Karl Marx, a thinker he
generally did not regard as much of an authority) that
"woman's greatest strength is her weakness."

My discovery of America was also a discovery of feminism—not only *Ms.* magazine and *The Feminine Mystique*
but also the open and straightforward manner of young
American women I met. This was in stark contrast to the
style that so many Russian women reverently equated with
"femininity"—a more-or-less affected air of capriciousness
and frailty, a flirtatious deference to men. I admired the easy
camaraderie between boys and girls on American college

campuses, the independence and self-confidence of young women who invited guys on dates and picked up the tab, drove when they were out with male companions, and wouldn't let anyone treat them like frail, helpless little things.

Those early impressions may have been too optimistic, perhaps somewhat superficial, perhaps incomplete. But I don't think they were wrong.

Becoming an American as a teenager in 1980, I joined the first generation of American women who had grown up assuming not only that they would work most of their lives but also that they were the equals of men and that they could be anything they wanted to be (except maybe a full-time homemaker). This was also the first generation, really, to have grown up after the sexual revolution—at a time when, at least among the educated, the nice-girls-don't sexual standard vanished almost completely. In a somewhat dizzying reversal of traditional norms, many girls felt embarrassed telling their first lovers that they were virgins (at least that's how I felt).

Of course new choices meant new pressures. I never thought a world of sexual equality would be a utopia of peace and harmony. I did believe that our generation of women, and men, was on its way to achieving a world in which people were judged as individuals and not on the basis of their gender; a world in which men and women worked and loved in equal partnership—even if, inevitably, they continued every so often to make each other miserable and furious.

And then something funny happened on the way to that feminist future. We were told that we were victims, with little control over our lives and our choices; we were told that we needed to be protected.

When the right said that women were victimized by career opportunities and sexual freedom, it didn't matter much—at least to the middle-class, college-educated women who were the main beneficiaries of these new opportunities. Who, in those social circles, was going to listen to people who said that wives should obey their husbands and stick to the kitchen and nursery—to Phyllis Schlafly or Jerry Falwell, notorious reactionaries with little impact on mass culture?

But the message of victimhood also came from the feminist left. Everywhere around us, we were told, was a backlash seeking to snatch from us the freedoms we had gained. We were told that we were the targets of a hidden war and had better start acting like ones, searching for subtle signs of enemy forays everywhere. If we believed that we had never experienced gender-based injustice and had never felt particularly restricted by our gender, we were not just naive but dangerous: we were turning our backs on feminism and fostering the myth that its major battles had been won.

Whenever a campus study has shown that young people of both sexes increasingly share the same values and aspirations and that most college women are quite confident of their ability to succeed in the workplace and to combine family and career, older feminists seem far from pleased. Their warnings—oh, just wait until these young women get a taste of the real world and find that they still face prejudice and discrimination—can sound almost gleeful.

Older feminists talk a good line about empowering young women and letting them speak in their own voices; but that goes only as long as these voices say all the approved things. At a university workshop on peer sexual harassment in schools I attended in the spring of 1993, some of the panelists complained that many girls didn't seem to understand what sexual harassment was; when boys made passes or teased them sexually they just shrugged it off, or they thought it was funny and actually liked it. "They need to be educated," one speaker said earnestly, "that the boys aren't just joking around with you, that it's harassment."

Ignored in all this discussion was intriguing evidence of the assertive, even aggressive sexuality of many of today's teenage girls, who apparently do a bit of harassing of their own. If girls seemed to revel in sexual attention, that could only be a sign of "low self-esteem" or inability to say no.

Judging by all those complaints about the unraised consciousness of the young, the preoccupation with the sexual and other victimization of high-school and college females is not coming, by and large, from young women themselves. Most of them, I believe, tend to regard all the extreme rhetoric as a sort of background noise; if they think about feminism at all, they often decide that they want no part of it— even if they're all for equal rights. The kind of feminists they usually see in their midst may further contribute to this alienation.

When I was still in college, I began to notice, alongside the spirited, independent, ambitious young women I admired, a different product of the feminist age: the ever-vigilant watchdog on the alert for signs of sexism. Occasionally, she made a good point; when our environmental science professor blamed overpopulation in part on Third World women "choosing" to have lots of babies, a student spoke up to note that for most Third World women, childbearing was hardly a matter of choice.

More typical, alas, was the young woman in my human sexuality class who was constantly pouncing on the professor for saying something like "People who suffer from premature ejaculation . . ." ("Are you implying that only men are people?"). When he had the audacity to cite data indicating that some rapists were motivated primarily by hatred of women and the desire to dominate them but others were driven primarily by sexual impulses, she went ballistic: "The ONLY thing that causes rape is men wanting to control and terrorize women, and you're trying to make it SEXY!" Later, this person bragged about having caused the poor prof "a lot of trouble" by filing a complaint with the dean.

Paranoid is a red-flag word to many feminists—understandably so, since it has been used all too often to dismiss women's rightful concerns about sexism. But what other word can come to mind when a woman claims that her writing instructor's selection of a sample of bad writing—a conservative Christian screed linking pornography and communism—was a personal insult directed at her, since she had sometimes worn a Women Against Pornography button in school?

And what can one expect when Naomi Wolf, a writer hailed as a trailblazer of a new "Third Wave" of feminism for the younger generation, urges women to undertake—

and men, to gracefully (and gratefully) second—"the arduous, often boring, nonnegotiable *daily chore of calling attention to sexism*" (emphasis mine)? In the essay "Radical Heterosexuality, or, How to Love a Man and Save Your Feminist Soul" (published in the twentieth-anniversary issue of *Ms.*), Wolf describes how even well-intentioned men tend to be blind to the horrific things women have to put up with:

> Recently, I walked down a New York City avenue with a woman friend, X, and a man friend, Y. I pointed out to Y the leers, hisses, and invitations to sit on faces. Each woman saw clearly what the other woman saw, but Y was baffled. . . . A passerby makes kissy-noises with his tongue while Y is scrutinizing the menu of the nearest bistro. "There, there! Look! Listen!" we cried. "What? Where? Who?" wailed poor Y, valiantly, uselessly spinning.

Like poor Y, I am baffled. God knows, I've been taking walks in Manhattan at least once or twice a week for nearly thirteen years now, and not a single invitation to sit on a face, not even a single hiss as far as I recall—nothing more dramatic than the occasional "You look gorgeous today" or "That's a pretty outfit," and certainly nothing like the constant barrage Wolf describes. Even the time I wore a new dress that exposed much more cleavage than I realized, all it cost me was one fairly tame remark (as I was stepping into a subway car, a man who was stepping off stared at my bosom and muttered, "Very nice"). Applied to everyday life and interpersonal relations, "eternal vigilance is the price of liberty" strikes me as a rather disastrous motto to adopt.

Like all would-be revolutionaries, the radical feminists seek to subordinate private life to ideology—an endeavor that I find, quite simply, frightening. You don't have to spend part of your life under a totalitarian system (though maybe it helps) to realize that social and political movements that subordinate life to ideology have a nasty way of turning coercive, whether it's the mass violence of communism or the neo-Puritan controls of "P.C."

This is not to say that there is no room for rethinking traditional attitudes, on things ranging from who picks up the check in the restaurant to who takes care of the baby. Millions of women and men are grappling with these issues at home and in the workplace, some more successfully than others. But that doesn't mean they have to walk around with their eyes glued to a microscope.

Eternal vigilance is a tempting trap for post-baby-boomer feminists. It has been often remarked that women of earlier generations had to struggle against visible and overt barriers, such as being denied admission to law school, or told that only men need apply for certain jobs or that married women shouldn't work. It seemed that once such barriers dropped, equality would come quickly. It didn't quite turn out that way; there were other, more insidious roadblocks, from a working mother's guilt over taking a business trip to a professor's unconscious tendency to call on the boys in the class. The problem, however, is that subtle sexism is an elusive target, with plenty of room for error and misinterpretation. If you complain to your professor that you find the course work too difficult and he says, "Well, I've always thought girls didn't belong in this class anyway," there's not a shadow of a doubt that he's a sexist pig. But suppose he says, "Hey, start working harder or drop the class, but don't come whining to me." Is he being insensitive to you as a woman? (An incident of this sort figured in a recent sex-discrimination suit at the University of Minnesota.) Or is he simply a blunt fellow who believes people should stand on their own two feet and who would have treated a male student exactly the same? And if he had been tough on a man but sensitive and solicitous toward a woman student, wouldn't that have been exactly the kind of paternalism feminists used to oppose?

But then, certain aspects of cutting-edge feminism do smack of a very old-fashioned paternalism, a sort of chivalry without the charm. At some campus meetings, it is considered P.C. for men who are first in line for the microphone to cede their place to a woman in order to ensure that female speakers—apparently too timid to just get up and get in line—get a proper hearing. Ladies first?

Definitions of "hostile environment" sexual harassment often seem like a throwback to prefeminist, if not positively

Victorian, standards of how to treat a lady: no off-color jokes, no sexual remarks, no swearing and, God forbid, no improper advances. Surveys purporting to gauge the prevalence of harassment lump together sexual blackmail—demands for sex as a condition of promotion, good grades, or other rewards—with noncoercive advances from coworkers or fellow students, with sexual jokes or innuendo, "improper staring" or "winking."

Well, guess what: women too make off-color jokes and risqué comments, and even sexual advances. Sure, many women at one time or another also have to deal with obnoxious, lecherous, and/or sexist jerks. But in most cases, especially if the man is not a superior, they're perfectly capable of putting a jerk back in his place. Of course, radical feminists such as Catharine MacKinnon tell us that there is *always* an imbalance of power between a man and a woman: even if you're studying for an MBA and have a prestigious job lined up, you're still powerless. Now there's a message guaranteed to build up self-confidence and self-esteem.

A video on sexual harassment, broadcast on public television twice in January 1993 and available free through an 800 number, includes a segment on a university experiment in which unwitting male students are assigned to supervise the computer work of an attractive girl. Before leaving them alone, the male research assistant pretends to take small liberties with the young woman (putting a hand on her shoulder, bending closely over her) while explaining the work process, and in most cases the male student proceeds to imitate this behavior or even push it a little further.

Then, the young woman—who, of course, has known what's been going on the whole time—talks on camera about how the experience has helped her understand what it's like to feel powerless. But doesn't this powerlessness have at least something to do with the fact that she was undoubtedly instructed not to show displeasure? Is it such a good idea to teach young women that, short of legal intervention, they have no way of dealing with such annoyances?

I don't believe that our views or our allegiances are determined solely or primarily by age. Still, one might have expected our generation to articulate a feminism rooted in the experience of women who have never felt subordinated to men, have never felt that their options were limited by gender in any significant way or that being treated as sexual beings diminished their personhood. This is not, of course, the experience of all young women; but it is the experience of many, and an experience that should be taken as a model. Perhaps those of us who have this positive view of our lives and our relationships with men have not lived up to our responsibility to translate that view into a new feminist vision.

In an *Esquire* article about sexual politics and romantic love on campus in the nineties, Janet Viggiani, then–assistant dean for coeducation at Harvard, was quoted as saying, "I think young women now are very confused. . . . They don't have many models for how to be strong females and feminine. Many of their models are victim models—passive, weak, endangered." In recent years, feminist activism has focused almost entirely on negatives, from eating disorders to sexual violence and abuse. Sadly, these problems are all too real, and they certainly should be confronted; what they should not be is the central metaphor for the female condition or for relations between women and men, or for feminism. What does it mean when the only time young women and girls think of feminism is not when they think of achievement but when they think of victimization?

The emphasis on victimhood has had an especially dramatic effect on attitudes toward sexuality. We didn't revel in our sexual freedom for too long; as if the shadow of AIDS weren't bad enough, sex was suddenly fraught with danger and violence as much as possibilities of pleasure, or even more so. A cartoon in the *Nation* shows a girl grooming herself before a mirror, with the caption, "Preparing for a date"—and in the next frame, a boy doing the same, with the caption, "Preparing for a date rape." Pamphlets on sexual assault warn that one out of every five dates ends in a rape, and that up to 25 percent of college women become victims: "Since you can't tell who has the potential for rape by simply looking, be on your guard with every man."

If these numbers are true, women would be well advised either to forswear dating altogether or to carry a can of Mace on every date. But what about these numbers? When one looks at how they are obtained, and how rape is defined, it becomes clear that the acquaintance-rape hysteria not only gives young women an exaggerated picture of the dangers they face in the company of men but essentially demeans women, absolving or stripping them of all responsibility for their behavior.

The question is not whether a woman's provocative dress, flirtatious behavior, or drinking justifies sexual assault; that attitude is now on the wane, for which the women's movement certainly deserves credit. It's not even a question of whether a woman should have to fight back and risk injury to prove that she did not consent to sex. The latest crusade makes a woman a victim of rape if she did not rebuff a man's sexual advances because she was too shy or didn't want to hurt his feelings, or if she had sex while drunk (not passed out, just sufficiently intoxicated so that her inhibitions were loosened) and felt bad about it afterwards. In a typical scenario, a couple is making out and then the woman pulls back and says, "I really think we shouldn't," and the man draws her back toward him, *nonforcibly,* and continues to fondle her, or says, "Oh come on, you know you want it," and eventually they end up having sex. If the woman feels that the intercourse was "unwanted," she can—according to the anti-date-rape activists—claim to be a victim, no different from the woman who's attacked at knifepoint in a dark, empty parking lot.

A few years ago, I was at the apartment of an ex-boyfriend with whom I was still on friendly terms; after a couple of beers, we started kissing. When his hand crept under my skirt, I suddenly sobered up and thought of several good reasons why I should not go to bed with the guy. I wriggled out of his arms, got up, and said, "That's enough." Undaunted, he came up from behind and squeezed my breasts. I rammed my elbow into his chest, forcefully enough to make the point, and snapped, "Didn't you hear me? I said, enough."

Some people might say that I overreacted (my ex-boyfriend felt that way), but the logic of modern-day radical feminists suggests the opposite: that I displayed a heroism that cannot be required of any woman in a situation like that because she could expect the guy to beat her up, to maim her, even if he hadn't made any threats or shown any violent tendencies. A "reasonable" woman would have passively submitted and then cried rape.

Even "no means no" is no longer enough; some activists want to say that yes means no, or at least the absence of an explicit yes means no. Feminist legal theorist MacKinnon suggests that much of what our society regards as consensual sex hardly differs from rape and that, given women's oppression, it is doubtful "whether consent is a meaningful concept" at all. Which is to say that, like underage children and the mentally retarded, women are to be presumed incapable of valid consent. MacKinnon's frequent ally, polemicist Andrea Dworkin, states bluntly that all intercourse is rape.

This reasoning is still very far from mainstream acceptance. Even MacKinnon only expresses such views when addressing fairly narrow and converted audiences, not when she's interviewed on TV. Yet a 1992 report by the Harvard Date Rape Task Force recommended that university guidelines define rape as "any act of sexual intercourse that occurs without the expressed consent of the person." What does this mean—that a consent form must be signed before a date? Or that, as a couple moves toward the bed after passionate and mutual heavy petting, the man should ask the woman if she's quite sure she wants to? (A friend who just graduated from college tells me that some men are actually beginning to act that way.) And perhaps he has to keep asking every time: the couple's prior sexual relationship, the advocates say, makes no difference whatsoever.

Clearly, this vision leaves no room for spontaneity, for ambiguity, for passionate, wordless, animal sex. What's more, it is, in the end, deeply belittling to women, who apparently cannot be expected to convey their wishes clearly or to show a minimum of assertiveness. It also perpetuates a view of woman as the passive and reticent partner who may or may not want sex and man as the pursuer who is naturally presumed to want it: *she* is not required to ask for *his* consent (even though, given some current definitions, plenty of women must have committed rape at least a few times in their lives; I'm sure I have). Sex is something men impose on women. We're back full circle to fragile, chaste, nineteenth-century womanhood.

And some people think that's good. Recently, I got into a discussion with a conservative Catholic male who vehemently argued that the campaign against date rape was nothing more than a distorted expression of women's legitimate rejection of sexual freedom, a thing so contrary to their chaste natures. Casual sex, he said, makes women (but not men) feel cheap and used, and what they're doing now is using the extreme language of rape to describe this exploitation; things were really better under the much-maligned double standard, when women were expected to say no to sex, and thus accorded more protection from male lust. To some conservatives, the outcry about sexual harassment confirms what conservatives have known all along: women want to be put on a pedestal and treated like ladies; they find sexual advances insulting because they are chaster than men.

I don't think that's true. Most young women have no wish to return to the days when they were branded as sluts if they said yes. It may be, however, that this generation's confusion over sexual boundaries has to do with the pains of transition from one set of morals to another, of contradictory cultural messages: the traditional ones of chastity as the basis of female self-respect and reputation and the new ones of sexual liberation and female desire. Sometimes, we may not think we're "cheap" if we go to bed with a man we just met—at least, we're no worse than the guy is for going to bed with a woman he just met—yet when we wake up the next morning we may find that *he* thinks less of us but not of himself. And we may find, to our chagrin, that feminine coyness is not quite as extinct as we might like to think. The other day, a very liberated fortysomething friend of mine breezily said, "Oh, of course no modern woman says no when she means yes." Alas, recent studies (done by feminist researchers) show that *by their own admission,* about half of college women sometimes do.

But there may be another reason, too, for this generation's

susceptibility to the victim mentality: overconfidence in the perfectibility of life. The sexual-liberation rhetoric itself overlooked the complexity of human emotions and fostered the belief that sexual relationships could be free of all manipulation or unfair pressure. More generally, there is the idealistic arrogance of middle-class boys and girls who have grown up in a sheltered, affluent environment, accustomed to the notion that getting one's way is a basic right. The old cliché "Life isn't fair" is not only unpopular nowadays but profoundly suspect, seen as a smokescreen designed by the oppressors to keep the oppressed—women and minorities, in particular—in their place. Yes, it has been used for such purposes often enough. But often it happens to be true, and to disregard that is to invite disastrous consequences—like the belief that anyone, male or female, is entitled to an annoyance-free life.

The danger in the new radical feminism is not only that it legitimizes what is, deep down, an extremely retrograde view of women; it also seeks to regulate personal relationships to a degree unprecedented since the Puritans roamed the earth. If you feel that a man has enticed or pressured you into having unwanted sex, you don't confront him and call him a manipulative creep; you run to a campus grievance committee and demand redress. If you don't like the way a coworker has been putting his hand on your shoulder, you don't have to tell him to stop it—you can go and file a lawsuit instead. Courts and law-enforcement authorities are being asked to step into situations where, short of installing hidden cameras in every bedroom and every office hallway, they have no way of finding out on whose side the truth is. Of course, many millions of women and men remain relatively unaffected by this relentless politicization of the personal. Still, the damage is being done.

Again, it may be my Soviet background that makes me especially sensitive to the perils of this aggressive, paternalistic interventionism. In the Soviet *ancien régime,* it was not uncommon to report one's unfaithful spouse to the Communist party bureau at his (or, less commonly, her) workplace, and conflicts between husband and wife—particularly if both were party members—were often settled at public meetings that satisfied both the voyeuristic and the viciously moralistic impulses of the other comrades.

What are we going to be, then? Assertive, strong women (and sometimes, surely, also needy and vulnerable, because we *are* human), seeing ourselves as no better or worse than men; aware of but not obsessed with sexism; interested in loving and equal relationships but with enough confidence in ourselves, and enough understanding of human foibles, to know better than to scrutinize every move we or our partners make for political incorrectness? Or full-time agents of the gender-crimes police?

Women's liberation is not yet a completed task. Sexism still lingers and injustice toward women still exists, particularly in the distribution of domestic tasks. We are still working on new standards and values to guide a new, equal relationship between men and women. But "Third Wave" feminism, which tries to fight gender bias by defining people almost entirely in terms of gender, is not the way to go.

We need a "Third Way" feminism that rejects the excesses of the gender fanatics *and* the sentimental traditionalism of the Phyllis Schlaflys; one that does not seek special protections for women and does not view us as too socially disadvantaged to take care of ourselves. Because on the path that feminism has taken in the past few years, we are allowing ourselves to be treated as frail, helpless little things—by our would-be liberators.

NOTES ON CONTRIBUTORS

Jenny Lyn Bader, twenty-four, is a writer living in New York City. Her play *Shakespeare's Undiscovered One Act* premiered at the Village Gate theater in 1992. She has worked as a theater director and book editor and has written for the *National Law Journal* and the *New York Times.*

Stephen Beachy, twenty-nine, is the author of the novel *The Whistling Song.* Short pieces of his have been included in the anthology *High Risk 2* and in various zines. He currently lives in San Francisco with his boyfriend, Jonathan Brunn, where they work as movers/haulers. He is also working on another novel.

Paul Beatty was born in Los Angeles in 1962 and now lives in New York. His second book of poetry, *Joker, Joker, Deuce,* was recently published.

David Bernstein, twenty-six, is the founding editor of *Diversity & Division* magazine. He lives in Washington, D.C.

David Greenberg, twenty-five, is a native of Newton, Massachusetts. He is assisting Bob Woodward of the *Washington Post* on a forthcoming book. He has written for *The New Republic* and other magazines.

Paula Kamen, twenty-seven, a Chicago writer, is the author of *Feminist Fatale: Voices from the "Twentysomething" Genera-*

tion Explore the Future of the "Women's Movement." Her work has appeared in the *New York Times,* the *Chicago Tribune, Newsday,* and the *Dallas Morning News.* She is working on a book about young women's sexual attitudes and is enjoying the research.

Ted Kleine was born in Lansing, Michigan, in 1967. His writing has appeared in the *Detroit News, Mother Jones, Utne Reader, Z,* and *In These Times.* He is not married, has no cats, and does not live in New York.

Karen Lehrman, thirty-two, is acting literary editor of the *Wilson Quarterly.* Her work has appeared in *The New Republic,* the *New York Times,* the *Washington Post,* the *Wall Street Journal, Mother Jones,* and other publications. She is writing a book on postideological feminism.

Eric Liu, twenty-five, is the founder and editor of *The Next Progressive,* a journal of opinion produced by writers in their twenties. He has served as a legislative aide to U.S. Senator David Boren and as a speechwriter for Secretary of State Warren Christopher and for President Clinton.

Lalo Lopez, twenty-nine, is spreading the Word of Pochismo from his art studio in East L.A. He is the cofounder of the comedy troupe Chicano Secret Service and of *Pocho Magazine,* Aztlan's Rudest Chicano Publication. He draws the satirical cartoon "L.A. Cucaracha" for the *Los Angeles Weekly* and has no day job.

Lisa Palac, twenty-nine, is the editor of *Future Sex* magazine and the producer of *Cyborgasm,* the first Virtual Audio sex C.D. Her work has appeared in *Playboy, Penthouse,* the erotic anthologies *Herotica 1* and *2,* and *Best American Erotica 1993.* She lives in San Francisco.

Robin Pogrebin, born in 1965, is an associate producer at ABC News with Peter Jennings's documentary team. She was formerly a staff reporter for the *New York Observer.* She spent three years writing for the *New York Times* and has also worked for the *Hartford Courant, New York* magazine, *Harper's* magazine, and the *Nation.* She is the daughter of feminist activist Letty Cottin Pogrebin and lives in Manhattan with her husband.

Ian Williams is a twenty-six-year-old writer who maintains an umbilical, almost Oedipal relationship with his college town, Chapel Hill, North Carolina. He was the sarcastic spokesman for the twentysomething generation in the book *13th GEN: Abort, Retry, Ignore, Fail,* although he hopes that if he were ever to *say* something like "spokesman for the twentysomething generation" that the audience would take him out back and shoot him like an old horse.

Naomi Wolf was born in San Francisco in 1962. Her essays have appeared in various publications including *The New Republic,* the *Wall Street Journal, Glamour, Ms., Esquire,* the *Washington Post,* and the *New York Times.* She speaks widely on college campuses and is the author of *The Beauty Myth* and, most recently, *Fire with Fire.* She lives in Washington, D.C.

Elizabeth Wurtzel is twenty-six, and is already considering early retirement. She is working on a book dealing with depression, youth culture, psychopharmacology, and other miserable topics. She has been the pop music critic at both *The New Yorker* and *New York* magazines, and her work has appeared in *Rolling Stone, Mademoiselle, Seventeen, Musician, People,* the *Oxford American, Hysteria,* and other publications.

Cathy Young was born in Moscow in 1963 and came to the U.S. with her family in 1980. Her book *Growing Up in Moscow* was published in 1989. Her writing has appeared in the *Washington Post,* the *New York Times, Newsday,* the *Philadelphia Inquirer, The New Republic,* and other publications. She is working on a book about contemporary feminism.